Language & Species

Language & Species

Derek Bickerton

The University of Chicago Press

Chicago & London

The University of Chicago Press, Chicago 60637
The University of Chicago Press, Ltd., London
© 1990 by The University of Chicago
All rights reserved. Published 1990
Paperback edition 1992
Printed in the United States of America
01 00 99 98 97   5 6 7

Library of Congress Cataloging-in-Publication Data

Bickerton, Derek.
    Language & species / Derek Bickerton.
      p.   cm.
    Includes bibliographical references and index.
    ISBN 0-226-04610-9 (clothbound); 0-226-04611-7 (paperback)
    1. Language and languages—Origin. 2. Human evolution.
I. Title. II. Title: Language and species.
P116.B522   1990
401—dc20   90-35922
                                                     CIP

 ∞ The paper used in this publication meets the minimum requirements
of the American National Standard for Information Sciences—Permanence of Paper
          for Printed Library Materials, ANSI Z39.48-1984.

for YVONNE
my soul's companion
in whose heart it is always summer

Nevertheless, the difference in mind between man and the higher animals, great as it is, is certainly one of degree and not of kind. . . . If it be maintained that certain powers, such as self-consciousness, abstraction etc., are peculiar to man, it may well be that these are the incidental results of other highly-advanced intellectual faculties; and these again are mainly the result of the continued use of a highly developed language.

—Charles Darwin, *The Descent of Man*

Contents

Preface

It gives me great pleasure to be able to reverse the normal order of acknowledgments, in which the author expresses boundless gratitude to everyone else, from his gurus to the people who licked envelopes, and at the very end briefly thanks his spouse for getting his meals on time and putting up with his moods. On any criteria, the person this book owes most to is my wife Yvonne. Its conception occurred while she was taking classes from Harry Drayton at the University of Guyana. Harry, a fine teacher, gave a course called 'Social Biology' at a time when sociobiology was hardly even a twinkle in Edward Wilson's eye, and she regularly kept me informed of its content, most of which was quite unfamiliar to me. I was fascinated yet baffled. Surely language should fit into all this somewhere, but exactly where? I talked to Harry about it, and at his invitation gave a couple of guest lectures the following year, the net result of which was to totally bewilder the poor students and to show me how little anyone (and how much less I!) knew about the subject.

My efforts to repair my ignorance were sporadic and often interrupted by other projects. The writing, when I could no longer think of anything to postpone it, was equally tortuous. The book went through several drafts and Yvonne carefully read each one. She was, I suppose, the reader I was aiming at: someone with a good general knowledge of the behavioral sciences, fascinated by humans and their relations with the world they inhabit, yet quite uninterested in linguistics, if not actually hostile to some of its more nit-picking aspects. If something wasn't clear to her, it was because it wasn't clearly presented and needed to be rethought and rewritten, she had, too, an infallible eye for delusions of omniscience. The book, whatever its merits, is infinitely better than it would have been without her.

I have also been fortunate in having a supportive work environment, due in general to the University of Hawaii and in particular to Byron

Bender, my department chairman, and Don Topping, director of the Social Sciences Research Institute, both of whom have benignly tolerated my idiosyncracies and encouraged me to develop my teaching and research in whatever directions I pleased. This included a generous leave that enabled me to spend two consecutive years away from my regular duties and to find equally tolerant and uninterfering havens, thanks to Pieter Muysken of the University of Amsterdam and Robert Chaudenson of the University of Provence.

Although this isn't a book about creole languages, my research on pidgins and creoles served as a catalyst in the formation of the ideas expressed in it. If I hadn't approached the issues from that somewhat unusual perspective, this would have been a very different book, if indeed it could have been written at all. I am therefore deeply grateful to the National Science Foundation, and in particular to Paul Chapin, head of its linguistics section, for supporting my research on these languages over the years.

A number of people have read all or part of one or another version of this book. I am grateful in particular to William O'Grady, Herb Roitblat, and an anonymous reviewer for the University of Chicago Press for comments on an earlier version. A later one was read in its entirety by Peter Manicas and a group organized by him which included Geoffrey Eisen, Bruce Morton, Ted Rodgers, Don Topping, Jim Unger, Michael Weinstein, and John Westphal; their lively and often heated discussion was invaluable and yielded, too, a variety of references that I should have consulted but hadn't. Ann Peters, Bob Hsu, and the students of Linguistics 615, who were exposed to the penultimate version, also made many helpful comments.

Over the years, too, there have been others, too numerous to list here, whose words or writings have contributed to the making of this book. The influence of Noam Chomsky, long resisted, will be obvious. More diffuse but at least equally potent is that of Kenneth Craik, a fellow of St. John's College, Cambridge, while I was an undergraduate there, but at that time totally unknown to me (and so foreign to what were then my interests that even had I met him I doubt if I would have profited thereby). Protracted though never rancorous arguments with Talmy Givon have helped to sharpen and clarify my ideas (how can you know what you think until you've disagreed with someone?). With all of these many and varied forms of assistance, for which again I would like to thank all concerned, I can have no excuse if there are still shortcomings in this book: the blame can only be mine.

Language & Species

Introduction

If at this moment you look around you, wherever you may happen to be as you read these words, the odds are that most if not all of what you can see has been built, made, or grown by members of our own species. Even if you look out on wilderness, that wilderness survives only because it serves our pleasures, or because the task of subduing it outweighs the profit to be reaped from it—we could subdue it if we chose to. We tend to take such things for granted, and do not normally contrast our circumstances with those of the gorilla, the orangutan, or the chimpanzee. These creatures seem as remote from us as the jungles they inhabit. Not until we begin to think about it does it strike us as in any way remarkable that our world should be, not only utterly different from and far more complex than theirs, but also, in large part, our own creation. Other species adapt themselves to the natural world—we adapt the natural world to us.

Yet if you consider our respective natures, you would never expect the gap between us and the apes to be as vast as it is. We share with the chimpanzee perhaps as much as 99 percent of our genetic material, and our common ancestor may be as little as five million years behind us. Yet if apes look around them, what can they see that their own species has made? At most, the beds of broken boughs that they built last night, already abandoned, soon indistinguishable from the surrounding forest. The contrast is no less striking if we look at how much of the world each species controls. The chimpanzee has a few patches of jungle, while we have the whole globe, from poles to equator, and are already dreaming of new worlds. Most species are locked into their own niches, ringed by unbreachable barriers of climate, vegetation, terrain. We alone seem magically exempt from such bounds.

Nor does the gulf between us end with what can be seen. Each of us has a lively and persistent sense that we are able not only to act in the world, but also to stand back, so to speak, and see ourselves acting; review our own actions and those of others, and deliberately weigh and judge them; seek in ourselves for the motives that inspire those actions; catalog our hopes, our fears, our dreams, and perform countless other operations that we subsume under the head of 'mental activities' or 'consciousness'. We do not know whether any other species has these particular capacities. We may well doubt it, for two good reasons.

First, many of us have lived at close quarters, on intimate terms, with other types of advanced mammal, yet no one has shown convincing evidence that any other species has a consciousness that resembles ours. It is true that failure to find something is no proof of its nonexistence. But the second reason lies in the likelihood that these two things—dominance over nature and a developed consciousness—are closely and indeed causally linked.

It is only because we can imagine things being different from the way they are that we are able to change them. But this imaginative capacity forms merely a part of our kind of consciousness. If that capacity were shared by any other creature, its fruits should surely be evident. Such a creature might be expected to share, even if only in a reduced measure, our own world-altering power. Since none does, we may take it, at least as a working hypothesis, that consciousness and power over nature are unique to our species, and that only through the first can the second come about.

These vast differences, qualitative as well as merely quantitative, between our species and those that are closest to it pose no problem for those who believe, as many still do, that we result from a unique act of creation, a supernatural irruption into the natural scheme of things. For those who do not believe this, and who find overwhelming the evidence that we developed, as all other species did, through the natural processes of evolution, these differences must remain puzzling indeed.

That evolution, over all-but-infinite time, could change one physical organ into another, a leg into a wing, a swim bladder into a lung, even a nerve net into a brain with billions of neurons, seems remarkable, indeed, but natural enough. That evolution, over a period of a few million years, should have turned physical matter into what has seemed to many, in the most literal sense of the term, to be some kind of metaphysical entity is altogether another matter. So, on the face of it, both sides seem to be left holding beliefs rather than theories: the one side, belief in a special creation, the other, belief in a no-less-miraculous transmutation of matter into mind.

Of course, things can't rest like that. The first side accepts miracles,

2

the second does not. Explanations must be sought, and have been sought, ever since Darwin wrote his *Descent of Man*. But somehow none of those explanations turns out to be really convincing. Each of them seems to slide away from the central problem into what are basically side issues: how the emotions developed, whether we are aggressive by nature, how much of our growth comes from culture and how much from biology, why our behavior should include altruism and incest avoidance. The real questions are, how did we get so much more powerful than anything else, and how at the same time did we get our peculiar kind of consciousness?

But, in confronting these questions, accounts of our species' development become embarrassingly vague. It was because of our big brains, some say. But if big brains were so adaptive, why had no previous species selected for them? Why only the hominid line? There have been a number of answers: because we used tools, because we made war, because we walked upright, because we were sexually competitive, because hunting on the savannas made our brains too hot. None of them, in and of itself, seems particularly compelling. Other species use tools, other species wage wars, other species hunt on the savannas, almost all species compete sexually; birds walk upright on two legs, and fly too.

An alternative possibility is that although none of these things alone was enough, their unique combination caused the brain to exceed some critical size, and it was the crossing of this Rubicon that radically altered our behavior. This proposal, like most 'bits-of-everything' proposals, sounds persuasive at first but proves less so on closer examination.

There are at least three things wrong with it. First, it lacks explanatory power. Was the particular set of factors that combined in early hominids the only set that could have created a species like ours, or were there—are there—perhaps others? If this question cannot be answered, it is simply because no one can yet explain how that set of factors worked to achieve its end. Second, it does not account for all the data. An expanded brain might give its owner greater powers to manipulate the environment, but why should it at the same time produce that characteristic doubleness of vision—'Here's me doing X, and here's me watching myself do X'—that consciousness gives?

In their book *Promethean Fire*, Charles Lumsden and Edward Wilson try to explain such a result with a graphic image: that of a mountain which, though only slightly higher than its grassy neighbors, becomes different from them by acquiring a cap of snow and ice. But this image, though vivid, does not really help. We know why the bigger mountain gets snow and ice on it; we don't know why the bigger brain gets consciousness in it.

The third thing wrong, one that affects all big-brain arguments, is that there is no evidence that brain size per se does anything for any species: Neanderthals had brains bigger than ours, and where are they now? Of course it is true that the larger a species's brain is, the more we would apply to it the convenient but ultimately vague and unhelpful label 'intelligence'. But that 'intelligence' (which is simply the capacity to perform varied and complex behaviors and to respond flexibly and efficiently to environmental input) is not a direct function of brain size, but rather of the number of sets of task-specific modules a creature has—modules each of which is devoted to some particular behavior or response—and the patterns of connections between those sets. In other words, it is the way in which the brain is organized, rather than its mere bulk, that leads to 'increased intelligence'. Of course the more task-specific modules a brain has, the bigger it will be, but size itself is a dependent variable.

This means that if the hominid brain got bigger, it did not do so by simply adding more 'spare' neurons. Indeed, it is questionable whether there is or ever can be such a thing as a 'spare' neuron (that is, a neuron that is not, initially at least, committed to any specific function). Rather, the brain got bigger by adding neurons that performed specific tasks. But what tasks? Having come full circle, we are back where we started—the additional neurons must somehow perform just those tasks of changing nature and generating consciousness that formed the original data to be explained. A century and a quarter after Darwin expounded the mechanisms of physical evolution, the mechanisms of mental evolution are still without a history and without a convincing explanation.

And yet the true source of our difference has been lying all the while, like Poe's purloined letter, hidden in plain view. There are not merely two things, consciousness and power over nature, that distinguish us from other species, there is a third thing: language. While it would be absurd to suppose that language in and of itself provided everything that differentiates us from the apes, language was not only the force that launched us beyond the limits of other species but the necessary (and perhaps even sufficient) prerequisite of both our consciousness and our unique capacities.

If this is so, why have people looked elsewhere for explanations? All along there have been those who recognized that language must have played an important role. Consider for instance the quotation from Darwin that serves as the epigraph for this book. But the precise nature of that role remained obscure because a number of factors conspired to make language itself an elusive and slippery object.

4

Language is, of all our mental capacities, the deepest below the threshold of our awareness, the least accessible to the rationalizing mind. We can hardly recall a time when we were without it, still less how we came by it. When we could first frame a thought, it was there. It is like a sheet of transparent glass through which every conceivable object in the world seems clearly visible to us. We find it hard to believe that if the sheet were removed, those objects and that world would no longer exist in the way that we have come to know them.

That, in turn, is because for most of us language seems primarily, or even exclusively, to be a means of communication. But it is not even primarily a means of communication. Rather it is a system of representation, a means for sorting and manipulating the plethora of information that deluges us throughout our waking life. How such a system came to be, how it functions, and what it accomplishes will form the themes of this book.

Another factor that has made the role of language hard to evaluate is that until relatively recently linguistics, the study of language, was very little developed. Most of what we know about language has been learned in the last three decades. Very little of that knowledge is readily available to the general public. Physics, chemistry, biology are routinely taught in high schools, but through some accident of educational history, linguistics is hardly taught at all outside graduate school.

Yet merely to know linguistics is far from enough. With few exceptions, linguists have refrained from any consideration of the origins of language or the role that it has played in the development of our species. Noam Chomsky, arguably the Newton of our field, has dismissed the origin of language as an issue of no more scientific interest than the origin of the heart. Strategically, this made sound policy. We would never have learned as much as we have about the purely formal, structural properties of language if some scholars had not concentrated on these to the exclusion of all else. But if we do not transcend this strategy we can never hope to learn what we are, and why we are what we are.

The alternative course, pursued here, is by its nature a risky one. It entails crossing disciplinary boundaries and trespassing on fields so various that no single scholar could hope to encompass them all. It is therefore inevitable that anyone who attempts such a course may, here and there, quite unintentionally oversimplify or distort the findings of others. The most one can do is to try to keep such errors to a minimum. In any case, the risks seem well worth taking. A book can not and should not even hope to constitute some marble mausoleum, enshrining the final word on the topics that it broaches. A book is a machine to think with.

5

This book is a machine for thinking about language and what language has done for our species and how it has made us different from other species. If it helps us to think about these things in new ways, it will have achieved its aim.

The organization of the book is as follows. The first three chapters concern themselves with the nature of language. Chapter 1 contrasts language with animal communication systems and outlines its representational function, while chapters 2 and 3 try to show how that function works, looking first at words, how they convey meaning, and what kinds of meaning they convey, and then at the principles that organize words into sentences.

The next four chapters examine the evolutionary history of language. Chapter 4 traces, from their earliest beginnings, the developments in neurological systems that formed the necessary prerequisites for a species to acquire any kind of language. Chapter 5 examines some existing behaviors (of our species and other species) sometimes described as 'language', but perhaps better regarded as something intermediate between a prelinguistic state and true language. Chapter 6 shows how such a 'protolanguage' could have come into existence under the pressure of circumstances peculiar to our ancestors of two to four million years ago, while chapter 7 suggests ways in which systematically structured language could have developed out of an unstructured protolanguage.

The last two chapters look at some of the consequences for a species that possesses language. Chapter 8 concentrates on our species' inner world, from individual consciousness of self to the construction of complex knowledge-systems; chapter 9 turns to the outer world of our relations with one another and with the universe we inhabit.

As this book is aimed at a broad general audience, it was felt that footnotes and textual references would only distract the reader and disrupt the flow of the argument. Accordingly, notes on the text are given at the end of the book in the form of a commentary on each chapter, including references to works listed in the reference section.

1

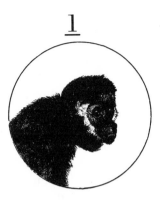

The Continuity Paradox

Anyone who sets out to describe the role played by language in the development of our species is at once confronted by an apparent paradox, the Paradox of Continuity. If such a person accepts the theory of evolution, that person must accept also that language is no more than an evolutionary adaptation—one of an unusual kind, perhaps, yet formed by the same processes that have formed countless other adaptations. If that is the case, then language cannot be as novel as it seems, for evolutionary adaptations do not emerge out of the blue.

There are two ways in which evolution can produce novel elements: by the recombination of existing genes in the course of normal breeding, or by mutations that affect genes directly. Even in the second case, absolute novelties are impossible. What happens in mutation is that the instructions for producing part of a particular type of creature are altered. Instructions for producing a new part cannot simply be added to the old recipe. There must already exist specific instructions that are capable of being altered, to a greater or lesser extent. What this means is that language cannot be wholly without antecedents of some kind.

But what kind of antecedents could language have? Since language is so widely regarded as a means of communication, the answer seems obvious: earlier systems of animal communication. It has long been known that many species communicate with one another. Some, like fireflies, have blinking lights, others, like crickets, rub legs or wingcases together, while many exude chemical signals known as pheromones. Of course such means are limited in their range of potential meaning and may signal nothing more complex than the presence of a potential mate. But the more sophisticated the creature, the more sophisticated the

7

means—from the dances of honeybees, through the posturing of sea gulls, to the sonar of dolphins—hence, the more complex the information that can be conveyed. Could not human language be just a super-sophisticated variant of these?

The trouble is that the differences between language and the most sophisticated systems of animal communication that we are so far aware of are qualitative rather than quantitative. All such systems have a fixed and finite number of topics on which information can be exchanged, whereas in language the list is open-ended, indeed infinite. All such systems have a finite and indeed strictly limited number of ways in which message components can be combined, if they can be combined at all. In language the possibilities of combination, while governed by strict principles, are (potentially at least) infinite, limited for practical purposes only by the finiteness of the immediate memory store. You do not get from a finite number to infinity merely by adding numbers. And there are subtler but equally far-reaching differences between language and animal communication that make it impossible to regard the one as antecedent to the other.

But the net result of all this is the Paradox of Continuity: language must have evolved out of some prior system, and yet there does not seem to be any such system out of which it could have evolved. Until now, arguments about the nature, origin, and function of language have remained inextricably mired in this paradox. Let us see if there is any way in which they can be released from it.

A Word about Formalism

We can at least clean a little of the mud from our wheels if we begin by tackling what might seem at first an unpromising and unrelated issue: the role that formal structure plays in language. Some linguists will tell you that the formal structure of language is very important. Others will tell you that it is relatively unimportant. Who is right?

There are two very odd imbalances between the formalist and antiformalist groups. The first imbalance is in what they believe. No formalist believes that a purely formal approach is the only way to study language. Any formalist would agree that there are many aspects of language— meaning, use, interaction with other social and psychological domains—that are all worthy of study. If you ask formalists why they insist on studying formal structure in isolation from all these other factors, they will probably tell you that significant advances in knowledge have always involved focusing on particular aspects of things and abstracting away from other aspects. They can see no reason for the study of our own species to reverse this sensible procedure.

But if you ask antiformalists why they ignore the formal structure of language, you will sometimes hear a much less tolerant story. They may tell you that it is quite senseless to study the formal aspects of language in isolation from its mode of functioning in society. Quite possibly they will go on to say that since those aspects are merely uninteresting mechanisms, or superficial trimmings, or even artefacts of the method of inquiry, they can be relegated to an inferior position, if not dismissed altogether.

The second imbalance between formalists and antiformalists is that since formalists have ignored all issues involving the evolution of language, that field has been yielded without a blow to the enemies of formalism. Subsequently there has been no significant interchange between the two sides, indeed they are barely on speaking terms. This has left the antiformalists alone to grapple with the Continuity Paradox.

Now to tackle a paradox, or indeed any research issue, from a one-sided position is not the best recipe for success. In large part, failure to resolve the Continuity Paradox has resulted precisely from what one might call the 'naive continuism' of the antiformalists, who have tried in a variety of ways to establish a direct line of development from animal communication to human language. Although all their efforts have signally failed to produce a convincing 'origins' story, their rejection of more formal approaches has left them without any viable alternative.

Accordingly the present work tackles the Paradox from a rather different viewpoint. This viewpoint takes as basic the assumption that formal properties of language do exist and do matter, and that without the very specific types of formal structure that language exhibits, it could not perform the social and communicative functions that it does perform, and could not convey the wealth of peculiarly human meaning that it does convey.

Those functions and that meaning should not—and, indeed, in a work of this nature literally can not—be ignored or even minimized. However, it seems reasonable to stand the antiformalist position on its head and say that it is quite senseless to study the origins and functions of language without at the same time studying the formal structures that underlie those functions. For these formal structures, abstract though they may appear, are exactly what enable language to communicate so efficiently. Nothing else that we know of (or can imagine) could have given language the unprecedented power that it proved to have: power that gave to a single primate line the mastery of the physical world and the first, and perhaps only, entry into the world of consciousness.

THE GULF BETWEEN LANGUAGE AND ANIMAL COMMUNICATION

Having established this perspective, we can now look a little more closely at the ways in which animal communication differs from language. Perhaps the most obvious is that of productivity. The calls or signs of other creatures usually occur in isolation from one another. There are as yet few, if any, clear cases where they can be combined to form longer utterances whose meaning differs from the sum of their meanings in isolation, in the way in which *look out!*, for instance, differs from the sum of the meanings of *look* and *out*.

It is not impossible that future research will uncover such cases. But then, if we were to parallel language, we would have to look for cases where the same calls in a different order can mean different things, like *Dog bites man* versus *Man bites dog*. Even this far from exhausts the possibilities of human syntax, which can also place similar words in different orders to mean the same thing (*John gave Mary the book, Mary was given the book by John*) or the same words in almost the same order to mean quite different things (*The woman that saw the man kicked the dog, The woman saw the man that kicked the dog*).

Note however that to achieve such effects we have to use elements like *-en, by, that*. Later on we shall look at such elements in more detail. For the moment it is sufficient to note that they differ from elements like *John* or *woman* in that the latter refer (if only indirectly) to some entity or class of entities in the real world, whereas the former do not really refer at all, but rather serve to express structural relations between items that do refer. The first class of elements can be described as *grammatical items* and the second, the class that refers, as *lexical items*. To which class of items do animal calls and signs belong?

Certainly there seems to be nothing in any animal communication system that corresponds even vaguely to grammatical items. But it is also questionable, in at least a large majority of cases, whether there is any true correspondence with lexical items either. We may find, for example, a particular facial expression, accompanied perhaps by a bristling of hair, that we might want to translate as *I am very angry with you*, or a peculiar cry that perhaps we would translate as, *Look out, folks, something dangerous is coming!* In other words, most elements in animal communication systems might seem to correspond, in a very rough and ready sense, with complete human utterances, rather than with single words per se. But note that the true correspondence is with utterance rather than sentence, because oftentimes a single-word utterance like *Help!* or *Danger!* would serve as well. The category *complete utterance*, however, is not a structural category in language, precisely because it can cover anything from a complex sentence (or even a series of such sentences) to a one-word exclamation.

It follows that, for the most part, the units in animal communication systems do not correspond with any of the units that compose human language. There is a good reason why this is so. Animal communication is *holistic*, that is to say it is concerned with communicating *whole situations*. Language, on the other hand, talks mainly about *entities* (whether other creatures, objects, or ideas) and *things predicated of entities* (whether actions, events, states, or processes).

The units of animal communication convey whole chunks of information (rough equivalents of *I am angry, You may mate with me, A predator just appeared*). Language breaks up those chunks in a way that, to the best of our knowledge, no animal communication system has ever done. In order to convey our anger, we must, as an absolute minimum, specify ourselves by a particular sign and the state in which we find ourselves by another sign (in English and numerous other languages we have, in addition, to use an almost meaningless verb in order to link ourselves with our current state, while in another set of languages, we would have to add a particle to indicate that our state was indeed current, not a past or future one).

If we think about it, this way of doing things may seem somewhat less natural than the animal way. Suppose that the situation we want to convey is one in which we have just seen a predator approaching. From a functional point of view, it might seem a lot quicker to let out a single call with that meaning, rather than *Look out! A lion's coming!* But the oddity is not just functional. In the real situation, it is simply not the case that we would see two things: an entity (the lion) and something predicated of that entity ('coming'). If we actually were in that situation, what we would perceive would be the frontal presentation of a lion getting rapidly larger. That is, we would experience a single intact cluster of ongoing perceptions. So the animal's representation of this would seem to be not merely more expeditious, but more in accord with reality than ours.

But there are, even in this limited example, compensating features. A generalized predator warning call, or even a specific lion warning call, could not be modified so as to become *A lion was coming* (as in the con-

11

text of a story), *A lion may come* (to propose caution in advance), *No lions are coming* (to convey reassurance), *Many lions are coming!* (to prompt still more vigorous evasive measures), and so on. To achieve this kind of flexibility, any utterance has to be composed of a number of different units each of which may be modified or replaced so as to transmit a wide range of different messages. And after all, if we want a rapid response, the possession of language in no way inhibits use of the human call system. In a tight corner, we can still just yell.

Still, you might argue, language had to begin somewhere, and where is it most likely to have begun than in some particular call whose meaning was progressively narrowed until it now covers about the same semantic range as does some noun in a language? Once the species had acquired a short list of entities—lions, snakes, or whatever—it needed only to attribute states or actions to those entities and it would then already have the essential subject-predicate core of language, to which all other properties could subsequently have been added.

You might then point to creatures such as the vervet monkey which have highly developed alarm calls. The vervet, a species that lives in East Africa, has at least three distinct alarm calls that might seem to refer to three species that are likely to prey upon vervets: pythons, martial eagles, and leopards. That it is the calls themselves that have this reference, and not any other behavioral or environmental feature, has been experimentally established by playing recordings of the calls to troops of vervets in the absence of any of the predators concerned. On hearing these recordings, most vervets within earshot respond just as they would to a natural, predator-stimulated call. They look at the ground around them on hearing the snake warning, run up trees on hearing the leopard warning, and descend from trees to hide among bushes on hearing the eagle warning.

We might therefore think that these calls were, in embryo at least, the vervet 'words' for the species concerned. But in fact, a warning call about pythons differs from a word like *python* in a variety of ways. Even though *python* is only a single word, it can be modified, just as we saw the sentence *A lion's coming!* could be modified. It can, for instance, be given at least four different intonations, each of which has a distinct meaning. With a rising intonation it can mean 'Is that a python there?' or 'Did you just say python?'. With a neutral intonation, it merely names a particular variety of snake, as in a list of snake species, for example. With a sustained high-pitch intonation it can mean that there's a python right there, right now. With an intonation that starts high and ends low, especially if delivered in a sneering, sarcastic tone, it can mean 'How ridiculous to suppose that there's a python there!'

Assuming that all these are used without intent to deceive, only in the third case is there a python there for sure. But with the vervet call, there is always a python there. At least, with one rare exception, the vervet involved genuinely believes there is a python there. (Just like human children, young vervets have to learn the semantic range of their calls, and again like children they tend to overgeneralize and sometimes give calls in inappropriate circumstances).

In order to understand further differences between humans and vervets, certain aspects of meaning must first be clarified. We might suppose that any relation between events in the world and meaningful utterances could be characterized as a mapping relation, that is to say, an operation that matches features of the environment with features of a (more or less arbitrary) representational system. We might begin by saying that a python in the real world is matched with a particular call in the vervet system and a particular noun in a given human language. This would be not very far from Bertrand Russell's theory of meaning and reference, for Russell believed, and got into terrible difficulties through believing, that nouns referred directly to entities in the real world.

Linguists, at least since Russell's contemporary de Saussure, have known that this is not so for human language. As noted above, grammatical items do not refer at all, and lexical items refer to real-world entities only indirectly. This is because not one, but at least two mapping operations lie between the real world and language. First our sense perceptions of the world are mapped onto a conceptual representation, and then this conceptual representation is mapped onto a linguistic representation.

Indeed, even in the animal case there cannot be a direct relationship between external object and call. Every now and then, even adult vervets will use, say, an eagle call for something that is not an eagle. It is no help to say that the vervet merely made a mistake. Why did it make that mistake? Because it thought that what it saw really was an eagle. In other words, if the vervet is wrong, it is wrong because it is responding to its own act of identification, rather than to the object itself. But are we then to say that the vervet responds to its own identification when it happens to be wrong and to the real object when it happens to be right? Obviously not. Vervets respond to their own identifications under all circumstances. But in that case there cannot be a direct link between call and object. The call labels an act of identification: the placing of some phenomenon in a particular category. In some sense, vervets too must have concepts.

That the things words refer to are not external entities is even clearer in our own case. One piece of evidence is the very existence of expressions like *a unicorn* or *the golden mountain* that gave Russell so much trouble. Since such expressions cannot refer to real-world entities, they must refer to a level of representation that is to some extent independent of the real world.

Indeed, it is sometimes inescapable that linguistic expressions are referring not to real-world entities but to our conceptions of these. It is surprising that Russell never discussed sentences like *The Bill Bailey I love and respect is very different from the drunken monster you depict him as being.* Here, obviously, two concepts of the same person are in conflict. Nor can we escape the situation by pointing to the indisputable fact that one does not normally preface proper names with the definite article, and claim therefore that while *the Bill Bailey I love and respect* may refer to a concept of Bill Bailey, *Bill Bailey* alone can only refer to Bill Bailey the real-world individual.

Suppose I say *Bill Bailey is honest* and you say *Bill Bailey is a rascal.* Since both qualities cannot be simultaneously predicated of the same person, the referent for the first use can only be my concept of Bill Bailey while that for the second can only be yours. But what about *Bill Bailey left early?* If we say that the name here refers to a real-world entity, we are in the uncomfortable position of claiming that names sometimes refer to real entities and sometimes to concepts. It seems safer to say that they refer to concepts all the time.

Yet even though both calls and words refer indirectly, there is evidence that they do not do so in the same way. For instance, it's a safe bet that no animal system has calls for unicorns or golden mountains or anything else of which there is no sensory evidence.

Another way in which calls and words differ is that words can be, and usually are, used in the physical absence of the objects they refer to, whereas calls hardly ever are so used. There is one exception: numerous observers have reported, for vervets and other primate species, what look like deliberate uses of alarm calls in the absence of any predator, designed to distract other monkeys from aggressive intentions or to remove potential competitors for some item of food.

If these can be proven to be genuine cases of deception, would they serve to undermine the distinction between words and calls? The answer is no, for two reasons. First, the strategy would not work unless all the other vervets believed, and behaved as if, there was a predator there. That is, it would work only if the deceiving monkey could rely on other monkeys to respond in the appropriate fashion. Second, in such observed instances the deceiving monkey itself failed to respond appropriately to its own call, even when it was in plain view of other monkeys. This suggests that the animal is not truly 'using a call in the absence of its referent' but simply exploiting one consequence of alarm calls (the disappearance of other animals from the vicinity) for its own personal ends.

Closely linked to these issues is the question of evolutionary utility. If human words were no more than the equivalents of animal calls, referring in the same way that animal calls referred, it would be remarkable that we have all the words we do. Vervets can 'name' pythons, leopards, and martial eagles. They cannot 'name' vultures, elephants, antelopes, and a variety of other creatures that do not have a significant impact on the lives of vervets. Why, in that case, is the human insect repertoire not limited to *fly, mosquito, locust,* and *cockroach* (plus any other insects that may significantly affect the lives of humans), and why is it that we have words—like *cockchafer, ladybird, earwig,* and *dung beetle*—for countless species that affect us minimally, if at all?

Here we differ from other creatures along a rather interesting dimension. All other creatures can communicate only about things that have evolutionary significance for them, but human beings can communicate about *anything.* In other words, what is adaptive for other species is a *particular set* of highly specific referential capacities. What is adaptive for our species is the *system* of reference *as a whole,* the fact that *any* manifestation of the physical world can (potentially at least) be matched with some form of expression. The fact that this difference is qualitative rather than quantitative (vervets could increase their repertoire by many orders of magnitude without even approximating the global scope of human reference) suggests again that quite different mechanisms are involved.

We should take account, too, of the fact that while animal calls and signs are structurally holistic, the units of human language are componential in nature. What this means is that animal calls and signs cannot be broken down into component parts, as language can. Words are, on one level, simply combinations of sounds. These sounds are finite and, indeed, small in number, not exceeding seventy or so in any known language.

Though in themselves the sounds of a language are meaningless, they can be recombined in different ways to yield thousands of words, each distinct in meaning. A word like *pat*, for example, can be broken down into three distinct sounds: /p/, /a/, and /t/. Those same sounds can be recombined to form *tap* and *apt*, two words of entirely different meaning. In just the same way, a finite stock of words (usually some tens of thousands, probably not much more than half a million even in the most 'developed' language) can be combined to produce an infinite number of sentences. Nothing remotely like this is found in animal communication.

To those already convinced that human language and animal communication are wholly unconnected, the foregoing paragraphs may seem like overkill. Yet contrasting animal communication and language has a purpose beyond merely convincing continuists that naive continuism won't work. It has the purpose of clarifying exactly what it is that makes language look like an evolutionary novelty. For if we don't do at least this, our prospects of explaining the evolutionary origins of language are dim. After all, anticontinuists have failed even more dismally than continuists at providing a convincing history of language and mind. Until we cease to regard language as primarily communicative and begin to treat it as primarily representational, we cannot hope to escape from the Continuity Paradox.

THE NATURE OF REPRESENTATION

It may be advisable to begin by clarifying some aspects of the general nature of representations. What do we mean when we say that X represents Y? Normally that Y, an event or an entity in the real world, bears some kind of correspondence relation to X, such that X somehow recalls or expresses Y, but not necessarily vice versa. This definition is informal and crude, and there may be several things about it that are questionable, but it will do as a starting point.

The first point to note is that in fact everything that we or any other creatures perceive is a representation, and not in any sense naked reality itself. That is to say, no creature apprehends its environment except by means of sensory mechanisms whose mode of functioning is everywhere the same. Particular facets of the environment excite responses (in terms of variations from their unstimulated firing rate) from particular cells that are specialized to respond to just those facets and no others. These neural responses in themselves constitute a level of representation. The firing of such-and-such a collection of neurons at such-and-such frequencies corresponds to the presence, in the immediate environment, of such-and-such a set of features. Almost simultaneously, in all verte-brates and many invertebrates, the original responses are synthesized and their synthesis, if functionally relevant to the creature concerned, is assigned to its appropriate category. This can be regarded as a further level of representation, in which the category assignment corresponds to a particular set of neuronal responses.

We do not, for example, directly see our surroundings. What happens is that sets of cells in our retinas programmed to react to specific features of the environment (lines at various angles, motions of varying kinds, different qualities of light, and so on) respond to those features on an individual basis, and this information is then relayed electrochemically to the visual areas of the cortex, where it is automatically reconstituted to provide a fairly, but not always completely, accurate simulacrum of what there is around us.

If this were not so, if our visual system merely presented us with a direct image of reality in the way that a mirror reflects whatever is before it, there would be no optical illusions. Optical illusions arise when prop-erties of the visual system are imposed on the raw data of the physical world. Nor can we dismiss such illusions as marginal phenomena. When we look around us we see an entirely colored world, but color is simply a property of the perceiving mechanism. All of us have seen mountains, gray or brown in the light of midday, turn to blue as the sun descends, then perhaps to pink or crimson as the last rays touch them, then finally to black as night falls. Of course the mountains have not really changed color, only the light reflected by them has changed, and these changes in turn interact with our means of perceiving and categorizing differences in wavelengths. But in that case, what are the mountains' *real* colors? Clearly they cannot have any.

We can now return to an earlier remark that may have seemed prob-lematic at the time. In the previous section, it was stated that expres-sions such as *the golden mountain* must refer not to the real world but to 'a level of representation that is to some extent independent of the real world'. How can we, one might ask, have a level that represents the real world but contains entities that do not exist in that world? If we treat 'representation' as meaning simply 're-presentation'—a wholly faithful one-to-one mapping from one medium to another—this seems absurd. But in fact, representation can never have such a meaning.

Consider the most basic facts about what a representation is and does. Although what follows applies to representations generally, let us, for the sake of concreteness, take as a particular example a painting of the

17

Battle of Lepanto; and let us for ease of exposition ignore for the present any intervening layer(s) of representation (sensory, conceptual, or other) that may come between the actual Battle of Lepanto and the painting with that title. It should immediately be clear that there are many properties of the Battle of Lepanto that the painting cannot represent. It cannot enable us, for instance, to smell the gunpowder smoke, or the sea spray, or the stench of blood below decks. The time that passed for an observer of the battle was determined by the length of the battle, but the time that passes for an observer of the picture is determined only by the observer's will. And there are many more properties of the actual Battle of Lepanto that are not, and indeed cannot be, represented in 'The Battle of Lepanto'.

But the converse is equally the case: there are many properties of the painting that never belonged to its original. 'The Battle of Lepanto', unlike the Battle of Lepanto, is made of paint and canvas, hangs on a wall, can be bought and sold, has properties of proportion that can be discussed by art critics, and so on. Yet even though 'The Battle of Lepanto' lacks much that the Battle of Lepanto possessed, and possesses much that the Battle of Lepanto lacked, we do not balk or express our derision when we read its title, instead we are perfectly prepared to accept it as a representation. Indeed someone who was actually present at the battle might have realized what the painting was meant to represent even without its title, by virtue of those features (names, types, and positions of ships, flags displayed, actual incidents depicted, and so forth) that the battle and the painting did share.

The relationship between a real-world event and a painting may look like an extreme kind of example to choose, since the level of real events and the level of pictorial representations might seem excessively remote from one another. However, it is hard to see how they are more remote than the level of real events is from the level of processing units in the brain, or than the level of processing units in the brain is from the level of spoken or written utterance. Moreover, remote or not, similar principles must apply wherever representation exists.

Both the properties of the Battle of Lepanto that must be excluded from the picture and the nonproperties of the battle that a picture must impose will be determined by the properties of static (as opposed to dynamic) representations, the properties of two-dimensional (as opposed to three-dimensional) objects, the properties of paint (as opposed to other media), and so on. In the same way, wherever representation exists, the properties of the medium in which the representation is made (or, to put it another way, the formal structures onto which the things to be represented are mapped) must both select from and add to the properties of the original.

In particular, the properties of neural systems, some of which are general but some of which are highly species-specific, and the properties of language, almost all of which are species-specific, must both add to and subtract from anything that they represent. Indeed, since everything we seem to perceive is in fact only a representation, these principles must apply universally. For there is not, and cannot in the nature of things ever be, a representation without a medium to represent in, any more than there can be a medium that lacks properties of its own.

Perhaps the only way in which pictorial representation might mislead us about the nature of representations in general is by suggesting that if any representation exists there must also exist someone to perceive it. Thus if we talk of nervous systems 'representing' reality in the brain, it seems natural to think of someone or something—ourselves, a little person, or the soul—who sits inside our head and looks at the representation. Such beliefs have been the cause of endless pseudoproblems. For the moment, all we have to do is note that a representation does not have to be perceived by any kind of discrete or conscious agent. If the particular set of neurons in a rabbit's brain that are triggered by the appearance of a fox should happen to fire, thereby representing a fox to a particular rabbit, that representation has only to be read by the motor neurons that control the rabbit's legs. If, under similar circumstances, we are somehow conscious of ourselves seeing the fox, that only appears to be a different story, one that will be dealt with in Chapter 8.

How veridical are representations? How much difference does it make that we can only perceive through a series of representations, rather than somehow perceiving directly? One might argue, with some justice, that representation at a lower level—what our brain derives from immediate sensory input—cannot stray too far from the reality it represents. If it did, the result would surely be dysfunctional from an evolutionary point of view. We would be continually colliding with obstacles, falling from high places, consuming poisonous substances, and performing a variety of other behaviors calculated to shorten our lifespan or even extinguish ourselves as a species. Indeed, you might argue that evolution must actively select for more veridical representations by eliminating those creatures that have less veridical ones.

But this line of reasoning cannot be taken too far. There is no indication that colorblindness, astigmatism, or tone-deafness are being bred out of us, nor that the range of our hearing is gradually extending, over succeeding generations, so that it will eventually approximate that of the dog or the bat. The sense of smell has not improved but has steadily deteriorated throughout the development of primates. Moreover, creatures like frogs or cockroaches with sensoria far poorer than ours have survived for tens of millions of years without apparent problems. Evolution does not hone and fine-tune representation to some point of near perfection. Rather it provides creatures with representational systems that are just about good enough for their immediate evolutionary needs. So long as a species can get by on what it has, there will be no selective pressure to improve.

What was said in the previous paragraph applies with even greater force to representation at the second level—the mapping from concepts to language. It was noted in the previous section that what gave our species its evolutionary advantage was not a capacity to represent in language just those things that had evolutionary significance for us, but a capacity (potential, at least) to represent *anything at all* in language, whether it was significant or not. The advantage this gave us was so enormous that members of our species can produce a great deal of dysfunctional behavior and still survive. Thus we would expect that the series of representational mappings from sense data to concepts and from concepts to language might carry us some distance from the world of reality, even to the point of representing entities that do not exist in that world.

We could even predict that a representational medium with the particular properties that language has would inevitably contain entities of the type of *the golden mountain*. A detailed account of those properties must await the next chapter, but one of them is that, subject to the constraints of a Sommers-Keil predicability tree (see chapter 3), any adjective can apply to any noun. This means that if there is an adjective, *golden*, it can apply without limit to any noun that represents the concept of a concrete object. If a mountain is such an object, *the golden mountain* becomes inescapable, regardless of the fact that there is no mountain made of gold anywhere in nature.

The remarkable thing is that the relationship between concepts and language is a two-way street. Normally we assume that a linguistic expression refers to a preexisting concept, but this is by no means necessarily the case. Linguistic expressions can equally well create concepts. Once we have heard of *the golden mountain*, we can imagine such a thing, and even what it might look like if it did exist. A friend once remarked, 'To evaluate that speech you'd really need your oxometer'.

On being asked what an oxometer was, he replied, 'It measures the percentage of bullshit'. There is, alas, as yet no oxometer in the real world. But you can imagine what it would be like, and maybe wish that you had one, too.

REPRESENTATION AND CONTINUITY

Having reviewed some of the ways in which representational systems work, we can return to the issue with which this chapter began. We have seen that between language and animal communication there exist qualitative differences, differences so marked as to indicate that no plausible ancestry for language can be found in prior communication systems. Yet evolution still requires that language have an ancestry of some sort. Thus if there is to be continuity, it must lie in some domain other than that of communication.

Communication is, after all, not what language is, but (a part of) what it does. Countless problems have arisen from a failure to distinguish between language and the use of language. Before language can be used communicatively, it has to establish what there is to communicate about.

If we perceived the world directly, this might not be so. Language might then indeed involve no more than the slapping of labels on pre-existing categories and the immediate use of those labels for communicative ends. But, as the last section showed, no creature perceives the world directly. The categories a creature can distinguish are determined not by the general nature of reality but by what that creature's nervous system is capable of representing. The capacities of that nervous system are, in part at least, determined by what the creature minimally needs in order to survive and reproduce. (They may also be influenced by what the creature's ancestors needed—but unneeded sensory powers tend to decay, witness the eyeless fish in subterranean caverns.) The categories distinguished by frogs, it would seem, do not extend very far beyond bugs they can snap at, ponds they can jump into, and other frogs they can mate with. The categories distinguished by vervets are more numerous, and those distinguished by our own species more numerous still, but the same principles apply.

Note that it is immaterial, for our purposes, how such categories are derived. They may be innate, they may be learned, or they may be acquired by the process of experience fine-tuning an innate propensity. There is good reason to believe, for instance, that some primates have an innate representation of snakes; when members of these species, raised

21

in isolation, are first confronted by a stuffed snake, or by anything that looks like a snake, they show signs of alarm or avoidance (in contrast to the high curiosity they exhibit towards certain other kinds of objects). At the opposite extreme, our representations of automobiles and airplanes are obviously learned.

Vervet categories seem to occupy an intermediate position. They cannot be wholly learned, for there are certain mistakes that young vervets seldom if ever make. They may generalize the martial-eagle call to owls or vultures, but they very seldom, if ever, use the eagle-call for snakes, or the python-call for leopards. In other words, they seem innately capable of distinguishing things that creep, things that walk, and things that fly. Experience is needed only to narrow those categories—of creeping, walking and flying things—to just those species that prey upon vervets.

Perhaps a word should be said about innateness, since many people still find the term objectionable. It may seem less so when one considers that all representations, whether innate, learned, or of mixed origins, share a common infrastructure. The medium onto which representations are mapped consists of sets of interconnected neurons, such that when enough of these respond to external phenomena, a particular behavioral response is triggered (the monkey's avoidance, the vervet's alarm call). Almost all creatures possess sensory cells that substantially vary their firing rate when particular features of the environment are presented to them; and they do so without benefit of experience. Let us suppose that in monkeys one set of cells responds to wavy lines, another set to rounded objects, a third set to the quality of light reflected from very smooth objects, a fourth to motions, and so on. It follows that most, if not all, of those sets of cells will vary their firing rates simultaneously when presented with a snake or similar object.

So far, there is nothing in the least marvellous about this. No one supposes that neurons are acquired through experience, or that we learn, in the traditional sense of learning, the difference between straight and wavy lines or between shiny and dull surfaces. The capacity to make such distinctions is simply part of our genetic inheritance, and it appears, if not actually at birth, at least early on in the development cycle (provided of course that those distinctions are observable in the environment). Nor does anyone express surprise if, as a result of particular experiences, the firing of all of the relevant sets of neurons should eventually trigger a particular response. Anyone would then be content to say that a learned response had developed.

Now it is true that learned responses cannot be transmitted to off-spring. However, if, by sheer chance, one out of countless billions of monkeys should happen to be born with a mutation that directly linked the sets of snake-responding cells to the cells that activated avoidance behavior, then that monkey would enjoy a selective advantage over its fellows. That monkey alone could be guaranteed to react appropriately to its very first encounter with a snake, while a small proportion of its un-mutated fellows in each generation might fail to survive that experience. Clearly, the genes that conveyed such an advantage would produce more offspring than those that did not. Thus, gradually, over time, the strain that lacked an automatic snake reaction would die out, leaving that reaction as a truly species-specific innate response.

On this analysis, it is hard to see what there could be to object to in the notion that there are innate concepts. Indeed, the issue would hardly need to be treated at such length were it not a fact that resistance to what are often rather oddly termed 'innate ideas' tends to grow stronger as one approaches the central citadel of language. That aspect of the innateness issue will be addressed in due course. For the present, it may be noted that, on the conceptual level at least, internal representations constitute a mosaic of innate and learned forms. If language is indeed, primarily, an additional system of representation found in a particular mammalian species, there seems no principled reason why it too should not consist of a similar mosaic.

But is language really a system of representation? If it is, then we should be able to resolve the Continuity Paradox. We could search for the ancestry of language not in prior systems of animal communication, but in prior representational systems.

But before this can be done, two things are necessary. The first is to show that language may indeed be properly termed a representational system, and to describe the properties peculiar to it. The second is to survey the development of representational systems in evolutionary terms, in order to show that at least a good proportion of the infrastructure necessary for language antedated the emergence of the hominid line. If these things can be done, we can then turn to the development of hominids and determine, first, what other properties were required to create language as we know it, and second, whether it is plausible that just those properties could have been developed by the few speciations that separate us from speechless primates.

Before we begin this quest, one point in favor of the chosen course may be noted. No attempt to derive language from animal communication could hope to tell us anything significant about the origins of consciousness. If language were no more than communication, it would be a process; consciousness is a state. But if language is a representational system, it too is a state. Moreover, if consciousness too is a way of representing to ourselves ourselves and the world around us, then it may be that the origins of the two are closely linked, and that by uncovering the one we may also uncover the other.

2

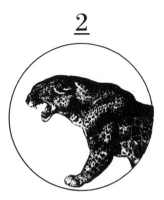

Language as Representation: The Atlas

If one is to show that the antecedents of language are representational, the first tasks should be to show that language is indeed a representational system, and to demonstrate the crucial properties of that system. It may be well to begin by clarifying just what it means to say that language is a representational system.

Two possible meanings can be distinguished from the start. Take, for example, an atlas and a handbook of itineraries. Both of these could be regarded as representations of a particular geographic area. The atlas contains a series of maps that correspond in sum to a representation of that area (although, as was noted in the previous chapter, many things that are in the area will not be in the maps, and many things that are in the maps won't be in the area). We might want to say that the atlas constitutes a fuller representation of the area than the handbook does. But this is not necessarily the case. We could in principle increase the number of itineraries in our handbook until they crisscrossed the entire area and effectively covered the same terrain as the maps.

But even if they contained identical information, the two would still represent that information in rather different ways. The atlas would contain the information in a static fashion, maintaining the proportional relations between towns, rivers, mountains, and so on that obtained in nature. But if we wanted to go from X to Y, or from Y to Z, we would have to construct the entire route for ourselves. Moreover, while the atlas might provide some of the necessary information, it would not provide us with any means to compute our itinerary. We would have to figure that out for ourselves. On the other hand, the handbook would not maintain proportional relations. Merely by looking at it, we could form no estimate of relationships between X, Y, and Z such as the distance between them or whether one lay east or west of another. Nor could we determine the general surroundings of X, Y, and Z—whether they lay on plains or in valleys, whether there were lakes or mountains nearby.

Is the kind of representation that language provides more like that of the atlas or more like that of the handbook of itineraries? The comparison of language to a map is, of course, by no means an original one, indeed it may seem rather obvious. But the ways in which language really resembles a map are not necessarily the ways in which language has been said to resemble a map. Perhaps the best known exponent of the map = language idea was Alfred Korzybski, the inventor of general semantics, who popularized the expression 'the map is not the territory'. Of course it isn't, but the ways in which the map differs from the territory are not the ways in which Korzybski thought it differed. There are at least three major problems with Korzybski's approach.

First, Korzybski seems to have believed that language mapped the world of experience directly. He certainly did not regard language as a remote or mediated mapping, a mapping of concepts that in turn derived from the processing of sensory inputs. Second, he seems to have believed, in common with many people who talk about representations, that representations can represent with an absolute verisimilitude, and that if they do not—if there are properties of the representation not shared by the thing represented, or vice versa—then this is a deficiency of the mode of representation that can and should be put right.

Korzybski failed to appreciate that *simply by virtue of being representations, representations cannot represent with absolute verisimilitude.* In other words, you cannot have a representation without its own properties, and these properties must be imposed on what is represented. It follows from this that it is a waste of time to try to tidy up language, to make it more logical and more realistic, as Korzybski and his followers did. Language is what it is. Since it is an adaptation specific to our species, we are not going to be able to replace it by anything different, and we would be better off simply trying to understand it, rather than trying to change it.

The third problem with Korzybski's approach is that language is not a map only. The answer to the question asked above—whether language most resembles an atlas or a book of itineraries—is that it resembles both. Although neither is or possibly could be an exact analogy (for every system of representation has properties unique to itself), there are aspects of linguistic representation that are weakly analogous to those of maps and other aspects that are weakly analogous to those of handbooks of itineraries. In this chapter we will consider the maplike representation.

MAPPING REALITY

In the previous chapter it was suggested that our knowledge of the world, or, for that matter, any creature's awareness of its environment, was derived by a series of mapping operations. The first of these, the level that we share with other creatures, is from objects in the real world, via the organs of sense, to specialized networks of cells and their connections in the brain. But can we say that these networks directly constitute a level of concepts that is then mapped onto language?

Put another way, the question is: Do creatures other than ourselves form concepts? This is not a straightforward question unless we suppose that 'a concept is a concept is a concept' for all species that have concepts. Consider again the vervet monkey and its alarm calls, specifically the one for 'leopard'. To use this call effectively, vervets must be able to distinguish (in a large majority of cases) leopards from nonleopards. Moreover, given that they might perceive leopards from a variety of angles, with a variety of degrees of occlusion (due to intervening grass, bushes, tree branches, and so on), it cannot be the case that only some single stereotyped presentation of a leopard triggers the leopard call.

But we cannot conclude from this that vervets have a concept of 'leopard' in the same way that we have. We noted that the call is given only in response to a leopard's actual appearance, whereas we can think and speak about leopards in their absence. Can vervets think about leopards (dread them, wonder how best to cope with them, and so on)? Or, to ask a perhaps slightly more answerable question, are all the possible manifestations of leopards individually linked to the alarm-giving areas of the brain, as in figure 2.1*a*, without being in any way linked to one another? Or are they linked to one another, as in figure 2.1*b*, so that any manifestation of leopards triggers the whole conjunction, which in turn triggers the alarm?

If we were talking about frogs or humans, there would be no difficulty in answering this last question—negatively for frogs, postively for humans. Frogs react quickly and effectively to bugs that fly past them, but this by no means implies that they have a concept of 'bug'. Indeed, we can be pretty sure that they do not, or at best that their concept of 'bug' both under- and overgeneralizes to a rather gross extent. For instance,

27

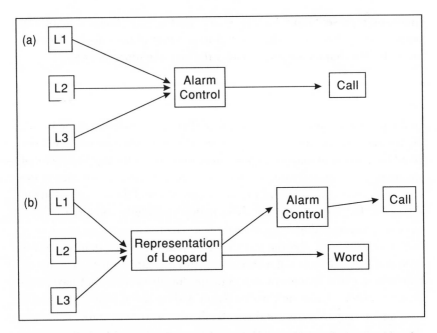

FIG. 2.1. Possible systems for categorization of sense perceptions by vervets (a) and humans (b). L1, L2, and L3 stand for different perceptions of leopards.

they will overgeneralize by snapping at bug-sized pellets that are flipped past them, but will undergeneralize by totally ignoring motionless bugs even when no other food source is available. The most parsimonious explanation of their behavior is that networks of cells that respond to rapid movement and small rounded objects are directly linked to the snapping reflex, and that there is nothing more sophisticated than this inside the frog's brain.

In our own case there is a very different story. Suppose that we are alone in a house late at night and hear a sound that we do not immediately identify. Unless we are in an abnormally anxious state we will not immediately respond to it. Rather we will listen intently, and try to identify the sound if it is repeated. In human terms, this means that we will *try to provide a linguistic description* for the sound. Only when we have done this (called it a *creaking shutter, cat trying to get out, possible burglar*, or whatever) will we take the appropriate action.

There can be little doubt that the case of the vervet is intermediate between those of the frog and our own species. At some stage in the evolution of species, some kind of linkage began to form among those perceptions that had evolutionary consequences (life-threatening or life-enhancing) for the creature that received them, given that the perceptions caused the creature to behave in similar ways. For instance, a leopard's spots, a leopard's roar, and a leopard's smell might originally have caused reactions in quite different parts of the brain, but the fact that all provoked a similar result (flight) may have helped to create a level of processing on which all three were neurally linked. For reasons that will become apparent later, saying this is better than saying that linkages developed among perceptions of the same object or class of objects. The result was the formation of categories; rapid and accurate identification of category-membership became a crucial factor in the survival of individuals.

In the case of mature members of our own species, it is pretty clear that we react to our perceptions of particular objects and events (a noise in the night, an object on Aunt Lucy's dressing table, an unexpected reaction by a neighbor to some innocent question) by trying to map them onto some pre-existing concept that has a linguistic representation (*a burglar, a scentspray, paranoia*). In other words, our moment-to-moment functioning in the world relies, unconsciously but quite implicitly and completely, on our having the equivalent of a map of reality which includes all the things that, at least for us as a species, are in it. This map enables us to orient ourselves rapidly to the fluctuations of the environment and to prepare appropriate responses to them.

But let's stop here and consider for a moment what kinds of things are in the map, what kinds of things are in reality, and what kinds of relationships exist between them.

'CONVENTIONS' OF THE MAP

In an ordinary map, we seem to find a direct symbolic relationship between objects in the mapped terrain and objects in the map itself. A church, for instance, may be represented by a cross, a railroad by a crosshatched black line, and a pond or lake by a blue blob. Note however that much variety in the terrain is erased in this process. A real church may be Catholic, Episcopalian, or Pentecostal, it may or may not have a tower or a spire, it may vary within wide limits with respect to its size, building materials, and style, but regardless of all this it will be represented by a cross, if it is represented at all.

But even on a map, representation may be much more indirect than this. Take a map that shows rainfall for a given area and indicates that the average annual rainfall at a particular point is exactly twenty-five inches. Now, there may never have been and there may never be a year in which the rainfall at that point measures exactly twenty-five inches. Similarly, the map may indicate that the population of a given county falls between thirty and forty persons per square mile, although if that county contains a few towns in the middle of a wilderness, every actual square mile may contain either more or fewer persons than the map suggests. What the map shows in these cases is not so much a representation of reality as an abstraction from it. It does not show what there is in an area (the cross/church relationship) but what relationships hold between one area and others—how some areas are wetter or drier, or more or less populous than their neighbors.

The relationships in such maps are conventional; they were arbitrarily and quite consciously and deliberately chosen by cartographers. This is, of course, no longer the case when we turn to species-specific mapping of reality. Here, the picture is also more complex, because, as already noted, at least three distinguishable mapping processes are going on: from reality to sensory perception, from sensory perception to categorization, and from categorization to language. The network of relationships that these processes entail can perhaps be made clearer if we consider four categories, already mentioned in this book, that are represented respectively by the words *leopard, burglar, paranoia,* and *unicorn.* These categories, in the order given, represent points which have an increasingly tenuous linkage with anything one might call 'the real world'.

Since we shall be obliged to keep switching among at least three levels (the level of what may be objects in the real world, the level of concepts, and the level of words), the discussion that follows will be confusing unless the three are systematically distinguished in some way. For convenience, then, objects that are normally regarded as being (and may actually be) in the real world will appear in an orthographically neutral manner (leopard); concepts (as well as 'categories', 'prototypes', and similar terms) will appear in quotes ('leopard'); and words will appear in italics (*leopard*).

You might want to say that *leopard* corresponds to a concrete reality. Even if this is so, the route by which the correspondence is established is not necessarily more direct than it is in more abstract cases. You might want to say that various perceptions of a leopard—characteristic smells, sounds, and visual presentations—were somehow fused into a conceptual category, and that this category was then labeled *leopard.* Now, pretty well any vervet has perceived a leopard, but how many of us have? Some of us may have first encountered *leopard* in a story or a school textbook without having any very clear idea of what it was. Indeed, the fact that we can say things like *What's a leopard?* shows that to use words in a meaningful way we don't need to have the faintest idea what they represent.

Suppose someone should answer such a question by saying, *It's an animal that eats other animals, it lives in Africa, it's related to the cat but much bigger, and it has spots,* and that only later on could we be shown an actual picture of a particular leopard. Then what might look like the 'natural order' of things is completely reversed. Instead of proceeding from object to perception, from perception to concept, and from concept to word, we have proceeded from word to concept (we may, after hearing the definition of *leopard,* have only the vaguest idea of what one might look like, but we would have a pretty good *idea* of one), and perhaps later, while reading an illustrated magazine, for instance, we might proceed from concept to perception. The final stage of the progress, from perception to object, need never happen. We may never actually see a real (or even a stuffed) leopard.

Of course this can only happen nowadays. Phylogenetically speaking, things surely followed a different course. In our speechless ancestors, phenomena of certain kinds gave rise to perceptions of those phenomena. Then, either clusters of perceptions were joined to set the parameters of a concept, which was subsequently labeled, or the emergence of language itself was what linked related perceptions together.

But the way in which things came into existence does not exhaustively determine either their nature nor their future relationships. All kinds and levels of representation acquire, simply through having come into existence, some degree of autonomy. They are things in their own right, as well as representations of something else—the picture of the Battle of Lepanto is a picture on a wall, not a battle. The autonomy of representational levels is at least as great in the brains of animate creatures, since the neural infrastructure that supports those levels is a biological mechanism that, unlike a painting, can grow and change.

The scope of this autonomy becomes apparent as we proceed to our other three concepts, 'burglar', 'paranoia', and 'unicorn'. No matter how indirect the representation, a clear linking relationship exists among leopard, 'leopard', and *leopard.* Much the same, you might say, is true of burglar, 'burglar', and *burglar.* But there are some very important differences.

As we saw, even things like leopards can be identified on the basis of secondhand information. But leopards can also be identified by the ways in which instances of them present themselves directly to our senses.

31

The same is not true of burglars. While a cartoonist may represent 'burglar' by a drawing of a burly yet furtive individual in a cap, black eyemask, and striped pullover with a bulging sack over one shoulder, and while we may recognize this stereotyped representation, none of us really believes that each, or even any, burglar necessarily looks like this.

Moreover, while identification of x as a leopard implies that x is, was, and always will be a leopard, identification of x as a burglar does not necessarily convey any comparable implication. A *burglar* is simply someone who has burgled, yet it is not just anyone who has burgled. Imagine an individual, respectable nowadays, who in his youth had committed one minor burglary for which he had never been convicted. Given our laws of libel, you would be unwise to refer to him as *that burglar, X*. Moreover, *burglar* can be qualified in ways that *leopard* cannot. You can have a *reformed burglar* or a *would-be burglar*, but not a *reformed leopard* or a *would-be leopard*. In other words, what lies at the heart of 'burglar' is not a bundle of sensory perceptions, but a particular behavior.

Is this not equally true of 'leopard'? So far it has been assumed that concepts arise from the linking of related perceptions, that are all, in some still rather vague sense, 'perceptions of the same thing'. Now this appears too simple, too unidimensional. Many concepts, perhaps all, are principally determined by function and by the evolutionary relationship that exists between us and their referents. Our concept of 'leopard' is a unified one, in part at least because we identify its referent as a competitor and a potentially dangerous predator. If there were an animal that looked and behaved exactly like a leopard except that it ate grass instead of flesh, we might call it a *false leopard* or *herbivorous leopard*, but we certainly would not call it simply a *leopard*.

However, there are still some differences between 'leopard' and 'burglar'. As noted above, there are *no* perceptual correlates of 'burglar'. Even if we saw someone break into a house and remove objects therefrom, we could not assume that that person was a burglar—he could be the owner who had mislaid his keys. Thus 'burglar' depends on a number of quite abstract concepts, such as 'ownership' and 'property', that derive uniquely from within human culture.

This means that while there may be things that are leopards quite independently of us, there are no things that are burglars except as we define them. There may be burglar, 'burglar', and *burglar*, but burglar is defined by 'burglar' and/or *burglar*, rather than vice versa—in contrast to 'leopard' and *leopard*, which can be defined in terms of leopard.

'Paranoia' takes this process a stage further. In the case of *burglar*, there are at least criteria, objective even if man-made, that allow us to determine whether the term applies. In the case of *paranoia*, this is not so. There are many, even among mental health professionals, who deny the reality of mental illness, or who regard it as a matter of arbitrary definition. Any two police officers, any two judges, any two members of the public even, would almost certainly agree as to whether *burglar* was an appropriate description of a given individual in a given situation, assuming that all the relevant facts were available to them. However, it is at least questionable whether any two lay persons, or even any two professionals, would agree whether a particular piece of behavior was indicative of paranoia or not. *Paranoia*, to the lay person at least, usually is taken as meaning 'an irrational fear of persecution'. But, in contrast to the case of *burglar*, there is no generally accepted or clearly articulated measure of what counts as 'irrationality'. It's a lot easier to define 'property' or 'enclosed premises' than it is to define 'reason'.

Thus there may be *paranoia*, and 'paranoia', but no paranoia. And yet, at least where the term is used in good faith, there should be *some* correlated phenomena, some abnormal behavior pattern that might seem to justify its use. In the case of *unicorn*, this is not so. There are 'unicorns' and *unicorns*, but absolutely no unicorns. *Unicorn* corresponds with no sensory input (except from our own artefacts) and has no functional justification. Even *paranoia* has a functional justification: just as the concept 'leopard' helps us to behave in particular ways towards leopards, and just as the concept 'burglar' helps us to behave in particular ways towards people who steal from enclosed premises, so the concept of 'paranoia' helps us to behave in particular ways towards individuals who express what we choose to regard as irrational fears. In the case of *unicorn*, there is not even this type of justification.

What all this shows us may be summarized as follows. The representational levels of words and concepts can be even more abstract and remote from sensory input than those of rainfall and population maps, even to the extent of creating, out of their own resources, words and concepts that have no correlates in perceptual terms or even in established cultural conventions. But if this is so, we may well wonder what it is that gives words and concepts the particular ranges of meaning that they have.

This is a question that has vexed philosophers and psychologists, even more than it has linguists, for a very long time. A traditional view is that each word represents a category and that for each category we have sets of criteria that must be met before membership can be assigned. Take *tree* and *bush*, for example: for something to be a tree it would have to have properties *a*, *b*, and *c*, whereas for it to be a bush, it would have to have properties *x*, *y*, and *z*. This does not work out too well in practice.

Size can't be involved, for a bonsai tree is smaller than any bush, nor can branchiness, for there are single-stemmed bushes and multiply-branching trees.

More recently it has been suggested that words represent prototypes rather than categories. A prototype is the most typical representative of its class. For instance, most people would agree that a thrush or a robin is more typical of the class 'bird' then, say, a penguin or an ostrich. The prototype then becomes a starting point and we determine what class something belongs to (and thus which word to apply to it) by deciding whether it is more similar to that prototype than it is to any other prototype.

This approach might seem promising, at least with respect to terms like *bush* and *tree*. It accounts, too, for the frequent fuzziness that we encounter at the borders of categories. There are vegetable objects, for instance, that we might be unsure whether to describe as *bushes* or *trees*. Prototype theory is deficient, however, in at least two ways.

First, it offers no principled account of why we have the prototypes that we do, and not others, or why we have a certain number of prototypes, and not more or fewer. For instance, why don't we divide largish vegetable objects into 'decs' (deciduous) and 'cons' (coniferous), rather than 'bushes' and 'trees'? Why do we have two terms, when we could have one, say *trush*, that would embrace both bushes and trees? Or why not a third term, *bree*, intermediate between *bush* and *tree?* For the fuzziness of the line between 'bush' and 'tree' results from the fact that there is no division between bushes and trees in nature. There is simply a continuum of vegetable forms, some larger, some smaller, some more or less branchy, upon which we superimpose the grid of our own classification. Why is that grid the way it is, and not otherwise?

The second deficiency of prototype theory relates to the limited nature of the domain it covers. It may seem helpful with regard to 'bushes' and 'trees', but when we turn to the four concepts examined above, it is less than helpful. Why would we need a prototype 'leopard', for instance? All leopards look and behave in a similar way. We are never, if we know anything at all about major predators, at a loss to determine whether something is a leopard, a tiger, or a lion.

With 'burglar' the prototype concept is superfluous in a similar way, even though membership of the class is assigned on a quite different basis: there is just one set of criteria, and one only, that has to be met for someone to be a burglar. The concept is also inappropriate, for since the criteria for being a burglar are notional rather than perceptual, it is hard

34

to see how the concept of 'prototype' makes any sense. With 'paranoia', again, there can hardly be a prototype in nature, since the class is a class by definition. In addition, the membership of that class may be at least partly controlled (unlike 'burglar') by idiosyncratic presuppositions on the part of the assigner. One man's paranoia is another man's rational suspicion.

A different approach will perhaps provide a coherent account of 'leopard', 'burglar', and 'paranoia' (as well as of 'bush' and 'tree'). This is based on the idea that words and concepts contain a dynamic element. They are not merely static symbols on a rigid, maplike sheet. They exist bcause they delimit classes each of which conditions a somewhat different set of behaviors on the part of our own species. 'Leopard' is a concept not because it represents a genetic species or a set of static attributes, but because the concept serves to trigger a set of expectations and hence potential behaviors.

For instance, if we have a concept of 'leopard' we will be prepared to meet one in a wooded place where there would be relatively little chance of meeting a lion. We will have a clear idea of its relative size and ferocity compared to other types of predator, the likelihood of its being alone, and other factors. These help to determine whether our response, should a leopard appear, will be cautious withdrawal, headlong flight, or vigorous self-defense.

In just the same way, the assignment of terms like *burglar* and *paranoia* helps to determine our response to certain phenomena in the real world. If we determine that the noise in the night is caused by a burglar, we will seek to arm ourselves and/or call the police. If the police agree that we have assigned the term correctly, they will arrest someone, and if a judge and jury decide that the police have assigned it correctly, that person will possibly go to jail. If we regard certain phenomena as constituting paranoia we will avoid the person concerned, unless that person is a friend or relative, in which case we may encourage him or her to see a psychiatrist. If the psychiatrist agrees with us that paranoia is present, then he or she may commence a course of therapy, or, if the case is severe, counsel hospitalization.

Examples such as these do indeed suggest that words and concepts are largely derived on a basis of *functional utility.* In other words, we distinguish only what we (as a species, or as a cultural group sharing common values) need to interact with in significant ways. In fact this is just what an evolutionary model of language would predict. In many creatures, objects that the senses are capable of detecting are limited to those with which the creature may interact significantly (recall the frog and its 'bug-detecting' vision). We, with our far vaster reservoir of sense impressions, still select out of these what will significantly affect our own behavior.

But this cannot be the whole story. Consider again *bush* and *tree*. One can indeed elaborate a plausible explanation: *bush* represents things humans can hide behind, or among, whether for stalking or predator-avoidance, while *tree* represents things humans can climb (to see further, to evade predators, or to steal wild honey or bird's eggs). This explains why there is no term *trush* covering both trees and bushes (the two involve quite different sets of human behaviors) and no intermediate term *bree* (there is no corresponding behavior pattern that something intermediate between a tree and a bush would evoke). But what about bonsai trees and year-old saplings, both quite unclimbable? Why don't we call these *bushes?*

There is a further factor in the mapping of reality that we might call the conservation-of-type principle. Things are distinguished with an eye to their utility, true, but also with an eye to their consistent identification. Both needs must be satisfied. A map in which objects identical in type are denoted sometimes by one symbol and sometimes by another is clearly undesirable. A sapling *will be* a tree if it grows long enough, and a bonsai tree *would have been* a normal tree if its growth pattern had not been deliberately interfered with.

And yet nothing so far proposed explains why there are words like *unicorn*. It may well be that 'you can't get there from here', and that to explain why there should be *unicorns* and 'unicorns' but no unicorns, it is necessary to start from a completely different direction.

COMPLETENESS AND AUTONOMY

Most efforts to explain the mysteries of meaning have begun by looking at the meanings of individual words. We tend to regard the lexicon of a language as a list of items, and indeed this is how dictionaries traditionally present it. In a thesaurus, true, words are grouped according to meaning, but they are still atomic entities, sharply demarcated from their neighbors.

Neither thesaurus nor dictionary conveys any suggestion that, perhaps, the range of meaning of a word can be defined only through the ranges of meaning of its neighbors. Yet for some time in the backwaters of linguistics there has been floating around the idea that there exists something called *semantic space*, an area of meaning that the lexicon simply carves into convenient chunks, according to principles yet to be fully understood. To some, these principles are quite arbitrary; to others, they directly reflect the perceptual equipment of our species. If we translate 'arbitrary' as 'following only the logic of the map', then perhaps both viewpoints are partly right.

If semantic space exists it should, as a minimum, represent all of real space, or at least as much of real space as our organs of sense make available. But how can a creature who is working on a plane at least two levels of representation away from reality know what real space contains? Philosophers sometimes write as if we somehow had privileged access to reality, as if we could peek at the back of the book in the way that one looks up translations of sentences in a home-study foreign language course. But there is, of course, no privileged access.

The only way we can know the world is through levels of representation, and if we seek to analyze the flow of information that our sensory representations offer us, if we seek to abstract from that flow the consistencies that might give it pattern, we depend wholly upon a further level of representation, our system of concepts. With the best will in the world we can only represent what we believe to be out there, and what we believe to be out there shades imperceptibly into what we want to be out there, or what would be convenient for us if it were out there. Suspecting from the start that our senses could not tell us the whole story of reality, we were not necessarily worried if our best guesses at what was out there were not immediately confirmed by those senses—if we did not see or hear *ghosts, souls, angels,* or *neutrinos,* or if a principle of heat, *phlogiston,* or a principle of attraction, *gravity,* should be apparent solely through its presumed effects, or if things apparently made of wood or stone or steel should in fact consist entirely of *atoms.*

In this list (*ghost, soul, angel, neutrino, phlogiston, gravity,* and *atom*) there should be for every person at least one thing that person believes in and one thing he or she totally disbelieves in. (Not everyone will agree as to which they are, of course.) The aim is to undermine the reader's faith in the level of words or concepts as being in any way a mirror image of reality. For all of these things were at one time of equal status: they were hypotheses about the nature of the outside world. Some seem to have been discredited, others seem to have been confirmed, some have not yet been confirmed and may never be confirmed or even confirmable, but when these terms first emerged they all represented exactly the same thing: educated guesses at what the world might contain, guesses that were not directly verifiable in terms of sensory data.

The *unicorn* represented just such a guess. The fact that most horned creatures had two horns did not logically entail that there should be no one-horned creature. There was, after all, the swordfish, and indeed a one-horned mammal, the rhinoceros, was rediscovered by Western Europe some time after the appearance of 'unicorn'. But by then even a perceptual object corresponding to 'unicorn'—a horselike creature with a spear like a narwhal's on its forehead—had become established, and a fullblown concept complete with behavioral attributes (extreme docility in the presence of virgins, for example) had crystallized around it. For levels of representation are indeed autonomous, and the units that compose them have a life of their own.

We are on pretty safe ground, though, if we assume that *leopard* preceded *unicorn* in the evolution of the lexicon. It seems only reasonable to suppose that the lexicon evolved over time, perhaps over a great deal of time, and that it began by abstracting those categories that were most immediately useful to our species. Subsequently it spread to cover the entire range of phenomena accessible to our senses, and beyond, since language is (among other things) a tool with which we rake through the debris of sense impressions in search of general principles or laws that will serve to guide our behavior. It is a characteristic of language that it enables us to describe anything in our experience. Even when a mystic talks of, say, 'experiences impossible to describe in words', the speaker has in fact just described such experiences in words (whether we regard such a description as adequate is another matter). But long before the lexicon could describe everything, it had developed in another direction that has yet to be discussed.

THE DYNAMIC ELEMENT

So far we have dealt only with those units that relate to entities. A system composed of such units might be adequate to represent the world, if the world were a museum and everything in it stuffed. In a living world, the behaviors of entities must also be represented. We may well want to ask why they are represented in the way that they are and not otherwise.

Take simple sentences like *A cow is grazing* or *A bird is flying*. If we look at the events these sentences convey, what we actually see in each case constitutes a single image, a-creature-and-its-behavior. It is possible to imagine a language in which things were arranged quite differently. In human sign language, for instance, it would be possible to make the handshape that corresponds to *bird* and simultaneously extend the same hand in an undulant motion to indicate *flying*. In fact (and the fact is significant) at least the American version of sign language does not avail itself of this opportunity. The handshape that indicates *bird* is followed sequentially by the handshape that indicates *flying*. In other words sign language, like spoken language, simply follows the patterns of the human faculty that, as will be shown, underlies all language, whether signed or spoken.

The subject-predicate distinction in language is so fundamental, and so much taken for granted, that it is perhaps worth emphasizing that it corresponds to nothing in nature. There is no sense in which we can perceive a creature without simultaneously perceiving that it is doing something—sleeping, grazing, walking, flying—and no way in which we can see a behavior like grazing, flying, sleeping, or walking without simultaneously seeing the creature that performs it. Constant behaviors of some sort are part and parcel of being a creature, and if language merely mirrored reality it would mirror this also. Why doesn't it?

You might want to answer that some principle of economy operates here. If one had to have separate words for cow-grazing, horse-grazing, sheep-grazing, deer-grazing . . . , and then for cow-running, horse-running, sheep-running, deer-running . . . , and so on, for every behavior of every creature, the lexicon would be very much larger than it is. But principles of economy are often only a luxury of hindsight. Whoever started the lexicon can hardly have envisaged running out of memory storage, and indeed it remains to be proven that humans could not learn the extra tens or hundreds of thousands of words that unitary terms for subject-predicate conjunctions would entail.

It seems likelier that language evolved the way it did because concepts of entities—and in particular, of other species—preceded concepts of behaviors. Some evidence relevant to this will be considered in later chapters. For the present we may note that behaviors are more abstract things than entities. We saw earlier that words purporting to denote entities covered a wide range extending from those that had a fairly solid foundation in experience to those that had absolutely no foundation in experience at all. But all behaviors involve some degree of abstraction, if only because they can be predicated not of just one kind of creature, but of any kind to which they can be attributed.

For instance, the things that birds, bats, butterflies, kites, airplanes, balloons, and flying squirrels do in the air are very different, but all of them are described as *flying*. A single feature, 'moving through the air', is abstracted away from countless variables ('with two/four/no wings', 'high/low', 'in a straight line/zigzagging', 'quickly/slowly', and so on).

You might think that this degree of abstraction merely mirrors our relative indifference to the way things fly (something we can't do naturally ourselves) as compared with, for instance, the way things walk. For a person can be said to *stride, lope, trot, amble, stumble, stagger, waddle, saunter, stroll, stalk, reel, shamble, shuffle, slouch, limp, hobble, tramp, trudge* or *strut*. But all this means is that the map is more detailed in some regions than in others, not that it is any less abstract.

For instance, *trot* may be predicated of people and horses, *waddle* of people and ducks, but people do not really move like ducks or like horses. In each case, only one or two features of duck or horse movements that happen to correspond in some sense to features of human movements have been abstracted from what are quite complex, and quite different, movement patterns. Or, in another type of case, the difference between *tramp* and *trudge* lies less in the physical movements that distinguish these kinds of walking than in the suggestion that more effort and/or less willingness is involved in *trudging*. In other words, the sense of such items is what we can infer from prior knowledge or subliminal clues about the walker's state of mind—an extremely abstract procedure.

A different kind of abstractness attends words like *bring*. In English we can say *they bring Mary presents* but in some other languages you have to say things like *they carry presents go give Mary*. Would you want to argue that *bring* was 'really' a single action that the other languages split up, or would you rather say that an action of bringing 'really' incorporates three distinct actions?

This issue has in fact been argued both ways, although it should be obvious that neither way is more or less natural than the other, since the semantic domain of any verb is relatively arbitrary. Take what might appear to be an uncontroversial single-action verb like *hit*, for example. In order to hit someone, it is necessary to clench one's fist, withdraw one's arm, and then extend that arm with some degree of rapidity and force so that the clenched fist meets its target. In other words, the 'simplest' action can be broken down into its set of component actions.

However, the word *arbitrary* was qualified by *relatively* because once again the criterion of functional utility will play its part. One could, in describing a fight, say that *Bill clenched his fist, withdrew his arm, and then extended it violently and forcefully so that the clenched fist connected with John,* and if we were holding up a mirror to nature that might be what we would see and thus perhaps what we should say. However, no significant meaning is lost, and much time is saved, if we simply say *Bill hit John.* Verbs represent those chunks of behavior (selected out of a much wider range of possible chunks) that are functionally significant for our species (or, at a later stage, for our culture), just as nouns represent those entities that have an evolutionary or cultural significance for us, selected again from a wider range of possible entities.

But behaviors (including states, and even states of mind) are not the only things that can be predicated of entities. There are also attributes— particular properties of size, color, temperature, age, and so on—that we may attribute to particular entities, and that serve the purpose, among others, of distinguishing two similar objects from one another (*the GREEN book, not the RED one*).

Colors constitute an interesting case, for the mapping relation between reality and language can be spelled out here in rather more detail than elsewhere. Brent Berlin and Paul Kay have shown that basic color terms (that is, color terms that do not derive from specific objects, like *orange*, and are not compounds, such as *dark green* or *navy blue*) are acquired by languages in a fixed order. If a language has only two basic color terms, these will mean roughly 'dark' and 'light'; if it has three, they will mean 'dark', 'light', and 'red'; if it has four, 'yellow' or 'green' will be added to these three, and so on.

These stages reflect the system of color discrimination common to all primates. Roughly, four paired sets of neurons respond to light of different wavelengths, the pair that responds to light/dark distinctions being phylogenetically the oldest. The pair that responds to red/green (one set firing with maximal frequency to the wavelength that gives subjective red and minimally to that which gives subjective green, the opponent set reversing these firing rates) is perhaps the second oldest, and so on. In other words, the distinctions that have been longest within the power of our remote ancestors to make are the most likely to be represented in language, while more recent ones are progressively less likely, and those that depend on cultural rather than biological factors (the *browns, pinks*, and so on) are rarer still.

The mix of liberties and constraints that this area shows is perhaps typical of the way in which the lexicon as a whole represents reality. Nothing in our neurological makeup determines absolutely how we shall divide up the spectrum. Anything from two to eleven basic colors may be represented, and, contrary to what is sometimes suggested by critics of this work, no one is claiming a necessary connection between levels of technological development and the number of colors represented. However, languages are not free to simply select what colors they will represent by basic terms. They can, of course, select any type of color-description for particular objects, but for general terms, applicable across the full range of lexical items, they are forced to decide among a set of alternatives that are, in part at least, neurologically determined.

In another respect, however, color terms are far from typical of attributes in general. Although they may derive from opponent pairs of cells, we do not feel any kind of binary opposition between *red* and

41

green, for instance, or between *blue* and *yellow.* These represent distinctions within a continuous spectrum. Other attributes, however, come in pairs (*hot* and *cold, young* and *old, rich* and *poor, long* and *short, wet* and *dry*) and yet, unlike color terms, they seem to lack any specific neural substrate. For instance, it would be bizarre indeed if we found that we had cells that fired with maximal frequency when confronted by rich people and with minimal frequency when confronted by poor ones.

Why are adjectives paired in this way? For most adjectives such pairs represent a continuum (those that do not, such as *married* or *single,* can be ignored for present purposes). It is not immediately obvious why a continuum cannot be represented by a continuum. In other species it often is. For instance, a robin indicates its willingness to defend its territory by the intensity of its song, a bee indicates the quality or quantity of a honey find by the vigor with which it dances, and so on. You might think that some language somewhere might have represented temperature, for example, by a continuous vowel sound, short for very low temperatures, gradually lengthening for higher ones. Such a process might seem at first sight to be much more informative than one of simply saying whether something is *cold* or *hot.* Yet no known language has ever chosen this process, and probably none ever will.

For the function of adjectives is not to place the attributes of creatures on any kind of absolute scale. To do so would be impossible, in view of the many and often very different entities to which a given attribute may be attached; for attributes, like behaviors, are not normally limited to single species, but are assigned across the board. This effectively makes the sense of adjectives dependent on the nouns they qualify. A small elephant is bigger than a big donkey, a long letter is shorter than a short novel, a cool oven is hotter than a hot summer's day. Attributes are predicated of things in order to place them relative to the norm for their class: *a small elephant* means something that is small for an elephant, rather than an elephant that is small, and so on.

The fact that for many adjectival pairs there may be intermediate terms (*middle-aged,* for instance, between *young* and *old*) or even pairs of such terms (*cool* and *warm,* between *hot* and *cold*) does not really affect the argument. These terms, too, merely divide a continuum into slightly smaller chunks, allowing for a closer approximation to the class norm, rather than representing that continuum iconically.

Thus the level of representation given by the lexicon abstracts away from and interprets (sometimes over-interprets) the flux of experience. By doing this, it derives a wide range of entities, together with the behaviors and attributes that can be predicated of these entities. This range of entities, behaviors, and attributes forms an inventory of all that appears to us to be in the world. But there are still important properties of the inventory that have not been discussed, and to these we now turn.

THE HIERARCHICAL ELEMENT

To say merely that the lexicon provides us with an inventory is still to suggest that, like a set of dictionary entries, its contents are unstructured. Such a lexicon is possible to imagine. Suppose you spoke a language such that, when someone asked you what the word *spaniel* meant, you could point at an actual spaniel, but if there were no spaniel in sight, you would be at a loss to define it. This is what would happen if the lexicon were merely a single-level mapping from reality onto words. Then the domain of each word would be defined only 'horizontally', by the bounds of its neighbors, much as the domains of different governments are represented on a political map of the world, and when asked what a spaniel was, we would have no recourse other than to say something like, *well, it's rather like a setter* or *not too far from a dachshund, only shorter and higher off the ground.*

In fact, we are able to say that *a spaniel is a kind of dog used in hunting*, and if our interlocutor (from another planet, perhaps) were to ask us what a dog was, we could reply *a smallish kind of mammal*, and if we were then asked what a mammal was, we could reply *an animate creature that suckles its young.* We are able to do this by virtue of the fact that the lexicon is hierarchically structured, that is, marked by levels of ascending generality, like *spaniel-dog-mammal*, with each term in it being superordinate to some terms and/or subordinate to others, along the lines illustrated in figure 2.2.

Note that this hierarchical structuring extends throughout the lexicon. Take any word, say *anger; anger* includes a range of other words like *fury, annoyance, rage, irritation*, and so on, but at the same time is itself a member of a set that includes *love, envy, gratitude*, and *disappointment*, all of which in turn fall under *emotion.* What this means is that any word in any language is not merely intertranslatable—that is to say, capable of being converted into a string of other words in the same language—but falls into its place in an intricately patterned structure of words that forms, as it were, a universal filing system allowing for rapid retrieval and comprehension of any concept.

There can be little doubt that this enormously efficient filing system, organizing as it does our entire knowledge of the world, forms one of the major factors in our success as a species. Yet it seems unlikely that this

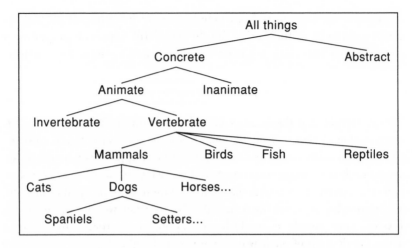

FIG. 2.2. Hierarchical structure of lexical items

system was automatically achieved simply by the emergence of language. As noted above, an entire lexicon did not emerge overnight. Moreover, there is considerable structural, cross-linguistic, and historical evidence that even in languages that exist today, what are claimed to be the oldest nouns among those referring to other life-forms, do so at the approximate level of the species (that is, words like *dog* were used earlier than words like *spaniel* or *mammal*).

This, again, is pretty much what we would expect, if meaning was originally based on functional interaction with other creatures. Lexicalization at the level of the phylum or order would have been too indeterminate, lumping together creatures that triggered different behavioral responses. On the other hand, lexicalization at the level of the subspecies or variety would have been overly repetitive, assigning different labels to creatures that all had to be dealt with by using a similar set of behaviors.

CONTIGUITY CONSTRAINTS

A further constraint on what can be lexically represented is one that involves spatiotemporal contiguity. It has often been noted that no language has words with meanings like 'a left leg and left arm' or 'every other Friday'. No language has a word that embraces the meanings 'red' and 'green', unless it includes the meaning 'yellow', for only contiguous sectors of the spectrum can be lexicalized. In other words, a minimal condition for word status is that the referent consist of an uninterrupted piece of matter or time or space. But contiguity constraints can be much subtler than this.

Consider figure 2.3, the four areas of which can be lexicalized in a variety of ways. Some languages use a single verb to express the concepts of 'existence', 'location', 'possession', and 'ownership'. Some use a separate verb for each concept. Some, like English, use one verb for 'existence', 'location', and 'ownership' (*there IS a book, your book IS over there, that book IS mine*) and another for 'possession' (*I HAVE a book*), and there are other possible patterns. So far, however, no language has turned up that uses the same verb for 'location' and 'possession' but a different verb (or verbs) for 'existence' and 'ownership', or that has the same verb for 'existence' and 'ownership' but a different verb (or verbs) for 'location' and 'possession'.

In other words, contiguity constraints seem to exist even within domains that are highly abstract. This lends support to the idea that semantic space may be real, may be represented in actual configurations of cells and connections in the brain. It has been known for some time that the brain contains a literal mapping of the motor and sensory areas of the

FIG. 2.3. Semantic space for four relations. Boxes indicate domains of individual words. Configurations of the lowest level are illicit.

body. The groups of neurons that receive and send messages to and from the various bodily organs are localized in the brain in a manner that largely replicates (although with considerable distortions of size) the spatial distribution of those organs within the human body, as shown in diagrams of the 'sensory homunculus' and 'motor homunculus' found in most introductory neurological textbooks. It is conceivable that some comparable form of organization may exist in the neural representation of concepts, but what such an organization might be like, and what principles might control it, are topics for the research programs of the future.

Thus language, at least as far as its component words are concerned, is indeed a system of representation in the true sense of that term. It is not a system that passively mirrors what it represents, but rather one that creates a new and parallel world constrained by the laws of its own nature just as much as by the nature of the phenomena that it represents. Within that world, meaning is largely determined by evolutionary (or cultural) significance, by type consistency, and by contiguity effects.

Correspondence with any kind of counterpart in the real world is not obligatory because language does not exist in order to give a rationalistic, textbook account of the real world. Language is an evolutionary adaptation of a particular species, and as such functions for the benefit of that species. If it seems convenient to members of that species that there should be witches or that human physiology and psychology should be based on four humors, then there will be *witches* and *humors* (as well of course as 'witches' and 'humors'). Otherwise, the world will be divided up in different ways. If language did not perform such tasks, we would quite literally have nothing to talk about.

Yet even now we have looked at only one side of linguistic representation. The other remains as a topic for the chapter that follows.

3

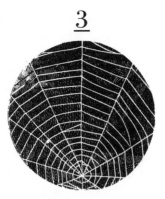

Language as Representation: The Itineraries

At the beginning of chapter 2 it was pointed out that if language is a system of representation, it functions as such a system in at least two ways, ways comparable to those of a map and a handbook of itineraries. For representation of meaning is not limited to the individual words that compose the lexicon, but is expressed in the ways those words are put together. A map tells you what there is in a terrain, but a book of itineraries tells you how to make journeys across that terrain. It will not be possible, ever, just to make your way across the terrain as your fancy pleases. Indeed, the area covered by the itineraries available to you will usually be only a minute fraction of the area covered by the map.

Our map is the lexicon, our itineraries are the sentences that we hear and utter. Like itineraries, they are constrained by the terrain they traverse. Crossing semantic space, they are impeded by boundaries as formidable as the beetling ranges and unfordable torrents that the map indicates, boundaries that if we try to cross them yield only uninterpretable garbage like *procrastination drinks serendipity* or *the hole in nescience precluded leopards*.

We may like to think that it is not the nature of the map but the nature of nature that renders these sentences meaningless, but that cannot be so. We are perfectly able to say things like *familiarity breeds contempt* or *procrastination is the thief of time*. If familiarity can breed contempt, why can't procrastination drink serendipity? Of course the answer is that familiarity does not breed contempt; 'familiarity' 'breeds' 'contempt'. The map is not a map of the world but a map of our concepts of the world. What is in it is not what is in the world but what we are capable of conceiving as being in the world. We have chosen that *familiarity breeds*

47

contempt should mean something. But we could equally well have chosen that *procrastination drinks serendipity* should mean something.

Suppose there exists a society in which all important decisions are made serendipitously, that is, by random and spontaneous choice, but only after a period of intense meditation, and only at certain propitious moments. Suppose that in that society the verb *drink* is used metaphorically for 'consume completely, destroy', just as we use the verb *breed* to mean 'create, be the immediate cause of'. *Procrastination drinks serendipity* would then simply mean that putting things off causes us to miss crucial moments of decision, just as *familiarity breeds contempt* means that getting to know things too well causes us to treat them too lightly.

But we must be careful here, or we shall fall into the trap of Wittgenstein's 'language games', the theory of 'meaning as use'. This approach holds that things mean what we choose them to mean, what society decides that they should mean—and it is a useful gambit against naive realists who believe that language merely labels what is already there. However, if it is taken too far it leads one to suppose that there are no constraints on meaning, that concepts can be created in any way we choose, and that words can be allocated whatever range of meaning we may decide to give them. That this is far from being so should become more apparent as this chapter proceeds.

Underlying the sentences we utter are three kinds of structural consistency: predicability, grammaticization, and syntax. We are free (to a limited extent) to tamper with only one of these, the first. These are the forces that shape our sentences, without which there would be no sentences. And although what they produce may seem equivalent to a list of itineraries through semantic space, they do not actually exist in the form of such a list. They do not directly state what sentences you can and cannot say. Instead, these three things together constitute a complex machinery that produces itineraries—sentences—quite automatically; as automatically as the various organs of the spider combine to produce its complex web.

And perhaps this is the most remarkable single fact about language. The machinery for producing sentences is so complex and subtle that after perhaps two hundred millennia of using it and nearly three thousand years of writing about it and several decades of studying it systematically, we are only just now beginning to understand how it works. You might think that to use such a complex instrument would cost some effort, and that, just as the most accomplished mathematician may have to employ conscious thought in the solution of a problem, so might we in the assembling of sentences.

But this seems hardly ever to happen. Although we may say that we often 'have difficulty in communicating' or 'don't know exactly how to say something', we hardly ever mean by this that we find any problem in the mechanical construction of sentences (unless, as occasionally happens, our sentences get so long and complex that we forget how they began before we can end them). All we normally mean is that we are unsure of the words we need to express our exact meaning, or of the order of ideas that will make what we have to say as comprehensible or as convincing as possible. The putting together of words, once they have been selected, is carried on so unconsciously, so automatically, that we are quite unaware of the mechanisms involved or even that such mechanisms exist. Yet if we did not have those mechanisms at our disposal, our vaunted 'system of communication', for all the richness of its conceptual map, would not be very much more expressive than the grunts and snarls of beasts.

PREDICABILITY

We can say *the story was interesting*, and *the story was true*, but not *the story was plump* or *the story was sorry*. We can say *Farmer Giles was interesting*, *Farmer Giles was plump*, or *Farmer Giles was sorry*, but not *Farmer Giles was true*. (The latter is not the same as saying *Farmer Giles was true to his wife* or *Farmer Giles was real*.) We can say *the fruit was interesting* or *the fruit was plump*, but not *the fruit was true* or *the fruit was sorry*. And we can say *the fight was interesting*, but not *the fight was true*, *the fight was plump*, or *the fight was sorry* (as distinct from *the fight was a sorry affair*).

Here we have four entities and four qualities that are related somehow. The relation between an entity and a quality is one of predication. What does it mean, to predicate something of something? We might say it means to claim that a quality somehow belongs to an entity, or at any rate to our concept of that entity. But right away it should be apparent that when we are talking about predication we are not talking about a truly unitary relation but rather about a cluster.

For instance, a story is not interesting in the same way that Farmer Giles is plump. We can quantify Farmer Giles's plumpness with the aid of a tape measure, but there is no artifact that will help us to determine, with any measure of intersubjective agreement, just how interesting the story is. Indeed, differences between predicates can be much greater than this. If we say *Farmer Giles was absent*, can we seriously suppose that 'absence' is a quality and that it belongs or belonged to Farmer Giles?

49

We might be tempted to say that predication is no more than the linking of an entity with something that may be said about that entity. But the process is by no means without constraints of some kind. If it were without constraints, then any of the four qualities under discussion could be predicated of any of the four entities—'the story', 'Farmer Giles', 'the fruit', and 'the fight'. But we saw that they cannot be.

Again it is tempting to suppose that there are 'natural kinds', that there is something in the inherent nature of real-world entities that allows certain qualities to be predicated of them while others are barred. You might say, for example, that anything may be interesting because anything is capable of arousing interest, while only concrete objects can be plump, only abstract objects can be true, and only human objects can be sorry.

But we alone can determine whether interest has been aroused, and there would not be abstract objects in the world if we had not created them. If there were no abstract objects, there would be no abstract/concrete dichotomy. Nor would there be human objects as a class, if we had not perceived ourselves as behaving differently from the rest of creation and attributed to ourselves qualities and behaviors that we denied to other species. If we think it reasonable to say *Farmer Giles was sorry to be beaten* but not to say *the fruit was sorry to be eaten,* that is after all only a matter of judgment. We may believe that it is a sound judgment—after all, we have cut the fruit open and found nothing we think it could be sorry with—and we may hope that some superior creature from the planet of another star would agree (while eating us, perhaps) that we were sorry to be eaten, but that fruit wasn't. However, it remains true that in this case we are the judges, the jury, and the detectives too.

As detectives investigating the world, we analyze what we think to be the nature of the world. As judges and jury we examine the results of our own investigation and, not surprisingly, pronounce them to be the correct and indeed the only possible ones. This refers of course to our tacit and preconscious investigation. Over the findings of our conscious investigation, our science, we sometimes squabble like a cageful of monkeys, and we never tire of updating them. But our unconscious findings—the fundamental analysis of nature that underlies all our conscious findings and that is determined not by our conscious decisions but by our species biology—are taken completely for granted, are never altered, and perhaps cannot be altered.

Those unconscious findings, that fundamental analysis, can in part be expressed in what Frank Keil, who developed the idea from work by Frederick Sommers, terms a 'predicability tree' (see fig. 3.1). The tree

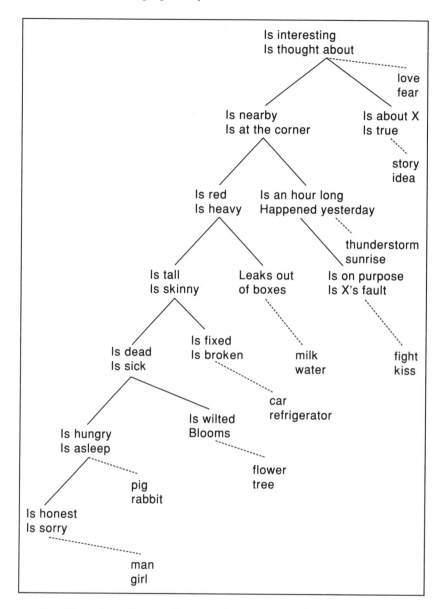

FIG. 3.1. The predicability tree. *Source:* Bickerton, *Roots of Language* (1981, fig. 4.7)

shows what can be predicated of what entities. A quality at the top of the tree can be predicated of any class beneath it. A quality on the main stem of the tree can be predicated of any class beneath it, but of no class above it. A quality on a side branch can be predicated only of a class on the branch below it.

Several things are worth noting about the predicability tree. First, it is binary branching. In principle, there is no obvious reason for this to be so. Why should the first node not have three branches, all leading to mutually exclusive classes of predicates and entities? We will encounter binary branching again, later on in this chapter.

Second, there is a contiguity constraint on the tree that is similar to the contiguity constraints discussed in chapter 2. There appears to be no quality that would apply to nonadjacent categories without also applying to categories between them. For instance, no quality can apply to humans and plants (the lowest and second from the lowest classes on the tree) without also applying to animals (the next to the lowest). Similarly, no word can take predicates from discontinuous sections of the tree, in other words, if we can say of something that it is both tall and hungry, we must also be able to say of it that it is sick.

Third, it seems unlikely that the nature of the tree is induced directly from experience of the world. That is, we do not seem to determine from personal observations that certain entities can, while others cannot, perform certain behaviors or possess certain attributes. Keil found that slightly truncated versions of the tree occurred among children as young as three or four. Whether the tree was learned from experience of language is another question. It's hard to test for this. The only way Keil could find out about the predicability trees of young children was by talking to them, by using language. But the fact that language obeys the constraints of the predicability tree would follow quite straightforwardly from the fact that language *as a classificatory mechanism* is constrained by the human, species-specific conceptual analysis of the natural world.

But, you may want to ask, what about 'familiarity breeding contempt', and things of this nature? If *familiarity* is an abstract noun, as it is, how can we predicate of it something that should not apply in the tree above *flower* and *tree?* The answer is that although we cannot change the structure of the tree, we can change the category membership of either entities or predicates. Keil was puzzled by children who told him that dreams could be tall until he questioned them further and found out that they regarded dreams as physical objects ("They're made out of rock," "They just got grass on them," "They turn white and go up in the sky"). Doing a similar thing from the opposite direction, so to speak, we can expand the meaning of *breed* so that it includes 'create, be the immediate cause of', thus turning it into an abstract predicate. Once this has been done, it can be applied to an abstract noun like *familiarity.*

At first sight you might think that this flexibility reduces the predicability tree to a mere tautology. So, only abstract qualities can be predicated of abstract nouns, only human ones of human nouns, and so on—what's such a big deal about that? Nothing, if you believe that the tree and its classes of entities and qualities exist in the external universe. But the categories into which we divide nature are not in nature, they emerge solely through the interaction between nature and ourselves.

GRAMMATICIZATION

Take any sentence that you might think of. Well, why not the one before this? It contains eight words. Only one of them expresses a concept that refers to something you could point at: *sentence*. Another, *take*, expresses a concept that you could at least try to demonstrate, although taking a sentence is not exactly like taking a drink or taking an umbrella (which are not like each other, either, but that is neither here nor there). A third word, *think*, expresses a concept that would be a good deal harder to demonstrate. But in what sense do the other five words in the sentence express concepts? At best they are very hard to define, and at worst they seem to be altogether devoid of meaning.

Take *any*, for instance. It doesn't, unlike *this* or *that*, specify which sentence is being referred to. Indeed, it *un*specifies: it says 'what is said here applies to all sentences'. But *all sentences* would not have worked in this context, since you were intended to take one only. So what *any* means is 'out of all possible sentences, one, but not any particular one'. But we have now included *any* in its own definition.

Now look at *that*. It is not the *that* of *that pen* or *I like that*. Those *that*s refer to something, but this *that* seems merely to link two parts of the sentence together. *You* looks more reassuring, but again it doesn't really have any definite reference. *You* can mean anyone who happens to be addressed, or one might say, 'the participant(s) in any dialogue that isn't the speaker' (but is this book, for example, a dialogue?). Besides, its reference shifts continually—it means B if A is talking, and A if B is talking.

As for *might*, it can express anything from a rather petulant request (*You might close the door*) through a rather remote possibility (*I might do it if I could only find the time*) to something quite predictable (*You might guess he'd say that! Yes, we might have known!*). And perhaps *of* is the vaguest of the lot. It is a preposition without a noun after it, at least without an overt noun, and yet contrary to what you may have been taught at school, it is not really possible to get it away from the end of the sentence. You can't say *Take any sentence that you might think* (you can *think a thought* but, for some reason, you can't *think a sentence*), while *Take any sentence of which you might think* somehow suggests that there is already a special class of thinkable sentences out there waiting to be taken. In fact, in the original sentence, the class was the class of all possible sentences, and the *taking* and the *thinking of* were somehow part of a single process. Moreover, *of* seems to mean no more than *that* in this sentence. It isn't even the *of* that indicates possession, itself far from transparent in meaning (*the handle of the door, the fundamentals of cognition, the friends of Eddie Coyle, the State of Massachusetts*).

It is a surprising fact that at least half the words we utter, hear, or read are like these: grammatical items (as opposed to lexical items that have some kind of demonstrable referent). Some of these items are not even full words but mere inflections, like the *-ing* in *working* or the *-ed* in *played* (many languages are much richer than English in such things). Occasionally a grammatical item can be omitted without loss of meaning (for instance, the *that* in *Take any sentence that you might think of*).

But in general, whether they are inflections or words, grammatical items cannot be omitted without changing the meaning of the sentence or making it somehow wrong (often both). No verb (except a handful like *cut* or *put*) can be used without overtly indicating whether its tense is present or past, and no noun (except for a few like *sheep* or *fish*) can be used without explicitly indicating whether it is singular or plural. Even here, agreement phenomena (*he cut it YESTERDAY, the sheep ARE grazing*) are there to show us that pastness and plurality are still present even when not overtly marked. Grammatical items, then, play as crucial a role in meaning as do lexical items, although unlike lexical items they are seldom within our power to pick and choose, and we cannot invent or add new ones.

And yet when philosophers talk about meaning they almost always talk about lexical items, usually about nouns, and most often about concrete nouns of one kind or another. The only exception is a small handful of grammatical items such as *if*, *and*, and *or* which happen to have logical significance. The rest they usually either recoil from or ignore. Willard Quine, for instance, was baffled by the fact that all finite sentences must express some kind of tense, a situation for which he could see no logical necessity.

If they don't mirror anything specific in the world of experience, what are grammatical items for? Do they have meaning, and if so, what kind? What do we mean, exactly, when we say that certain concepts are grammaticized? There are two things at issue here which we should try to separate.

Looked at from one point of view, grammatical items are simply structural pieces that hold the more meaningful parts of a sentence together, rather in the same way (to return to our 'itinerary' metaphor) as stretches of road we often find boring link together the towns or resort areas that are all we really want to visit. But just as those well-engineered yet dreary freeways enable us to drive with minimal attention, developing our own thoughts as we travel, so grammatical items enable us to pay almost no conscious attention to the construction of our own sentences, or to the deciphering of the sentences of others, while allowing us to devote ourselves entirely to the content of what we say and hear. We do not have to be continually peering for road signs and cutoffs to find out where we're going, or who did what to whom. The broad highway of grammaticization grabs us and takes us effortlessly where we want to go.

We will return to the structural-functional side of grammatical items in the section on syntax. It is not their only side, however, for though they may never have referents to which you could point, they are by no means devoid of meaning. They constitute, as it were, the coordinates of the linguistic map, a kind of topological grid whereby the positions of objects and events can be plotted relative to the observer and to one another.

This relativity is a critical attribute of grammatical items, as it is of adjectives. Just as *small* is always relative to the category under discussion, rather than to absolute size, so items like *up* or *down* are used without any reference to absolute distance. You can go *up the tree* or *up Mount Everest*, and there is no implication in either case that you completed the ascent. Even if you have only ascended to the second or third tier of branches you have gone *up the tree*, and the sentence *He went up Everest but couldn't make it to the top* is in no way contradictory. Moreover, there is no word *flup* such that *I went flup the mountain* would mean, say, 'I ascended the mountain to a height of five hundred feet'. Similarly there are no tenses that would differentiate between, say, past events that happened within your lifetime and past events that happened before you were born. The same past tense is used for things that happened seconds ago and things that happened billions of years in the past.

The relations that grammatical items can express include relative location (*above, below, in, on, at, by, next to*), relative time (*before, after, while,* and the various indicators of tense), relative number (*many, few, some,* the *-s* of plurality), relative direction (*to, from, through, left, right, up, down*), relative familiarity (*the* for things the speaker thinks the hearer will recognize, *a* for things the speaker thinks the hearer won't recognize), relative possibility (*can, may, might*) and relative contingency (*unless, although, until, because*), as well as a variety of relationships such as possession (*of,* possessive *-s, have*), agency (*by*), purpose (*for*), necessity (*must, have to*), obligation (*should, ought to*), existence (*be*), nonexistence (*no, none, not*), and so on and so forth.

Only relations found in English have been listed here. Other lan-

55

guages may not always express all those relations, or may express ones that English does not. For instance, languages as diverse as Turkish and Hopi have verbal inflections that indicate whether a statement is based on personal experience or on information obtained at second hand. But by no means every relation in the real world can be grammaticized.

Indeed, what is remarkable is that the list of grammaticizable relations is so short, especially when you consider that the number of possible qualities and relations in the world is certainly immense and perhaps infinite. Why do languages grammaticize a few of these relations quite consistently, but never grammaticize the vast majority of them?

One guess might be that what languages grammaticized were the things that had proved most useful to us in evolution. If this is correct, it is far from being obviously so. If it were, we might expect to find at least some language that attached to every noun a grammatical item indicating whether the thing it referred to was edible or not, hostile to humans or not, or some other quality of a similar nature. Yet apparently no such languages exist.

There seems no obvious reason why distinctions like one/more-than-one or past/nonpast should have played a more important role in our evolution than distinctions like edible/inedible or hostile/friendly. For reasons not yet understood, language forces us to express *automatically* a very restricted subset of all the possible qualities and relations in the world. If we want to express others, we can of course do so. If we want to say that something is friendly, or edible, or whatever, we can, but that will take up a whole sentence. We can't build these things into the very structure of our discourse, as with tense, plurality, and so on we are obliged to do.

It is worth noting, too, the extent to which limitations on what can be grammaticized affect the way in which language represents the world. It is even possible to think of cases where it might seem highly advantageous to have a grammatical item that doesn't actually exist—one that would express the relation between wholes and parts, for instance.

Take an expression like *a tree has leaves*. In passing we may observe the oddness of this verb *have*, which can appear in a wide variety of contexts, and express a variety of very different relations: *You have a cold, Mary has a sick grandmother, Bill has a good job, Who has the exact time?* and so on. All of these at least share the feature that if you were to take away your cold, Mary's grandmother, or Bill's job, you, Bill, and Mary would still be there intact. But in addition to a *a tree has leaves*, we can say *a tree has branches, a tree has roots, a tree has a trunk, a tree has bark*. Take away all the things that a tree 'has', and there is no tree left to 'have' them.

It might be extremely convenient if a language could express the relations that exist between wholes and parts by means of grammaticization, rather than by recruiting unsuitable lexical items like *have*. One might then substitute grammatical items like *inc*, meaning 'including as part of itself', or *onc*, 'forming a part of'. This would allow us to say things like *a tree inc leaves* (instead of *a tree has leaves*) or *leaves onc a tree* (instead of *leaves of a tree; of* is as bad as *have* in this context, since if you take away everything that is OF the tree, once again you have no tree left). But no language yet discovered does things this way. When it comes to lexical items, we can invent as many new ones as we want or need, but we cannot add to the store of grammatical items. We are stuck with the ones we've got, so that we have to stretch concepts that *are* grammaticizable, like 'possession' with its *ofs* and *haves*, in order to express even something as basic as the part-whole relationship.

You may dismiss such things as mere 'conventions of language'. But conventions are made and can be broken. Things like our ways of expressing the relation between a thing and its parts are quite automatic and cannot be altered, replaced, or even added to. Lexical items are open-ended and can always be added to, but grammatical items constitute closed sets. It is as if nature has provided us with a black box containing a machine that enables us to orient ourselves in the semi-simulacrum of the real world that language-as-representation creates. But the box is sealed; we can neither alter it nor (so far) explain it.

SYNTAX

Having looked, all too briefly, at predicability and grammaticization, we must now turn to the third and most formidable pillar of language structure, syntax. The reader is warned that without some previous exposure to linguistic argumentation, much of the remainder of this chapter will be heavy going. There is however no alternative. As will become apparent in the chapters that follow, syntax, rather than referential meaning, may be what most decisively separates us from other species. If this is so, then we can hardly hope to understand what is most remarkable about our nature if we do not have at least some understanding of what syntax is and how it works.

Try to rearrange any ordinary sentence consisting of ten words. There are, in principle, exactly 3,628,800 ways in which you could do this, but for the first sentence in this paragraph only one of them gives a correct and meaningful result. That means 3,628,799 of them are ungrammatical. How did we learn this? Certainly no parent or teacher ever told us. The only way in which we can know it is by possessing, as it were, some recipe for how to construct sentences, a recipe so complex and exhaustive that it automatically rules out all 3,628,799 wrong ways of putting together a ten word sentence and allows only the right one. But since such a recipe must apply to all sentences, not just the example given, that recipe will, for every language, rule out more ungrammatical sentences than there are atoms in the cosmos—and there are at least five thousand different languages!

What kind of handbook of itineraries could allow us to pick our way across the atlas of language in so delicate a fashion, avoiding so many possibilities, selecting so few, and yet doing all of this so automatically that we are aware only of the mote we can say, and not of the mountain we cannot?

Constraints on predicability and grammaticization are only a part, probably the smallest part, of the story. The part of the sentence machine that enables us to make an infinite number of new meanings out of combinations of words is itself quite meaningless, a purely formal structure. Moreover, for all its complexity, we acquire that structure without the least conscious effort. More surprisingly still, we learn it, to all intents and purposes, without making mistakes. For of all the apparent 'mistakes' a child may make in learning English, there is hardly one that would not be correct in some other language. The following brief account of this syntactic machine will stick fairly closely to the descriptive model currently being developed by Noam Chomsky and his associates—a model that differs in some radical respects from his earlier work.

Let's start with the shortest possible kind of declarative sentence, such as *Fred left* or *Night fell*. We saw in chapter 2 that some force, perhaps the way concepts developed in antecedent species, resulted in a distinction between entities and the behaviors (actions, states, processes) that can be predicated of these entities. Thus the prototypical sentence consists of an entity and a behavior, or rather of the labels for the concepts of these. These two kinds of label are termed, respectively, 'noun' and 'verb', and they are perhaps the most basic building blocks of language, from which everything else is somehow or other derived.

Some readers may recall the old definition 'a noun is the name of a person, place, or thing'. This is obviously wrong, since there are nouns like *absence* or *nonexistence*. Moreover, nouns are not names (although a name is a kind of noun). *Cow* is neither the name of any particular cow, nor the name of all cows. We might better define a noun as something of which something can be predicated. If you can predicate of absence that it makes the heart grow fonder or of nonexistence that it constitutes the goal of some Eastern religions, then *absence* and *nonexistence* are nouns, whether or not they denote anything. If nouns and verbs are the most basic elements of syntax, then predication is its most basic act.

For *Fred* or *night* we can substitute pronouns, we can say *he left* or *it fell*. If we couldn't, we would be forced to say things like *The young boy told the older sister of the young boy that the young boy didn't know what the older sister of the young boy wanted for the older sister of the young boy's birthday*. It is much quicker and easier to say *He told her that he didn't know what she wanted for her birthday*, provided of course that we can reliably identify *he, she,* and *her* (more about that in a moment).

Notice however that we can't say things like *the young he left* or *his heavier it fell*. From our examples so far one might conclude that pronouns replace nouns, but in fact they replace noun phrases: *he* replaces *the young boy*, not just *boy*. The fact that you can replace *Fred* by *he* in *Fred left* but that you can't replace *boy* by *he* in *the young boy left* shows us that even where we see only a bare noun, like *Fred* or *night*, there is really a full noun phrase present—the phrase just doesn't happen to contain any elements other than the noun.

In fact, pronouns replace not merely noun phrases, but the largest available noun phrase. If they replaced just any noun phrase, it would be quite normal to replace *Bill and Mary left* with *he and she left*. In fact, this sounds very odd; we naturally say *they left. Bill and Mary* constitutes a kind of super-noun-phrase that contains two other noun phrases.

Of course noun phrases like *Fred* and *night* can be expanded to form larger phrases like *The Fred you were talking about* or *any night in the next few weeks*. Here, the noun may be preceded by a specifier, a grammatical item like *the* or *any*, and followed by a complement, a clause or another phrase of some kind. Nouns and verbs may be the most basic building blocks of language, but the most important are phrases. If we know how to construct phrases, and how to join phrases to one another, we know most of what we need to know in order to construct sentences.

PHRASE STRUCTURE

But *how* do we know how to construct phrases? Because we have—somehow—a kind of template or model of what a phrase must be like. Not just a noun phrase: any kind of phrase. For the remarkable thing is that phrases of all kinds, including whole sentences (for a sentence turns out to be just a big phrase with lesser phrases in it), are constructed in the same way. A phrase consists of three parts or levels. The most critical part, the only part that can be there on its own, is the head. The head of a phrase cannot be larger than a single word and that word must belong to the same class as the phrase. Noun phrases have nouns as their heads, verb phrases have verbs, and other types of phrase (adjective phrases, prepositional phrases, and so on) follow the same pattern.

A head is first linked to its complement. For example, in the noun phrase *the cow with a crumpled horn*, *cow* is first linked to *with a crumpled horn*, and the node that joins them is specified as N'. N' is simply the level of structure intermediate between that of the head noun, the N level, and that of the full phrase N" (see Figure 3.2). Note that while a head cannot itself be a phrase, a complement may consist of a phrase or even several phrases embedded in one another (here, *with a crumpled horn* is a prepositional phrase, which in turn contains another noun phrase, *a crumpled horn*).

This embedding is possible because phrases are not, as they might appear to be, strung together serially, like beads on a string. Phrases are like Chinese boxes, stacked one inside another. The importance of this point can hardly be overestimated. Many people concerned with the origins of human language, or with the alleged language capacities of non-human species, have been led to propose grossly simplistic hypotheses about how language could have emerged, simply on the basis of a mistaken assumption. They assume that words are serially chained into phrases and phrases into sentences in pretty much the same way that steps are chained into walking, or (in a slightly more complex fashion) the same way that a variety of motor functions are chained into a series of actions—for instance: grasping, raising, drinking from, and then lowering a cup. Nothing could be further from the truth.

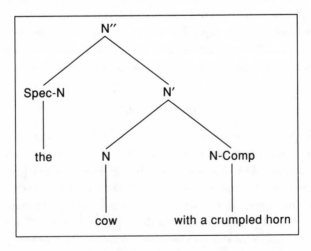

FIG. 3.2. Basic noun phrase structure

This can be seen by considering a phrase like *the cow with the crumpled horn that Farmer Giles likes*. Although no single word in this phrase is ambiguous, the phrase as a whole is, because we do not know whether it is the horn or the cow that Farmer Giles likes. The ambiguity is purely structural, due to the fact that the clause *that Farmer Giles likes* can be attached in either of two places. If it is the horn he likes, then the clause is a complement of *horn*. If it is the cow, the clause is a complement of *cow*, not *horn*, even if, in utterance, it comes directly after *horn* rather than directly after *cow*.

This is possible because a head may have more than one complement. It would be possible to take the idea of 'level' with dead literalness and branch all complements of N from a single N' node, as in figure 3.3*a*. However, there are strong reasons for supposing that no more than two branches can spring from a single node, so that the structure of the phrase is better represented by figure 3.3*b*. In other words, the N' level simply represents an abstract level intermediate between the noun and the full phrase. Normally a head will have only a single complement, but if there is some other element that meets somewhat strict conditions for serving as complement of that particular head, then the abstract X' level may be represented by more than one literal level.

Finally, we complete the phrase by linking the highest N' to the specifier, *the*, as in figure 3.2. The overall pattern of that figure can be repeated for any other kind of phrase, and constitutes, so to speak, the very core of universal syntax (figure 3.4).

X in Figure 3.4 stands for any lexical category (noun, verb, adjective, preposition, etc.) that can be expanded to form a phrase. The n in parentheses after X' indicates that this level, unlike X" and X, can be repeated, provided that there is more than one complement that genuinely can pertain to X. The parentheses around Spec and Comp indicate that these items are not obligatory, although everything else is. The horizontal two-headed arrows indicate that the relative positions of Spec and X', and of X and Comp, can be exchanged.

Contrary, again, to the idea that language is some kind of serial stringing process, syntactic principles have nothing at all to say about the order things come in, except insofar as this is determined by their hierarchical positions relative to one another. (As figure 3.3b suggests, the serial order of words can be determined by starting from the top left-hand side of a tree and then working down it to the bottom and up again to the top right-hand side.) In other words, X-bar theory (the theory of phrase structure briefly sketched above) specifies vertical, but not horizontal, relations.

It is partly because general principles fail to determine word order that the syntaxes of the world's languages look as diverse as they do. Languages fully exploit the possibilities of variation permitted by the schema shown in figure 3.4 (as well as certain movement possibilities to be discussed below). Thus in many languages one finds verbs preceding their subjects, or following their objects; adjectives and relative clauses

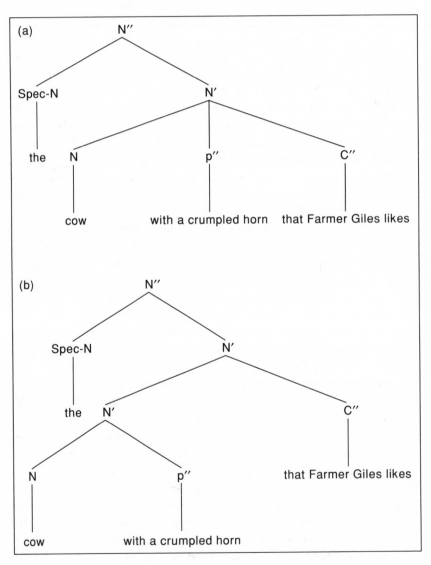

FIG. 3.3. Nonbinary versus binary branching

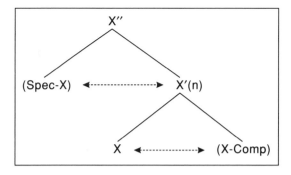

FIG. 3.4. Universal phrase structure

'in the wrong order' with respect to the nouns they modify; and so on. This is a daunting experience for the learner, and one that has led some linguists to suppose that 'universal grammar' is an impossible dream. However, the regularities of figure 3.4 underly all this superficial variety.

As noted in that figure, specifiers and complements are optional, but heads are obligatory. This is why single nouns that are the heads of noun phrases (NP-heads) can occur in isolation, like *night* in *Night fell*. But a specifier or complement can never appear without a head. You could say that a head is necessary in order to 'govern' its specifiers and complements.

However, sometimes nothing actually appears in a place where you would expect to find at least a head. Compare *I expected Bill to leave* with *I expected to leave*. In the second sentence there is no word that corresponds to *Bill* in the first, yet somehow we know that it is I myself, not Bill or Mary or people in general, who was expected to do the leaving. Should we assume that there's nothing there, or that there was something there that has been taken out?

Compare *I called Bill e to ask him about it* with *I told Bill e to ask him about it*, where *e* indicates the positions of null (not overtly expressed) noun phrases in both cases (someone, some subject must be doing the asking). These sentences look at first sight as if they are identical in meaning and structure except for the choice of verb. But this cannot be so, for in the first sentence, *him* can refer to Bill and would normally be taken as doing so, whereas in the second, *him* cannot possibly refer to Bill. And if we look a little closer, we will see that we have to make different assumptions about *e* in each case. In the first sentence, it refers to *I* and in the second it refers to *Bill*. Now a genuine 'nothing' can't have two different references, nor could it change the reference of *him*. We can therefore conclude that there must be 'something' there. For in language, as in physics, there are things that aren't perceptible to our senses but that are known to be present because of their differing effects.

Let us turn now to structures larger than the single phrase. It was noted above that all language is phrasal in structure, but, on the face of things, this remark may seem odd. What about our very first and simplest example, *Fred left? Fred,* though appearing on the surface to be a single noun, has been shown, by the 'pronoun replaceability' test, to be in reality an N" structure, a full noun phrase. In a similar way, it might be assumed that *left* is the head and only constituent of a V" or verb phrase. But what then becomes of the statement that phrases are always inside phrases, like Chinese boxes? Here we seem to have a noun phrase and a verb phrase, enough to give us a complete sentence, with nothing left over. How can these statements be reconciled?

Contrary to appearances, *Fred left* does contain 'something left over': an additional element that has not yet been noted. The head of V" is not really *left.* The verb is *leave; left* is simply *leave* + past tense. Recall Quine's bewilderment at the fact that every sentence had to have tense. Now we can see why this is so, and at the same time we can appreciate the two-faced nature of grammatical items: on one side, they are conveyers of meaning, on the other, indispensible parts of syntactic structure.

Tense constitutes part of the inflectional system of verbs. Another part, one not very apparent in English but much more so in a language like Spanish, is agreement, usually agreement of the verb with the subject of the sentence. Agreement and tense are not parts of either the noun phrase *Fred* or the verb phrase *leave.* Tense sometimes attaches to the verb, but it has scope over the whole sentence, not just the predicate. For instance, if, in the sentences *His wife left him* and *His wife is leaving him, him* has the same referent, then the sentences can only be about a man who has had (at least) two wives; *his wife* will have two distinct referents and only tense (past versus present) will indicate which one is referred to in each case. Agreement may be determined by properties of the subject ('male', 'plural', or whatever) but it, too, often attaches to the verb, and may be regarded as what ties subject and predicate together.

If tense/agreement is neither a specifier nor a complement of anything, it can only constitute a head. If we assume that it does then a simple subject-predicate sentence falls into exactly the same pattern as do all other phrases. Since tense and agreement are generally inflections, call that head INFL or I for short. Then the subject noun phrase is

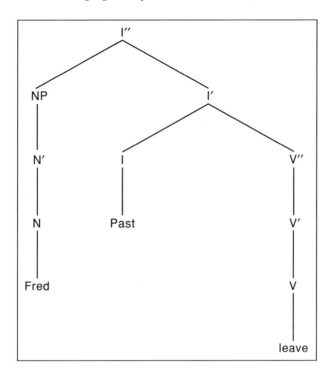

FIG. 3.5. Structure of *Fred left*

the specifier of I, while the verb phrase is its complement. (A predicate like *left immediately* is quite indeterminate unless you specify *who* left.) A sentence, then, is simply I".

It follows that the full structure of *Fred left* is that shown in figure 3.5. Note that this figure follows exactly the model of figure 3.4. But because in *Fred left* INFL is less than a word, it cannot remain in its original position, but must attach itself to the nearest word of a similar class, a verb. You may ask how we know that the original position of INFL is between subject and predicate when INFL usually attaches to the ends rather than the beginnings of verbs (*they partED, Bill snoreS*). The answer is that if INFL is attached to some special word of its own, it can and does stay in place, witness *Fred DID leave!*

ARGUMENT STRUCTURE

But most sentences are longer and more complex than *Fred left*, and one variable that affects the complexity and length of a sentence is the number of entities that it makes reference to. (*Fred leaves*, of course, mentions only one.) That variable depends to a large extent on the verb chosen, for each verb subcategorizes for (more or less obligatorily selects) a fixed number of 'arguments', each of which will be an N" or sometimes a P" or even a whole clause (I"). By an argument of a verb is meant simply a phrase referring to any participant involved in or directly related to the action, state, or event that the verb expresses.

Thus *arrive, sleep, fall, expire,* and *trickle* take only one obligatory argument; *beat, trap, drop, inspire,* and *tickle* take two; and *give, order, promise, bring,* and *tell* take three. We cannot say *I arrived him* any more than we can say *I beat.* Note that *to leave* in *I ordered him to leave* is just as much an argument of *order* as is *him*—you cannot just say *I ordered him,* although of course there is another verb *order* (as in *they ordered steak*) that takes only two arguments. As will be apparent, there are cases where even subcategorized arguments can be omitted, or rather, may be null elements with unspecified reference: *they sang, we ate, he drinks.* However, if we say *she likes to tickle,* no one would take this to mean 'she likes to tickle doorknobs, ferns, kitchen equipment, etc.', but only 'she likes to tickle entities that can respond to being tickled'. In the same way, *they sang* means 'they sang songs', *we ate* means 'we ate food', and so on.

In addition to subcategorized arguments, there may be optional arguments relating to time (*on Thursday next*), place (*right outside the door*), instrument (*with a hammer*), and a few other members of a very limited set. As this suggests, arguments are not chosen arbitrarily. We can, if we like, conceive of a sentence, notionally, as being like a little play or story, one in which each of the characters has a specific role to perform. There is a finite and indeed very short list of these roles. Not all linguists are agreed as to exactly what they are, but most, if not all, would include the roles of Agent (*JOHN cooked dinner*), Patient or Theme (*John cooked DINNER*), Goal (*I gave it TO MARY*), Source (*I bought it FROM FRED*), Instrument (*Bill cut it WITH A KNIFE*), and Beneficiary (*I bought it FOR YOU*), as well as Time and Place.

Again, note that the function of grammatical particles is a double one involving both meaning and structure. The 'meaning' function is that the grammatical item shows us what is the thematic role of each argument: *to* indicates a Goal, *from* a Source, *with* an Instrument, and so on. The 'structure' function is to govern arguments that cannot be governed by the verb, and we will return to this shortly.

What has been very briefly sketched above is something called 'argument structure'. One remarkable thing about argument structure is its universality. When we learn a foreign language, initially we make all kinds of mistakes; we assume that structures in the target language resemble structures in our own, or that the semantic ranges of its words are identical with those of words in our language, or that its tense system relates to time in the same way that ours does. In practically every department of language we are confronted by pitfalls such as these. In only one area do we never make mistakes, indeed our success is so complete we probably never realize how effortlessly we are 'learning'.

That area is argument structure. If a foreign language has a verb that means 'sleep', we can be sure it will have only one obligatory argument. If it has a verb that means 'beat', that verb will have two, and if it has a verb that means 'give', that verb will have three. Moreover, the roles of those arguments will in every case be the roles that English verbs assign.

Argument structure, then, is universal. It is a form of structure that runs parallel with, yet separate from, the phrase structure discussed in the previous section. In order for sentences to be made, one kind of structure has to be mapped onto the other. A systematic mapping is necessary because if we are to correctly arrive at the meaning of a sentence, we have to be able to determine, automatically and quite unambiguously, 'who did what, and with which, and to whom'. That is, since not all thematic roles carry distinguishing prepositions, we may have to be able to determine the thematic role of an argument from the structural position of that argument in the sentence.

An example will make this mapping process clearer. Most verbs, as shown above, regularly take one, two, or three arguments. However, there are some verbs, like *melt, boil, sink* and so on, that sometimes take one argument and sometimes two. Whether one or two are present, there is always a Patient, but the position of the Patient is not always the same. If there are two arguments, then the Patient will follow the verb (*Mary melted the ice, The Navy sank the ship,* and so on). If there is only one, the Patient precedes the verb (*The ice melted, The ship sank*).

The reason for this is that argument structure is mapped onto phrase structure according to a hierarchy of thematic roles. This hierarchy is roughly as shown in figure 3.6. Usually only the roles above the line in that figure are subcategorized for, although there are one or two exceptions (*put*, for instance, subcategorizes for location, so that we can say *put the dish on the table* but not simply *put the dish*). Mapping onto phrase structure proceeds by putting the highest available role in the highest position (Spec-I, the position of *Fred* in figure 3.5). If the verb subcategorizes for an Agent role, Agent will be highest, and either Patient or Goal will take the next highest position (often, though not always, these two can commute, as in *give John money* versus *give money to John*). Any remaining roles will take still lower positions.

This process is not without exception. Occasionally a nonsubcate-

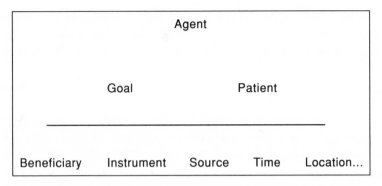

FIG. 3.6. Hierarchy of thematic roles

gorized role can be found higher than a subcategorized one. For example, one can say *a key will open the door* (where *key* is an Instrument) alongside *the door will open with a key*. Also, what has been said applies only to active verbs. If the verb is passive, the highest role, Agent, can never appear in the highest position, although it may optionally appear in a lower position as part of a *by* phrase. But in active sentences there are no cases where a lower thematic role *obligatorily* takes a higher position than a higher thematic role. That is, there will always be an alternative that obeys the hierarchy (for example, *the door will open with a key*) and in most cases the form that obeys the hierarchy will be the only form.

It was noted just now that prepositions such as *for*, *to*, and so on perform two kinds of role. The first role is that of determining an argument's thematic role, the second a more purely structural one. Recall that in discussing phrase structure a head was said to govern its complements. Part of what we mean by this is that arguments cannot simply wander around loose in a sentence. Every argument has to be governed by something, which is just another way of saying, every argument has to be within some X", and every X" has to have a head.

But every argument cannot be governed directly by V, because a verb cannot take an unlimited string of complements. For one thing, we would have a lot of trouble in processing things like *wrote letters Mary Bill his computer his study night* (at least, a lot more than we would have in processing *wrote letters to Mary for Bill on his computer in his study at night*). For another, a verb can only give thematic roles to the arguments it subcategorizes for, in other words those we can expect if we simply know the verb's meaning. So prepositions are necessary (in English—in other languages their function might be performed by postpositions, or other types of particle) not only to assign thematic roles, but also to head up a new X" structure within which they, as heads, can govern the argument and also give it case.

The idea of case has had a checkered career in syntax. At first, English was said to have case because Latin had case and all good languages ought to be like Latin. Then it was observed that (outside of pronouns) there are no overt signs of case in English, so it was claimed that case was nonexistent in English. Later still, fairly recently in fact, when a universal grammar no longer based on Latin began to seem not only possible but real, case came back. Take a simple sentence like *Mary met the girl*. Neither *Mary* nor *the girl* has any overt marking of case. But if you replace these by pronouns, you have to say *she* (nominative) *met her* (accusative). You can't say *her met she, she met she*, or *her met her*. If, when you replace a noun phrase by a pronoun, that pronoun automatically gets case-marked, this suggests that the noun phrase, too, must have been receiving case even if no overt case-marking was visible.

Also, if case was only a fiction, it is rather odd that one could specify exactly the conditions under which that fiction would be assigned: direct adjacency of case-marked argument and case-assigning constituent, and only one case to be assigned by each assigner. Granted, there is one apparent exception to this, which no one has yet satisfactorily explained— double-object constructions like *gave him change*, where both *him* and *change* seem to get case from the verb—but it is the only one. Whatever the process is, it doesn't extend to overtly case-marked items, at least not in American English. *Give him it* is unacceptable, we have to say *give it to him*.

The need for nouns to get case explains a lot of puzzling things about language. It explains, for instance, the mysterious *of* in the sentence *Take any sentence that you might think of*, discussed earlier in the chapter, which seemed totally meaningless. So it is; it is there simply because *think* does not subcategorize for N", but only for a clause (*They think it's time to leave*). Otherwise, it is intransitive (*I think, therefore, I am*), or it is a question of *thinking thoughts*. (Since there is nothing that can be the object of *think* except *thoughts*, the latter counts as an idiom, and therefore falls outside syntactic theory proper.)

Think must be able to govern a complement, otherwise it could not govern *it's time to leave* in *They think it's time to leave*. But complements that are clauses don't require case, so the reason that *think* can't have a noun phrase as its complement may be that it can't assign case to it. (This has something to do with the fact that it doesn't subcategorize for a noun phrase complement, but which is cause and which effect isn't entirely clear.) *Think,* therefore, has to be followed by some grammatical item that will assign case. *Of* happens to be chosen for the job nowadays, but *about* may be used too, with slight or sometimes nonexistent differences in meaning. At an earlier stage of English, *on* could be chosen (*Think on these things*). What is chosen, and what that something means, is secondary to getting the purely formal work done.

But *of* is generally chosen when verbs are turned into nouns. If we say *Columbus discovered America* we don't need an *of* before *America*—indeed, if we say *Columbus discovered of America,* the sentence is bad. And yet we can't talk about *Columbus's discovery America,* only about *Columbus's discovery OF America, of* being essential in this context. But what does *of* add to the meaning? Nothing at all. It is there simply to give *America* accusative case. *Discover,* unlike *think,* can give case to a noun phrase complement, but nouns, even nouns formed from verbs, can't do this.

If something didn't give *America* accusative case, the case that verbs normally give to their objects, we wouldn't *automatically* know that *America* is still related to *discovery* in exactly the same way as it was related to *discover* in *Columbus discovered America.* That is, we would not know that *America* is still a complement and Patient argument of a deverbalized noun. Without *of,* we wouldn't *automatically* be able to distinguish the sequence of *Columbus, discovery,* and *America* from the same sequence in, say, *Since Columbus's discovery America has never been the same,* where *America* and *discovery* are totally disconnected from one another.

In other words, case and government function (among other ways) as backup systems for processing and interpreting the products of the argument-structure/phrase-structure system. Their principled predictability makes it possible for us to interpret sentences quite automatically, without paying any conscious attention whatsoever to HOW things are said, freeing us to devote all of our consciousness to WHAT is said. Case and government achieve this result by acting, so to speak, as a kind of glue that sticks sentences together, ensuring that everything has a place and is in that place, or at least can be related to that place.

MOVING AND KEEPING TRACK OF THINGS

If the system described so far were the whole of language, language would be a very unresponsive instrument, rigid and restrictive. With trivial exceptions, we would not be free to move words around in our sentences so as to emphasize certain things while de-emphasizing others, nor to direct our hearers' attention to the exact shades of meaning we wished to express. We need that freedom, but we have it at the risk that, if movement is unprincipled, we may no longer be able to reconstruct meaning, to determine 'who did what to whom'. If things are to move, we must be able to keep track of them, to see where they have moved from.

The actual status of 'movement' is still controversial. There are those who hold that, in sentences like *What did you see e?*, *what* really did move from the position marked by *e*. *What* is, after all, the direct object of *see*, it bears the thematic role of Patient normally assigned to things at the position of *e*, and indeed the position of *e* is actually occupied by *what* in the question expressing surprise, *You saw WHAT?* Others hold that there is no such thing as movement. Things are where they are, they would say, although mechanisms will still be required to link certain elements, like *what* in *What did you see?*, to certain empty positions, so that they can be interpreted automatically.

For, regardless of whether we hypothesize movement or not, we have to have some way of explaining how we know, for instance, that a sentence like *How do you know who he saw?* is a possible question, but not a question about how someone saw someone or who you know, while *Who do you know how he saw?* is not a possible question at all, even though there would be a perfectly logical and possible answer for it (*I know he saw Bill by looking through a telescope, but I've no idea how he saw Fred*).

Chomsky has suggested that these two approaches, 'movement' versus 'nonmovement', may turn out to be merely notational variants of one another, and the issue is certainly not worth the paper that has been used in arguing about it. Perhaps it is best to think of movement as a convenient metaphor to help us grasp processes that are still far from being thoroughly understood. The importance of movement may lie in helping us to realize that, with almost every second sentence we utter, we deal, blithely unaware, with at least two kinds of 'nothing'. If someone says *What did you tell me to do?* there is a nothing that represents a gap that something has been moved from, and a nothing that represents something that is definitely still there. In other words, in the sentence *What did you tell me e_1 to do e_2?* e_2 marks the space from which *what* has moved (or, to which it must be related), and e_1 the space where an invisible first-person pronoun still sits, because it's 'I' not 'you' who is expected to do something.

But to distinguish one kind of null element from another is not enough. We need some way of finding how far we have to look, from a

71

space left by movement, in order to locate the thing that moved from it. Moreover, since this looking has to be as automatic and unconscious as breathing, that way has to be both highly specific and infallible. The way is also quite complex, but in brief, things can move quite a long way if they can hop, so to speak, from one space to another.

Take a sentence like *Bill heard that Mary said that John knew what Fred did e*, where *e* marks the place that *what* moved from. You can also say, *Bill heard that Mary said what John knew e that Fred did e*, or *Bill heard what Mary said e that John knew e that Fred did e*, or even *What did Bill hear e that Mary said e that John knew e that Fred did e?* This is possible because, for each I", each cluster consisting of a verb and its arguments, there is usually (not always) an additional phrase, a kind of superphrase that includes I" as its complement. Since in many cases such a phrase is headed by an overt complementizer (a grammatical item like *that* which introduces a clause), we call this C" (see figure 3.3), and the space to which things move is actually the specifier of C. When there is a chain of such positions, as in the *Bill heard* . . . sentence, things can hop from one position to the next.

The reason we can't have *Who do you know how he saw e?* is if *who* moves from the position marked by *e*, it has to pass through the space already occupied by *how*. *Who* can't simply jump over it, because the boundaries of phrases, the N"s and V"s and C"s, act as barriers to prevent things from getting 'too far from home', so to speak. If something 'got too far', you could no longer know *for sure*, and *automatically and unconsciously*, where it came from. So movement, even when it seems to go a long way, is really a very local phenomenon.

You could also say that it has in some sense to be an 'expectable' phenomenon. Things can really only move either out of simple one-clause sentences, as in *What did you see?*, or out of clauses that are subcategorized complements of some verb, as in the *Bill heard* . . . sentence just discussed. That is to say, you can move something into the next highest clause, if the clause where it originates has to be there. But other kinds of clause, such as relative clauses, adjunct clauses, and coordinate clauses, don't have to be there. A subcategorized clause is one that the sentence would be incomplete without; these other kinds can be omitted at will and still leave a complete sentence.

It follows that if the clause is a relative clause, you can't extract a question-word from it. You can say *We know the boy who comes from Texas*, or *Who do we know?*, or even *Where does the boy who we know come from?*, but not *Where do we know the boy who comes from?* If the clause is an adjunct, you can't extract a question-word from it. You can say *John read the paper while waiting for the bus* or *When did John read the paper?* or *What was John waiting for while he read the paper?*, but not *What did John read the paper while waiting for?* If the clause is coordinate with another clause, you can't extract a question-word from it. You can say *Mary washed the dog and John cooked spaghetti*, but you can't say either *What did Mary wash and John cook spaghetti?* or *What did Mary wash the dog and John cook?*

Now none of these facts are facts that we were ever taught by teachers or by parents. Nor are they things that are dictated by logical necessity, or social convention, or any language-external factor that we might think of. It should be apparent that we are in the presence, not merely of a system that determines what we can and cannot say, but of a system wholly below the level of consciousness that cannot have been acquired through instruction, induction, or any of the other recognized processes by which learning takes place.

The Necessity of Syntax

The reader who is not accustomed to thinking about language from a purely formal viewpoint may find the whole system of syntax, as described above, excessively abstract and complex. In fact, such readers should feel relieved rather than put-upon, since this account has been drastically shortened and simplified (oversimplified, in some cases) for reasons of space and ease of exposition. Furthermore, again for ease of exposition, this account has dealt with only one language, English. Although the principles described are universal, and have been shown to be operative in a wide range of languages, some of which are very different from English, the fact that other languages include different types of grammatical item (clitics, noun classifiers, switch-reference particles, topic markers, and so forth) as well as different processes (scrambling, ergativity, verb serialization, and so on) means that these principles will inevitably be expressed in different ways.

Language *seems* simple and transparent to its users because its processes are quite automatic and unconscious. There is, perhaps, a tendency to believe that automatic and unconscious operations are associated with 'lower' faculties (breathing, digestion, circulation of the blood) while 'higher' faculties ought, simply by virtue of being 'higher', to be somehow within the reach of introspection. If we can't introspect them, we may think, they can't be there. For this reason, many people, including even some linguists, continue to suppose that the complexities of syntax represent some kind of arcane chop-logic indulged in by a handful of ivory-tower grammarians, or the superficial top-dressing of some literary 'high' language remote from the ways in which ordinary people speak.

In fact, the more closely you examine syntax, the more complex you find it to be and the more widely its complexities show up, even in the allegedly 'simple' speech of everyday usage. For instance, all of the crucial examples in this chapter are sentences such as might be heard in any casual conversation. Yet all of the complexities described here, and more besides, were essential if our species was to achieve a communicative system with the power that language has.

A rich and subtly-layered vocabulary, such as we saw in chapter 2, might be sufficient to represent our environment and what we thought might be in that environment. But, if we were to be able to exchange those representations with one another, if we were to gain the vast increment in cognitive capacity that came from being able to manipulate and transmit our thoughts, and if we were to do all of this without having to spend an instant's reflection on the 'how' of it all, then the triple structuring derived from predicability, grammaticization, and syntax (the greatest of which is syntax) was essential. Indeed, no matter how rich the vocabulary, those thoughts could not even have been formed unless at the same time we had had some specific system for organizing them—precisely the system of formal properties described in this chapter. In later chapters, when we try to see how human language could have come into existence, it may become clearer *why* those formal properties were essential to it.

4

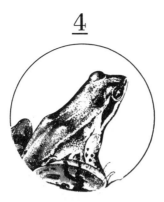

The Origins of Representational Systems

In chapter 1 we encountered what has seemed to many a paradox. On the one hand, language could not have evolved out of animal systems of communication. On the other, language must have evolved, since, for all its complexity, it is simply one of the countless adaptive mechanisms that have developed in species in the course of evolution. But we can escape from this paradox if we accept that language was first and foremost a system of representation. It was therefore, like all other such systems, a mechanism that to a large extent created its own output—rather than merely replicating, in another mode, what was fed into it. Precisely because of this, language was able to increase, by several orders of magnitude, not just the things but the *kinds* of thing that creatures could communicate about. No mere communicative mechanism could ever have done this.

Thus, if we are to seek for the ultimate origins of language, we cannot hope to find those origins by looking at the means by which other creatures communicate with one another. To find out how language, with all its complexities, evolved, it is necessary to look at how systems of representation evolved.

It should be made clear at this point exactly how the term 'representation' is being used. It has sometimes been used in psychology in an unduly narrow sense, to refer to fixed knowledge systems (whether derived innately, or from experience, or by interaction of experience and innate mechanisms). Of course fixed knowledge systems are representational systems, of which language is just one. But the most fleeting perceptions are equally representations. On the highest level of abstraction, at which we must work to get any sense of how creatures in general function in the

75

world, 'representation' will mean simply 'responding or having a permanent propensity to respond to x, an entity or event in the external world, in terms of y, a particular pattern of neural activity'.

Suppose for instance that some form of human interaction, a greeting, say, or an act of worship, is represented in two different modes. Suppose that one of these modes is the tessellated pavement of a Roman bathhouse, where the representation has lain buried for almost two thousand years, and, having now been excavated and artificially preserved, may endure for thousands more. The other is a subliminal image, projected on a video screen so rapidly that our conscious mind cannot apprehend it, although subsequent behavior may strongly indicate that it has indeed been seen. Surely both of these are representations, regardless of the very different lengths of time for which they persist.

Moreover, in the case of human perceptions and knowledge systems, the representations involved, whether fleeting or quasi-permanent, are, unlike the mosaic and video image, generated in ways similar to each other. Whether they are simple or complex, innate or learned, triggered and then immediately lost or permanently stored, they will all be somehow instantiated by patterns of actual or potential activity in selected cells and circuits of the central nervous system (CNS).

In the case of sensory perceptions, those neural actions and interactions may be, relatively speaking, extremely brief and simple, whereas in the case of knowledge systems they may be prolonged and complex. Moreover, in the case of perceptions, the neuronal activity fades rapidly, often leaving no discernable trace, whereas knowledge systems may endure even when their neural infrastructure is relatively inactive for long periods, much as the mosaic endured under earth and rubble when for centuries no human eye could observe it.

The relative endurance of mosaics and subliminal images is of course determined by differences between the properties of stones and light-waves. However, no such difference can account for the varying durability of percepts and knowledge systems, since both are products of the CNS. Although it is still far from clear how long-term memory works, the difference between storage and immediate representation can involve only differing conditions within the CNS, conditions in which the strength of synaptic connections may play a critical role.

But is it really legitimate to speak of activities such as seeing, hearing, and smelling as consisting basically of representation? And can we really gather activities as disparate as seeing, hearing, and smelling, on the one hand, and believing, thinking, and knowing, on the other, under the same heading? For if the answers to these questions are positive, this is equivalent to saying that representations are simply ways of knowing the world—perhaps the only ways in which the world can be known.

Questions such as these can be answered positively only if it can be shown that what seem to be highly structured and complex states and behaviors were derived, through evolutionary processes, from far simpler ones. This is the task that the remainder of this chapter will attempt. Before beginning, however, a word of warning is in order. Any such account has to deal with neurological systems and their modes of operation. Neurological systems, even quite simple ones, are among the most complex things known to us, and it will be hard to keep the main thread of the argument intact without grossly oversimplifying their modes of operation. Hopefully, although some details may be distorted and many others will have to be ignored, the general principles involved will remain clear and will not be falsified.

SIMPLE REPRESENTATIONS

One essential difference between animates and inanimates is that the former are continually acting in their own interests to maximize their chances of survival, whereas the latter aren't. Stones just lie there until heat and frost crumble them to dust, but animate creatures, even plants and amoebas, may react repeatedly without losing their structure. But before any creature can react there must be something for it to react to. That is, some kind of information must pass from environment to creature. Information is, in Gregory Bateson's term, 'a difference that makes a difference'—news of some change in some dimension of the environment that has a potential effect, life-threatening or life-enhancing, on some particular creature. But of course, the fact that some such change takes place does not mean that the information will automatically be transmitted. The creature concerned has to be able to gather the information. That means that it must have some mechanism capable of representing the information through some particular pattern of neural impulses. Moreover, the creature is unlikely to be able to gather the information unless it has some capacity to react appropriately to that information.

Many plant species are capable of reaction to changes in temperature, humidity, or available light which cause them to contract or expand the area of leaf surface that is exposed to the surrounding air. However, only a very few plant species (the so-called 'sensitive plants') respond to being touched by other animate creatures. This is not because the information conveyed by touch is any less crucial to the plant than the information conveyed by climatic changes. Being touched is often only a prelude to being eaten. It is because the plant has very limited resources for responding to touch. Indeed, it has only the same response that plants in general have to climatic changes, which is that of varying their leaf area. Plants cannot pull up their roots and hike off when some herbivore starts munching on them.

In the case of most plants, sensitive or otherwise, it is hardly appropriate to speak of representation, since the cells that receive the information are the same as, or at least of the same type as, those that respond to it. This is true even when, as with some sensitive species, touching the tip of a single leaf sends a ripple of associated activity through the whole plant. The case of insectivorous plants, such as the sundew, is rather different. Typically, a sundew has leaves covered with sticky hairs. When a fly becomes attached to one of these hairs, the leaf gradually closes around it, imprisoning the fly, which the plant 'digests' at leisure.

Here the cells that gather the information are distinct from the cells that cause the leaves to close. Cell A (together perhaps with others like it) registers the fact that a fly (or something) is on it, and then transmits that information to cell B. Cell B, together with other cells of a similar type, then closes the leaves. Could we describe the reaction of cell A, a primitive sensory cell, as a representation of the fact that a fly (or something) has landed on it?

To most people this might seem excessive. Admittedly, both the purely unconscious response of a sundew and our own conscious and highly detailed vision of a fly may have very similar outcomes: the leaves close on the fly, the human reaches for a fly-swatter. But the first outcome is more automatic than the second. Instead of swatting it, the human may write a poem about the fly, or simply ignore it. This difference comes about because in the sundew there is nothing between the representation and the reaction, whereas in the human there is infinitely much.

Another, more immediate difference between our representations and the sundew's lies in degree of definition. We can distinguish flies from other insects and even different species of fly, whereas the sundew cannot distinguish flies from other insects or even insects from bits of earth or stick that the curious observer may place upon it. The sundew's cell A is capable only of distinguishing between two states, a state of no contact and a state of contact with something.

Thus we cannot really say that the reaction of cell A to a fly is the sundew's representation of a fly, or even of a fly-landing event. And yet, which constitutes the most crucial step: distinguishing two states where others distinguish none, or distinguishing infinitely many instead of merely two? Certainly the first step was an indispensible prerequisite for the second. So, to call the firing of cell A a kind of protorepresentation of the state 'assumed presence of potential prey' should not seem altogether unreasonable. For the development of more truly representational mechanisms came about, in large part, through the mere addition and interconnection of equally simple sensory apparatus.

It is perhaps not accidental that the earliest forms of internal representation should be found among the most primitive of predators: sundews, sea anemones, and the like. This is because photosynthesis can be carried on over sustained periods, but live prey is only fleetingly present, and the most basic prerequisite of there being predation at all is the capacity to spot and react to potential prey. This capacity in turn requires the existence of cells specialized to respond to features of, or events in, the creature's immediate environment.

We may suppose that the sensitivity of such cells began in a quite random fashion. Through normal genetic variation and mutation, cells could have developed a wide range of potential sensitivities. However, sensitivities that did not materially increase the lifespan and therefore the breeding potential of their owners would neither spread through a population nor undergo further development. Other types of sensitivity (whether to light, sound, touch, or other factors) might give their owners access to some aspect of the environment that would either provide them with nourishment (say by making them aware of the presence of potential prey), or enable them to escape some danger (by recognizing a potential predator). These other types of sensitivity may be regarded as primitive organs of sense.

Imagine the process of enlarging a photograph. The final output of this process is a blurred and grainy image in which only gross differences of light and shade can be discriminated. Then imagine the process in reverse, beginning with the grainy image and proceeding towards the original photograph. The development of a sense, such as sight, across large numbers of species and over countless millennia of evolution is rather similar to this reverse process. Among earlier species, discrimination is minimal. Gradually, vague shapes coalesce, and some details resolve themselves into identifiable objects even while others, along with most of the background, remain a blur. Only at the end of the process will the photograph resemble the detailed world that our own species sees.

Plants, as compared with animals, have a sharply limited range of sensitivities. More critically, they lack (so far as one can determine) any means for storing information. It follows from this that plants, unlike some quite humble animals, cannot learn.

But lack of storage space is not the only reason plants can't learn. There is also their lack of alternative behaviors. Normally, for any given stimulus plants have only one possible type of response. By comparison, the humblest animals have the option, if touched by some other organism, of approaching or withdrawing from it. You might feel that these are not real alternatives, that the animal is programmed to respond automatically to certain stimuli. But the nature of so-called 'automatic responses' needs closer examination.

Take a species of sea anemone known as *Stomphia coccinea*, whose habitat is frequented by eleven species of starfish, two of which prey upon *Stomphia*. If a member of one of the nine inoffensive species should happen to touch a *Stomphia* specimen, the anemone takes no notice. However, if a member of one of the other two species touches it, it withdraws immediatley. You might say that this is a simple reflex, but it demands a recognition process that was absent in the sundew's case. To execute the reflex, the anemone must be able to distinguish between members of different starfish species, something that even a member of our species could not do without training. Of course the anemone does not train, learn, or in any sense consciously recognize. All it presumably does is to perform some sort of automatic chemical analysis. Yet this analysis suffices to distinguish organisms potentially harmful to it from organisms that are harmless.

Even this simple level shows the intimate link between information and behavior. Behavior of any kind depends on information. If the necessary information is available, the behavior can be performed appropriately (at the right time, to the right creature, and so forth). If the necessary information isn't available, the behavior will not happen or will happen in dysfunctional ways. The senses of creatures in general are such as will give them not random quanta of information, but the information they need to perform those behaviors that they are equipped to perform.

Thus the back legs of cockroaches have fine hairs on them, hairs that contain cells sensitive to changes in air pressure, so that the cockroach can easily dodge your descending shoe. Thus the pit vipers that live in the deserts of the American Southwest have heat-sensitive organs that enable them to distinguish between a toad and a mouse even when the creature is concealed from their vision. A heat sense would give the cockroach more information, and pressure-sensitive cells would give the pit viper more information, but these developments haven't come about and aren't likely to. The cockroach's chances of survival would not be improved if it could tell warmblooded from coldblooded creatures, nor would the viper's if it became sensitive to a buildup in air pressure.

If a sense does not enhance a creature's fitness in some way, that sense will not develop or will not develop past a certain point. Indeed, existing senses may decay if they are not needed (most creatures that dwell in caves are blind). We should bear such things in mind, because our own senses, particularly our sense of sight, tend to mislead us about what senses are and do.

Human vision, for instance, may feel like a magic window on the world, directly revealing to us all that is really there. Of course this is an illusion. What happens in any act of seeing something is that, first, certain cells in the retina react to selected features of that something by varying the normal rate at which they fire. Some of these cells may be little more sophisticated than those of the sundew or sea anemone, reacting merely to the presence or absence of some feature (such as light or movement). Others may respond to a range of features, say lines of a similar orientation, firing at peak rate only in the middle of the range and declining sharply on either side of it. It is as if the object 'seen' were broken down into all its component features and then each feature were given a digital code.

In this coded form the information is sent to subcortical visual centers as well as to the visual cortex, where it is reassembled, so to speak. However, this reassembly does not create a literal replica of what is before the eye, but introduces a variety of subtle rearrangements. It compensates for our own movements and preserves consistencies of size and shape despite movements of the objects concerned, among other things. It is only when these complex yet all-but-instantaneous procedures have been carried out that we 'see' the object before us, that is, integrate and interpret the information that is represented for us by a unique pattern of neural activity.

Compare this with our sense of smell. While we can distinguish an infinite variety of objects by sight, there is only a handful of smells that we can distinguish, and we distinguish them quite crudely. We tend not to be aware of these limitations. We assume that most objects have no smell, an illusion that would not last long if dogs could talk.

Contrast this with some other senses. An absence of information from our ears, which we call 'silence', can be quite disturbing if it is complete enough. An absence of information from our eyes (unless we have closed them deliberately) brings immediate panic. An absence of information from our nose, however, seems the natural, normal condition, whereas 'a nice smell', 'a nasty smell', or 'a funny smell' are somehow unusual and noteworthy events. Imagine what it would be like if for most of the time we saw nothing and only occasionally some random object, funny, nice, or nasty, loomed within the scope of our vision. Yet even our sense of smell, with its few and narrow tunnels through a wall of olfactory blindness, is subtler than the mechanisms with which senses originated and on which all senses are founded.

No creature, including ourselves, receives from its senses more than a selection from the range of information that is potentially available. Creatures get the senses they need for the behaviors they are capable of. If they cease to need them they lose them, as cave-dwelling species lose sight and as the primates, culminating in us, have been losing smell. It follows that what is presented to any species, not excluding our own, by its senses is not 'reality' but a species-specific view of reality—not 'what is out there', but what it is useful for the species to know about what is out there.

This species-specific view constitutes what we may call the primary representational system (PRS) of any creature. A PRS may be very simple or very complex, but regardless of their degree of complexity all PRSs belong to the same type. No species, not even ours, has any privileged access to reality, although some species, and in particular ours, may perceive more aspects of it than do others. But the most complex PRS (as distinct from the secondary representational system that language provides for us alone) derives from the same source as the simplest, and simple representations arose naturally from the conjunction of three things: cells that could discriminate between two states, the distinction between sensory cells that gathered information and motor cells that acted on it, and motor cells that could perform more than one type of behavior in response to a given stimulus. What most sharply differentiates simple from complex PRSs is the degree of processing that outputs of sensory cells undergo.

PROCESSING OF SIMPLE REPRESENTATIONS

In the kinds of creature we have considered so far, there is no intermediate level of processing. Stimulus and response—the touch of the 'bad' starfish and the anemone's withdrawal—are directly linked. When such a creature perceives, no one would suppose that it needs a homunculus in its head to read its perceptions. Yet even at this stage, increases in the size of creatures were sufficient to cause the appearance of cells intermediate between sensory and motor cells, although at first these were required merely to boost the messages of sensory cells over intervening distances.

However, if more than one type of sensory cell develops, and if nerves extend and branch rather freely, as they do, it is only a matter of time before two types of sensory cell become linked to the same intermediate cell. A new dimension now appears: the intermediate cell incorporates the outputs of both sensory cells. On the simplest assumption, which is that both sensory cells transmit only either-or messages like the sundew's cell A, the intermediate cell can transmit four messages, rather than the two it could previously transmit: cell 1 is firing alone, cell 2 is firing alone, both 1 and 2 are firing, neither cell is firing.

In fact, cells 1 and 2 need not both be sensory cells. One may be interoceptive or proprioceptive, reporting on the creature's internal states or providing feedback from its movements. Even among creatures that can do little but move and eat, the fact that they are autonomous energy sources and actively seek their own energy supply means that there must be some mediation betwen stimulus and response that incorporates both external and internal information. Quite simple predators have to decide not merely, is this object prey or not? but also, am I hungry or not?

Creatures best conserve energy by hunting when hungry and resting when replete. If they snatched at all prey with automatic reflexes, the only lasting result would be indigestion. Accordingly, information from different sources has to be collated. Nervous systems translate both internal and external states into quantitative terms, represented by variations in the firing rates of the relevant neurons. Messages from other cells may cause them to fire faster than, or slower than, their normal 'resting' rate. These variations form, as it were, an abstract schema that represents what is happening elsewhere, both inside and outside the creature. The intermediate neuron(s) that merge these two sources will determine the creature's behavior in accordance with the following equations:

$$+ \text{ 'belly full' } - \text{ 'prey present' } = \text{ 'no action'}$$
$$- \text{ 'belly full' } - \text{ 'prey present' } = \text{ 'no action'}$$
$$+ \text{ 'belly full' } + \text{ 'prey present' } = \text{ 'no action'}$$
$$- \text{ 'belly full' } + \text{ 'prey present' } = \text{ 'action'}$$

For simplicity's sake, it has been assumed that the 'belly full' signal, like the signals that we have previously considered, is an 'all-or-nothing' signal. But this is by no means always the case. Some stimuli are of their very nature binary: a fly (or a bit of earth) touches the sundew's hairs, a 'bad' starfish touches or fails to touch the anemone. But in many cases stimuli are gradient in nature.

Take the hypothetical case of a grub that lives in cracks in the bark of trees and responds to an increase in light intensity, which may mean that some predator is opening up the tree's protective bark. Changes in light intensity are on a continuum. A slight change should not have any effect on the grub, since it might arise from innocent causes. The grub will be more efficient if it wastes little time running from nonexistent dangers, but responds quickly to real ones. Its nervous system will then include some type of threshold mechanism, some level that the stimulus has to reach before the reflex is triggered. The grub remains inactive till this threshold is reached, then moves. A scale of gradience in terms of light intensity is somehow translated into two states, inaction/motion.

But a threshold does not represent a fixed point on such a scale. Consider what is known as habituation. The first time a creature receives a novel stimulus, its reaction is usually quick and extreme. However, if no ill effects follow, and the stimulus is repeated, each recurrence elicits a weaker response. The common crayfish has an escape mechanism that causes it, if touched from the rear, to pitch forwards abruptly, so that it looks as if it is standing on its head. However, if you touch it at one-minute intervals, you will eventually reach a point at which it doesn't react at all. It might seem excessive to say that the crayfish 'has learned' or 'remembers' that your touch is harmless. But processes such as these are the precursors of learning, and show that even the most rigidly pro-grammed behaviors are malleable under the hammer of experience.

The information a creature receives may be, and often is, gradient in nature, consisting of relatively gradual changes in the size and shape of objects, for instance, rather than sudden appearances and disap-pearances. This gradience is reflected by variations in the frequency with which given neurons fire. But in general creatures will distinguish gradience only if they possess a graded range of responses to match the gradient information. This in turn will depend on how sophisticated par-ticular motor organs (and the cells controlling them) have become. Can those organs only respond with a grab? Or can they make a variety of motions from all-out grab to tentative, stealthy extension? Other things being equal, behavioral plasticity—the capacity to make more and more varied responses to slightly differing stimuli—will give an adaptive ad-vantage to the creature that possesses it.

But plasticity alone is not enough. The more plastic a creature be-comes, the more sophisticated it must be, both in its senses and in its ability to collate information from more than one sensory source. This latter process involves far more than merely summarizing data, for sometimes information from different sources may suggest different forms of action.

Consider a lizard on a wall stalking a fly. You might say that its moves are preprogrammed, a fixed action pattern. The moves themselves, its forward or slantwise darts and long pauses, are indeed stereotyped. Yet the *execution* of this routine cannot be preprogrammed. The angle at which the lizard moves, the distance it covers on each forward movement, and the amount of time that elapses between movements are all variables, sometimes clearly dependent on the activity, or lack of it, shown by the fly.

For the lizard must continually monitor the fly's movements and in particular its degree of restlessness, since this may indicate that it is in a state of high awareness. The lizard's hunger and its knowledge that it is within striking distance of the fly will urge it forward, while its observation of the fly's extreme restlessness will hold it back. A balance has to be struck: a complex (and of course quite automatic and unconscious) computation has to be made that will hopefully yield the exact right moment for the lizard to strike.

Thus the process of collating inputs can perhaps best be described (if we can purge the term of its connotations of consciousness) as an evaluation procedure. The lizard, or any creature of equal or greater complexity, weighs the information and on the basis of that information determines its next move.

The ability to evaluate conflicting data strongly suggests that the creature is already far more than a passive puppet of its environment. For it weighs not only inputs from different senses and its own internal and external states, but also elements of experience that are exclusively its own. That this is so is manifest even in a process as basic as habituation, where the creature looks back, so to speak, at its past experience and uses this to evaluate its current experience.

In this way creatures begin to acquire autonomy. Autonomy does not mean 'free will', although autonomy is clearly a necessary precursor of the state we ourselves enjoy, a state in which we can at least wonder whether or not we have something called 'free will'. It merely means that, although decisions may still be unconscious and automatic, the place where decisions are made no longer lies somewhere between the creature and its environment (which is where we might suppose that the decisions of amoebas, or anemones, or sundews take place). Rather it rests firmly within the brain of the creature concerned.

What this means may at first sound paradoxical. The opening of the gates of consciousness is in fact a progressive distancing of the creature from the actual world of external objects and events. For a stone, no level of representation intervenes between it and the rest of nature. At the lower levels of organic life there are simple representations consisting of the activities of sensory cells. From the higher invertebrates on up there have to be representations in terms of the processing mechanisms that increasingly intervene between sensory and motor cells to summate and evaluate the input of the former. As in the case of the fly-catching lizard, it is these representations, rather than external events, that trigger action. Eventually, language will constitute yet another level of representation, further distancing the creature from its environment even as it brings that environment further yet under the creature's control.

At this stage, the reader may ask how we can talk about sensory and brain processes 'distancing' a creature from the external world, when they are in fact the only things that give the creature access to that world. If the view of that world they gave were not a true one, how could creatures avoid flying into walls, walking into the embrace of predators, or trying to mate with members of the wrong species?

In fact it is meaningless to talk about 'a true view of the world'. To attain such a view, a minimum prerequisite would be for the viewer not to belong to any particular species. For every species has a unique view of the world. All of these views may seem defective in some respect when compared with the views of other creatures, let alone in any absolute sense, but this state of affairs is inescapable. Each species's view, what we have termed its PRS, is determined by its species-specific equipment. This equipment is in turn determined, in part by biological accident and in part by what has proven useful or beneficial to that species over the course of evolution.

Moreover, the paradox of consciousness—that the more consciousness one has, the more layers of processing divide one from the world—is, like so much else in nature, a trade-off. Progressive distancing from the external world is simply the price that is paid for knowing anything about the world at all. The deeper and broader consciousness of the world becomes, the more complex the layers of processing necessary to obtain that consciousness. The more complex the layers of processing, the greater the chance that the properties of those layers, like the properties of all representational systems, will be imposed on what is represented, causing distortions of which the processor can hardly be aware. Indeed the clarity and detail that complex representations provide are so great, so convincing, that it is hard to believe they could ever be defective or misleading as a guide to the real.

Finally it is absurd to speak about 'a true view of the world' because it is not even true for any creature that what is perceived is the world itself. What constitutes any creature's view is essentially a system of categories. The sea anemone, for instance, divides the world into 'prey' and 'nonprey', then divides the latter category into 'potential predators' and 'others', while the frog divides the world into 'frogs', 'flying bugs', 'ponds', and perhaps a few other categories like 'large looming object (potential threat)'. All that changes, as creatures grow progressively more complex, is the number of categories into which things can be divided.

FROM REPRESENTATIONS TO CATEGORIES

Suppose you say to me, 'I saw a golden eagle yesterday'. What this really means, cumbersome though it may sound, is 'An object presented itself in my visual field that seemed to correspond to an internal representation labeled *golden eagle*'.

Now suppose that you are alone in a house at night and hear a noise. Your first reaction is to try to assign that noise to a category. Only if you can do this can you make an appropriate response: ignore it, fix the screen door, let the cat out, call the police, or whatever. You have categorized it as 'a noise'. This means that you have not really categorized the experience itself, but have merely identified the sensory channel that brought it to you.

Finally, suppose that something awakens you from a deep sleep but you have no idea whether that something was a noise, a flash of light, a touch, a change in temperature, or something in a dream. You have not even identified the sensory channel through which the experience came to you (or even identified its source as being a sensory channel, since a dream cannot be excluded). Have you then perceived or experienced anything at all? The answer would seem to be no (unless you count the awakening itself as an experience).

If we say we have perceived something, we are simply saying that we have responded to some stimulus that seemed to arise in the external world and have assigned that stimulus to some category or other. We have determined the appropriate category by a process of selection, selecting what seems the best fit out of the set of all categories available to us. That assignment might, of course, be wrong. What we thought was an eagle might turn out to have been a buzzard, what we thought was the cat could be an intruder who will cost us our lives. The fact that our assignments may more often than not prove correct does not alter the fact that no 'perception' is anything more than a category assignment, a best guess at what may be out there.

The set of categories from which a creature can select is largely determined by its species membership, and will vary according to whether the creature concerned is an anemone, a frog, a rat, or a human. The fact that these categories vary according to species follows naturally from the fact that they have no separate existence in the external world. They exist only as internal representations, specialized mechanisms for apprehending that world.

If knowing the world consists of sorting it into categories, how are such categories derived? In some cases there can be little doubt that the representations on which they are based are innately given. We saw in chapter 1 how a captive monkey raised in isolation will respond to its first sight of a snake with fear and avoidance. It cannot have had a previous bad experience with a snake, nor can its mother or some older monkey have somehow told it about snakes. Yet, as we also saw, there is nothing either mystical or mysterious in claiming that the monkey has some kind of innate representation of a snake. If those neurons that would be excited or inhibited by the various aspects of a snake's appearance happen already to be linked either to the fear centers or directly to cells controlling avoidance behaviors, then the monkey will react with fear or avoidance to his very first experience of a snake.

Yet, useful as such mechanisms are, there is a limit to their utility. One weakness is that innate representations tend to be fuzzier than learned ones—if this were not so, it would not be so easy to fool a monkey by waving a piece of rope or a length of rubber hose. But a more crucial weakness is that each innate representation must be matched with a single response.

In simple cases this doesn't matter. If someone tries to jab a pencil in your eye, there is nothing more useful you could do than blink. If you feel sudden heat on any part of your body, there is no sensible alternative to jerking that part away from the heat source. But relatively few things need quite such unequivocal responses. Indeed, in many cases responses of this kind would be dysfunctional.

Suppose a species such as the wildebeest was so programmed that its members took to their heels whenever they saw a lion. Such a species would have less feeding time than its competitors and would exhaust itself more. Wildebeest would then fall prey to lions much oftener than members of other species, and might soon become extinct. It is obviously in the interests of wildebeest to differentiate between those lions that constitute a direct and immediate threat to them and those that do not. Such distinctions, involving much subtle if tacit analysis of lion behavior, can only be made on the basis of experience—in other words, must be learned.

But a problem arises here. Creatures whose activities are based on fixed action patterns have stereotyped representations to which they automatically respond, because a triggering of the representation directly triggers the action. But if the advantage of learned representations is greater plasticity of response, how can the link between representation and appropriate response be maintained? Say that the wildebeest has learned to recognize lions in a wide variety of presentations (perhaps in much the same way as, in intelligence tests, we are able to recognize whether an abstract figure rotated in space is 'the same' or 'a different' figure). How is it to know when lion behavior is getting dangerous? What is to stop it from just standing there and saying to itself, as an intelligent robot might: 'Hmm, that lion appears to be getting bigger, which indicates that it is approaching me, how interesting!'

The most subtle analysis of lion behavior will not profit the wildebeest unless it is afraid of lions. Mere sight of the lion does not trigger an immediate response, as it might in a less complex creature, but it does trigger a particular state of awareness, a state that becomes intensified if the lion approaches. Indeed, at a certain point we might say that the state changes qualitatively as it in turn triggers a behavioral response. If the wildebeest were possessed of our own faculties, we would have no hesitation in saying that alarm had turned into fear, or in more acute cases, that fear had turned into terror or panic.

In fact it may not be at all anthropomorphic to say that the wildebeest, or any other creature of adequate complexity, has just such a range of emotions. Emotions are bridges between representation and response that become essential as learning increasingly replaces fixed action patterns. They are probably even less well understood than representations or behavioral responses, so relatively little will be said about them here. But it is essential to note their emergence, for they mark a further stage in the development towards consciousness.

Emotions are the unique properties of the creature that experiences them. All normal members of a species may react in the same way to the same hard-wired representation—it is not the case that some of us jump back from a red-hot object while others do not. But emotional reactions to a given stimulus vary notoriously and unpredictably from one person to another. This variation will be less in less complex species. But there will always be some degree of variation, because emotions are triggered by learned representations, and since no two creatures have exactly the same experiences, no two creatures will have exactly the same set of learned representations.

Thus emotions contribute to the autonomy of individual creatures. They flee from their own particular fears, and react with aggression to incidents that make them angry but might leave another conspecific unmoved. They pursue their own wants and desires on the basis of what has been pleasurable to them as individuals in the past. The more varied the experience, the greater this emotional autonomy. We will find, in chapter 8, that these facts play an important part in the greater mysteries of mind and consciousness.

At least one fairly direct link between learned representations and consciousness can be briefly mentioned here. It is learned rather than innate information that is accessible to human consciousness. If you doubt this, try describing how you write, or sew, or swim, and then try (without consulting a physiology textbook!) to describe how you metabolize food, produce hormones, or grow hair—or, for that matter, how you produce sentences in your native language. Why consciousness should be circumscribed in this manner remains mysterious. The general wiring system of the brain, which links certain areas much more fully than others, is perhaps largely responsible, and this system in turn may be influenced by some kind of 'need to know'. Our bowels constitute a closed system that can adjust automatically to most factors affecting it, whereas our behavior in the world requires constant feedback if it is to be properly adjusted; input from as many sources as possible should be evaluated if that adjustment is to be optimal.

Yet, whether representations are innate or learned, they all have certain things in common. Both innate and learned representations lead to category formation, but do not form categories unaided. We saw above that for the monkey to form its category 'snake' required more than just snakes and an internal representation of long, thin, nonstraight objects. What linked object to category was the particular emotion that a certain representation aroused and the particular behavior that that emotion activated. In other words, three things, not two, have to be present for a category to be formed: an object in the external world; patterns of cell activity, in an observer's brain, that are directly or indirectly triggered by that object; and the observer's responses, both internal and external, to these patterns.

Because we look at category formation as a part of meaning, and meaning as something exclusive to ourselves, we tend to see categories as the result of some kind of analytic process in which an observer looks objectively at the world and somehow decides what is what. In so doing we ignore the possibility that our categorizations may owe much to the categorizations of earlier, prelinguistic creatures. For them, category formation surely resulted not from some abstract form of analysis but rather from a dynamic interaction between themselves and their environment. Rather than creating a list of features or estimating distances from prototypes, their categories were built on sets of phenomena to which they responded in similar ways.

It seems likely therefore that we too do not build categories merely by analyzing sensory input, by counting points of similarity, or by extrapolating from some prototype, as discussed in chapter 2. Categories may be influenced by such factors, and certainly, after the event, we can make up plausible stories about how we could have arrived at them by these means. But a further and perhaps more crucial factor in category formation is the grouping together of representations that require similar behavioral responses. Thus, a bird is not merely something with two legs and feathers that flies, nor is it simply a quality that radiates from a robin. It is something that lays round things you can eat if you can find them. A tree is not just something that is taller or straighter than a bush, but it is something that is a source of wood (if mature) and that requires an axe or saw of some kind to cut it. It is also something that you can climb, if pursued, rather than merely something you can hide in (like a bush).

In other words, the set of categories that constitutes the PRS of any species is determined by the evolutionary requirements of that species: what it eats, what other things it needs, what it fears, what its preferred strategies for survival are, and how those strategies interact with the strategies of other species. The PRS as a whole constitutes, as it were, a model of reality that serves to guide behavior.

But what exactly constitutes a category? As should be apparent from the foregoing discussion, a category is simply a tacit concept. Or, to put it another way, 'concept' is simply the name we give to a category when we know that it is a category and that we have it at our disposal for the sorting of raw experience. The categories by which other creatures operate—of whose existence they have (we may assume) no conscious awareness—may perhaps be more appropriately referred to as protoconcepts.

In this way we may resolve an issue that was left vague in earlier sections: Did concepts arise prior to language, or was language the catalyst that produced them? In all probability, language served in the first instance merely to label protoconcepts derived from prelinguistic experience. Of course, in the long run it did far more than this, generating its

91

own concepts, like 'absence' or 'unicorn' or 'golden mountain', that had no basis whatsoever in the PRS. But initially, at least, language may have contributed little to conceptualization beyond a means by which its results could be more easily manipulated.

The exact mechanisms by which categories are formed are still very far from being understood, though fortunately their precise nature is immaterial to the present discussion. We may suppose, for example, that a creature as simple as a frog has a category of small, round, dark objects that are in a state of rapid motion. If the frog could label its own categories, it would probably label this one 'bug'. However, the fact that frogs can be deceived into snapping at small round pellets flipped past their heads shows that the trigger for the snapping action cannot be equated with real-world bugs. In the same way, the willingness of young thrushes to gape at a figure that is quite abstract (consisting basically of a small circle atop a considerably larger one) shows that the trigger for gaping behavior cannot be true recognition of the birds' own mother.

These systems seem to us naive and easily fooled. But in fact, no system of categorization would work if it could not operate across quite broad ranges of objective phenomena. For, in the real world, objects of the 'same kind' seldom present themselves to us in exactly the same way. They may appear frontally or obliquely, with varying degrees of occlusion, at varying distances, and under widely differing light conditions. Unless a creature can reliably categorize over most, if not the whole, of this range, its chances of survival may be sharply reduced.

What this means is that any creature whose sensory capacities exceed those described in the first section of this chapter somehow perceives relations of unity between objects that in superficial detail appear quite different. Consider for example the diversity of those objects that we would classify as 'trees', including as they do palms, pines, maples, baobabs, olives, and poplars, from which, somehow, a common identity is abstracted. Something very similar happens in our processing of speech. Any utterance of a given speech-sound may differ acoustically, even if only slightly, from any other. This is a problem for automated speech-recognition devices that has still not been completely overcome. The human ear, however, automatically equilibrates these differences, at least for dialects with which the hearer is familiar.

In all probability, successful categorization depends as much on negative as on positive factors—on saying what things are not, as much as on saying what they are. When we identify several different things as being all pictures of trees, it is unlikely that we really abstract from them some common quintessence of 'treeness'. It is more plausible to suppose that—since our minds work as they do, with large numbers of weak parallel processors rather than a single strong linear processor—we simultaneously eliminate possible alternatives.

If this is so, it derives from a feature of PRSs that has so far gone unnoticed. As was shown in chapter 2, in language—our secondary representational system—a system of categories divides the universe exhaustively. But the same is surely true of the primary system also. If the only categories a frog has are 'frog', 'pond', 'bug', 'large looming object', and 'what's left (irrelevant to frogs)', then these categories compose the frog's world, and everything the frog perceives must be assigned to one category or another.

If categories are indeed constituted in this way, they should be quite easy to define negatively. Perhaps the most basic category, for any species that reproduces sexually, is that of 'own species'. This would initially give the frog, for example, the two categories of 'frog' and 'nonfrog'. The second could then be further subdivided so that any category could be defined in terms of nonmembership of other categories: a frog definition of 'pond' might be 'nonfrog, nonbug, non-large-looming-object, (but not irrelevant)'. And this is only what we would expect if indeed all senses derive ultimately from cellular structures which, like lightswitches, distinguish only two states. In the beginning, there was the undifferentiated void. Then came 'x' and 'not-x' (the sundew's 'contact with something' versus 'no contact'). Then 'not-x' was divided into 'y' and 'not-y' (the sea anemone's 'good starfish' and 'bad starfish'). Eventually, representations proliferated. The resemblance to the 'origins' story of Taoism may not be altogether coincidental.

There is evidence that relatively 'unintelligent' creatures have (or can develop) categories that are quite sophisticated. For instance, experiments by Richard Herrnstein and his associates have shown that pigeons possess well-established protoconcepts of such things as trees and people. Pigeons were first trained to peck at a button when a picture appeared that contained a given class of object (tree, human, or whatever). When they had acquired this behavior, they were presented with a wider variety of pictures, some of which contained representatives of the category being tested, while others did not. The pigeons were able to respond with a high degree of accuracy, pecking for 'tree' pictures, for instance, even when only a few branches appeared within a predominantly urban scene. It is hard to see how such behaviors could be performed if pigeons had not acquired protoconcepts that allowed, as do human concepts, for very wide variation in the objective phenomena associated with them.

But are such protoconcepts innately specified, requiring only some form of environmental triggering to activate them, or are they acquired inductively? That they are all hard-wired is implausible in view of the fact that pigeons have also been trained to behave in similar ways using pictures of fish or Snoopy cartoons—things no pigeon can have had prior knowledge of. Yet, since things looking more or less like people have probably been a threat to pigeons for at least five million years, and since trees have been a haven for pigeons as long as there have been pigeons, it seems unlikely that the brains of pigeons are complete *tabulae rasae* on which experience must laboriously rewrite such crucial environmental factors for each individual in each of millions of pigeon generations. It is at least as likely that over the course of evolution there emerged pigeons whose neural equipment provided almost immediate recognition of things (like trees and people) that had specific significance for pigeons, and that the neural capacities required for such a task (capacities still hardly understood, and hard, if not impossible, to instantiate in machines) were subsequently transferred to the analysis of novel objects in the environment, regardless of whether these objects were significant or not.

Any evolutionary model predicts that, if this supposition is correct, such capacities, once present in any individual, will spread and develop until they became characteristic of whole populations. Moreover, given the conservative nature of genetic blueprints, one would expect a particular protoconcept to be found among descendents of the species in which it first occurred, provided that the referent of the protoconcept continued to be significant in the lives of descendent species. In this way, protoconcepts would tend to accumulate over evolutionary time.

REPRESENTATION OF SPACE

So far, for simplicity's sake, but at the cost of some artificiality, we have been treating creatures as if each of them perceived only single, isolated phenomena and as if each phenomenon was some kind of static entity. This, of course, is far from the truth. What creatures perceive and experience is a gestalt, a holistic view that includes, at the very least, the behaviors of objects and the relations between different objects, as well as the objects themselves.

Take, for example, the spatial relationships that exist between fixed objects. These and similar relations are internally represented, just as the objects themselves are. If we are familiar with a room, we can move around in it even in total darkness or with our eyes closed. Or, if we walk through a region that is strange to us, we can, with a little attention, find our way back again even though we will be approaching all landmarks from an opposite direction. In order to do such things, we have to construct some kind of internal representation of the areas concerned. This representation constitutes in effect an internalized map of the room or the region, a map that at least some of us could transfer to paper if we were required to do so.

The general capacities in use here are not unique to us or even to 'higher' species. There are species of insect that carry in their heads maps of the immediate environment within which they nest and feed. One species of hunting wasp, *Philanthus*, locates its nest not by using an automatized homing instinct but by memorizing the location of various landmarks around it. If the landmarks are disturbed, it laboriously searches out its nest and then learns a new set of landmarks. An even more striking example is provided by another wasp species, *Ammophila*, which rears its larvae in burrows and provisions them with caterpillars. *Ammophila* may have as many as 15 larvae hidden away at any given time and it must remember where each one is and what stage of development it has reached in order to tend it appropriately.

Both insects, then, have in their brains internalized maps of their environments. Note how the need for such maps arises as soon as creatures develop the strategy of obtaining a secure base to operate from. Unless, like hermit crabs, they carry that base around with them, or, like mussels or whelks, they are attached to that base, all such creatures have to find their way home. Since the location of 'home' may vary over time, fixed action patterns alone are useless here, and the ability to learn becomes essential.

But a creature cannot construct a cognitive map on the basis of sensory information, learning, and memory alone. What it learns has to be embedded in a preexisting framework that is in effect a transform of external space. Without some such transformational link between map and environment, the creature could not know that point x in the internalized map bore a constant relation to point x' in the environment, and that the proportion borne by the distance x-y to the distance x-z in the map is the same as that borne by x'-y' to x'-z' in the environment.

Cognitive maps do not, of course, have to be based on sight. Mental mechanisms, including language, are modality-free (signed languages obey the same principles as spoken languages). Bats, operating by night, rely principally on echolocation to determine their whereabouts. If you raise bats in a vacant barn and then crisscross the empty areas with wires, the bats will learn the locations of the wires and will consistently avoid them. But if, during the bats' sleeping period, you rearrange the

95

wires, the bats on waking will repeatedly blunder into the wires until they have learned the new arrangement.

What this means is that bats do not normally operate on direct sensory impressions of their environment. If they did, then the bats' 'sonar system' would immediately inform them that the wires had been moved to new locations, and there would never be any accidents. Rather, bats build an internal model of their environment and then operate on the basis of that model.

Under most circumstances, such a course has evolutionary advantages. Rather than expending all its energies on continually verifying and reverifying facts that are unlikely to change, as might a robot with no prior knowledge of the world, a bat is best served by assuming that features of the environment do not change and by concentrating all its energies on those factors that do change and change rapidly, such as the location of the insect that it is currently pursuing. Occasionally this concentration may be excessive and may lead to disaster, but most times it will not.

There is no reason to suppose that this degree of model-dependence is limited to bats. For most, if not all, species, many environmental features are relatively stable, so that the same considerations of economy apply. Moreover, there is no reason to suppose that model-dependence is limited to spatial maps of the environment. Such models are best conceived of as merely parts of the much more comprehensive models of the environment that are created by the PRS of each species.

REPRESENTATION OF ACTION

So far, we have spoken as if the categories into which models of the environment divide the world were limited to types of object or entity. But this cannot be the case, since the brain contains not merely cells tuned to respond to colors, light-intensities, edges, and other static features, but also cells tuned to respond to motion—motion of various types and speeds, and in a variety of directions. Recent work by David Perret and others has shown that different cells in the temporal cortex of monkeys respond to different movements—forward, backward, to the left, to the right—of a primatelike figure. Such cells, moreover, are highly specialized. For instance, a cell excited by the motion of such a figure toward it remains quite unaffected by motion away from it or to one side. Indeed, there are even specific cells that are excited only by specific motions of the (human or monkey) hand: grabbing, picking, tearing, and so on.

In light of what has already been surveyed, there is nothing essentially mysterious about such processes. Given a set of sensory cells A, B, C, D, and E, summatory cell X fires only when all members of the set are excited simultaneously. But suppose that what A, B, C, D, and E each respond to is some property of angle, or size, or motion inherent in, say, a left-to-right movement of a primate body, or a grabbing gesture of a primate hand. Let us suppose, too, that X is not affected either by the firing of other cells or by the firing of any subset of the set A–E. The firing of X might then be said to have the 'meaning' of 'primate body moving rightwards' or 'primate hand grabbing'.

It may be tempting, at this stage, to see in the responses of higher-level neurons to complex stimuli the neurological infrastructure of those lexical items that would eventually form the building-blocks of language. Where these responses, imply the existence of categories like the pigeon's 'tree' or 'human', such a move may be legitimate. These may well be embryos of the concepts that in us are represented by nouns. It is harder to regard the monkey's 'primate moving rightwards' or 'primate hand grabbing' as examples of protoverbs. For one thing, their referents are not actions but agents-plus-actions. If language were read directly off outputs like those of cell X, then we would surely have a 'cow-grazing' kind of language that expressed an entity and its behavior with a single term.

As we saw in chapters 2 and 3, this is something that never happens: the subject-predicate distinction is perhaps the most basic in language. But this can hardly be due to any deficiency in the PRS. It may be due instead to an inevitable imbalance between the representation of entities and the representation of behavior.

Imagine two sets of pictures. One set shows a tiger sleeping, a tiger waking, a tiger stalking, a tiger running, a tiger attacking prey, and so on. The other set shows a tiger running, a rhinoceros running, an ostrich running, a cockroach running, a man running, and so on. Notice how much more constancy there is in 'tiger' than there is in 'running'. 'Tiger' will preserve many consistent features across all of its behaviors. Ears, stripes, tail, and so forth will remain much the same regardless of what the beast is doing. The representations of these constant features in the PRS will take the form of constellations of neurons a very high percentage of which will fire on every presentation of a tiger.

'Running', in contrast, will preserve relatively few constant features across all of its performers. Sometimes there will be two legs running, sometimes four, sometimes six, the legs themselves will vary greatly in size and shape, and so on. The existence of these objective differences between the different tokens of 'running' means that there will be no single set of neurons all or almost all of which will fire for any event of 'running'. Indeed, relatively few neurons will be fired by both the running of a cockroach and the running of an elephant, while relatively many will be fired for the first but not the second, and vice versa.

It was pointed out in chapter 2 that verbs are much more abstract than nouns, and we can now see why this is so. Nouns could have as their substrate the kind of generalizations available to creatures no more sophisticated than pigeons. But perhaps this does not apply to verbs. Indeed, since the same action by different species would excite quite different sets of neurons, it is hard to see how, without language, there could be any primary representation of actions that abstracted away from different performers of those actions, as verbs like *run* or *attack* or *hide* do. (One could easily test this by seeing if pigeons could be trained to recognize pictures of 'running', and if so whether they could subsequently distinguish between 'running' and 'nonrunning' pictures as reliably as they distinguish 'tree' from 'nontree').

However, this line of argument breaks down if we limit ourselves to behaviors that only certain species are likely to perform. Perhaps 'primate hand grabbing' is the key here. For only primates have anything quite like a primate hand, and it follows that only primates can perform an action like 'grabbing with the hand'. Hence nothing can be conceived of as 'grabbing with the hand' that would not trigger sensory neurons A–E and summatory neuron X. Moreover, since members of a given species of primates seldom interact with primates of other species, but almost always with members of their own species, the firing of those neurons would have come to be associated exclusively with behaviors of their own species. If prototypical nouns represented species that interacted significantly with hominids, then prototypical verbs perhaps represented actions that only hominids could perform.

The very concept 'action performed only by one's own species' suggests a dimension that has not been examined thus far. If any creature has what amounts to an inbuilt recognition device for such actions, and if, moreover, the species performing the actions is the observer's own species, this can only be the result of high attention paid to the behavior of conspecifics with whom the creature interacts on a regular basis. In other words, there are certain kinds of representation that are unlikely to arise outside of social species.

REPRESENTATION OF SOCIETY

Throughout evolution, there have been social animals and solitary animals. But as complexity increased, the social tended to be favored over the solitary.

The connection between complexity and sociability is a complicated one. Broadly speaking, the survival of a species may be secured in either of two ways: by sheer numbers or by complex adaptations. Creatures that depend on fixed action patterns can afford to "take the numbers route," to lay vast quantities of eggs and then leave them to hatch on their own. A vast percentage will be destroyed by predators but those that survive are, practically from birth, as fit to cope with the world as they will ever be.

But creatures that depend more heavily on complex adaptations involving learning cannot be left to the vagaries of chance, otherwise a whole generation could be consumed by predators before it reached breeding age. Such creatures require the active nurturance of at least a mother (and for many species, both parents or several older females). This means that, at least during the early part of their lives, they form part of a tightknit social community. For those species that have developed communal foraging patterns, this social community may persist through their entire lives.

Here we find a paradox similar to that of distancing. Just as creatures had to be distanced from the world in order to know the world, so creatures had to live socially before they could learn what it meant to be an individual.

Of course, not all creatures that live communally learn individuality. Although the societies of ants, bees, and termites are highly complex, the individuals that compose them are too simple, and depend too heavily on fixed action patterns, to develop any kind of awareness of others as individuals. (Or so we assume—we have no way of asking them!) But social mammals, especially canids and primates, evolved at a time when the substrates of consciousness (sharp and diverse senses, memory, learning, information-based internal states, and internalized models of reality) had developed far further than they ever could among insects. Once such creatures began to live together, it was inevitable that they would derive a sense that their companions were not merely members of the same species but a set of individuals, each with its own distinctive character.

Recognition of others arises, in the first place, from the circumstances under which social mammals mature. Over a period of at least several months, the members of a single litter interact intensively with one another. Often they are confined together for long periods in a lair or burrow, where they compete for food and the attentions of their mother. Later they may be incorporated into a small group the membership of which changes only through the death of old members and the birth of new ones.

Under these circumstances, each individual learns the strengths and weaknesses of each of the others: what pleases them, what makes them angry, whether they are quick or slow to respond, whether they are friendly, distant, or aggressively hostile, and a host of other personality features. It is only by learning such things that the young animal finds out just how far it can go in pursuit of its own ends. Thus, to each individual in such a group, every other individual constitutes a sharply defined and detailed personality.

It is impossible to determine where, or even whether, in this process a creature realizes that it figures in the lives of others in just the same way that others figure in its own life. Perhaps it can never truly do this until language has provided it with a secondary representational system from the platform of which, so to speak, it can observe both others and itself. But the awareness of others as unique individuals forms a necessary, if not a sufficient, prerequisite for the discovery that one is oneself just such an individual. And this awareness of the self as an individual in turn forms a cornerstone of the world of language and consciousness that is, so far as we are aware, the property of only one of the countless species that evolution has produced upon earth.

THE LONG YET STRAIGHT ROAD TO LANGUAGE AND CONSCIOUSNESS

With the more advanced primates we have arrived at a stage immediately antecedent to that of language. When that stage was reached, a great part of the infrastructure of language had already been laid down. Since language is primarily a representational system, its antecedents are to be found not in primitive forms of communication but rather in the means by which earlier and simpler species represented to themselves the universe they inhabited.

The first step toward language was taken when there evolved cells that were responsive to features in the environment. The second step was taken when cells that responded to the environment became distinct from cells that controlled motor action. The third step was taken when different information from the sensory cells could trigger different behaviors by the motor cells. And the fourth step was taken when cells intermediate between sensory and motor cells began to function as processors of information, merging and summating the outputs of different cells.

Further steps were taken as these mechanisms proliferated, gathering more and more diverse information, and processing that information to generate a set of categories that constituted the PRS of a given species. The capacity to represent a spatial matrix, physical behaviors, and the personality features of conspecifics formed yet more steps in the same direction. All of these steps increased the autonomy of creatures. Decisions were no longer simple, unmediated reactions to outside stimuli, but became increasingly the outcomes of internal computations that merged information from the external world with information from the creature's current state and past experience.

Protoconcepts that could serve as referents for nouns and even verbs—nouns and verbs being the basic units from which other linguistic categories are derived—were in place by the time the higher primates had developed. All that was then required for the emergence of at least some primitive form of language was appropriate selective pressure and a viable modality: that is, some set of factors that would make the development of secondary representations advantageous, and some means through which such representations could be made both concrete and communally available.

It will be apparent that the view of evolution briefly summarized here conflicts in certain respects with views of evolution that are widely held today. Those views have very little to say about representation. Moreover, many of their expounders refuse to speak of any form of consistent development. Those who do admit such development usually describe it not in terms of representation but in terms of 'intelligence'.

The term 'intelligence' is put in quotes because neither its validity nor its value are obvious. Within our own species, it has either its vague lay sense, or the somewhat circular meaning of 'the capacity to do well on intelligence tests'. Correlation of this factor with other capacities is often unclear. Between our own species and others, 'intelligence' is sometimes treated as 'success at problem solving'. However, since the problems for other species are always set by us, never vice versa, this definition is hardly unbiased. Yet, vague and unsatisfactory as the concept of intelligence is, and despite the absence of any systematic measure, many persist in believing that there is some kind of *scala naturae* of intelligence, on which flatworms rank very low, frogs a little higher, dogs much higher, and humans highest of all.

On a conservative reckoning, intelligence is no more than the power to form associations, whether between stimulus and response or between two stimuli. One psychologist, Euan McPhail, has argued that in fact all vertebrates and many nonvertebrates share this power and are therefore on an identical level of intelligence. Our species alone rises above this level, and does so solely through its possession of language. From this viewpoint, the apparent differences in intelligence between the various vertebrate species arise simply because these species differ in the plasticity of their behaviors and the variety of their niche-adapted motor skills.

From the present viewpoint, the picture looks a little different from this. There is indeed a *scala naturae,* but it is based on the degree to which creatures are capable of representing the world around them. As has already been noted, this degree correlates closely with the variety of behavioral responses that each species has at its command. Only in science fiction are there protoplasmic blobs equipped with advanced intelligence. In real creatures, the advance of representational powers is paced by the capacity to react differentially to differing representations, so much so that the two seem to develop in tandem, with reciprocal feedback effects.

This view, compared with other current views of evolution, has two noteworthy consequences.

First, it places language in the mainstream of evolution. From other viewpoints, language is an alarming and embarrassing accident, as much from its apparent lack of evolutionary antecedents as from its unexpected power and complexity. It is perhaps partly for this reason that it is dealt with in such a cursory manner in most accounts of our species' origins. From the present viewpoint, however, language is merely a single (if admittedly rather a large) step in an orderly process, the development of more and more sophisticated ways of representing (that is, knowing) a world external to the creature. When the level of primary representation had reached a certain degree of sophistication, it made possible the creation of a second level upon which the output of the first level could undergo processes of still greater refinement.

Looked at in this way, language would constitute a development not unlike that which took effect when, in place of direct linkage between sensory and motor cells, there came into existence a layer of intermediate cells to process the output of sensory (and other) cells. We might indeed choose to speak of three levels of representation, rather than two: a primary level (for example, those cells in the retina that respond directly to stimuli); a secondary level (those cells in the visual cortex that process the output of the sensory cells); and a tertiary level (those cells that compose the utterances with which we describe what we see).

But the 'secondary level' might be yet further divided, since evidence suggests the existence of several layers of processing in the system of vision. Moreover, subjectively speaking, we cannot differentiate between direct sensory perceptions and the processing of these. What we perceive can only be the output of the latter, never of the former. Thus, rather than quibbling over the number of representational levels, it seems better (especially since our main interest is in the linguistic level of representation) to lump together all kinds of prelinguistic representation into a single primary level, and to reserve the term 'secondary representational system" (SRS) for that created by language.

The second consequence of the present approach has to do with the directionality of evolution. It is fashionable to regard evolution as an entirely random process. This view arose, in part at least, as a reaction against the view (shared by some Victorian thinkers, and by Teilhard de Chardin in the present century) that evolution was some kind of irreversible 'onward and upward' process, of which our own species represented the logical and inevitable apogee.

In contrast, it was urged that there was no consistent pattern to be observed in evolution. In one epoch, aquatic forms might be favored over terrestrial. In others, there might emerge creatures with lungs, or wings, or long necks, or big brains. However, the process was ruled entirely by chance, and it would have been impossible to predict, at any given stage, what the next stage would be like.

Now it is true that, at the level of genetic change, processes are entirely random and unpredictable and that the conditions imposed by the environment may seem equally random and unpredictable. (Think of droughts and floods, glacials and interglacials, the parting and rejoining of landmasses, and the rises and declines in predator and prey populations). However, one great constancy prevails through it all. As long as there are creatures whose motor capacities and environmental conditions allow them to benefit from it, evolution will always favor an increment in representational power.

The nature of this claim should be made quite specific. It would be absurd to suppose, for instance, that creatures must continue to get better representational systems in order to survive. Amoebas would not still be with us if this were so, nor would cockroaches be among the most successful types of creature in terms of distribution and age (some hundreds of millions of years). Nor would anyone want to claim that improved representational powers guaranteed the survival of a species. Australopithecines and other species closely antecedent to ours became extinct, even though their representational powers were surely greater than those of all earlier mammals.

However, once cells with sensitivities to the external world develop, random genetic variation is sooner or later going to produce cells that have wider or more complex sensitivities to aspects of the environment. Anything that gives a creature a fuller view of its environment will, if only in a few cases, enable it to survive perils that would otherwise be fatal or to recognize and exploit food sources that it would otherwise miss. In this way, creatures whose PRSs are even fractionally more sophisticated than those of their conspecifics will tend to outbreed them, and over lengthy periods of time the genes that carry such adaptations will spread through the breeding population. Similarly, if two species are competing for the same ecological niche, it will never happen that the species with the weaker PRS occupies the niche while its competitor goes extinct. The last five million years of primate history suggests quite a contrary outcome.

Moreover, so long as the PRS adequately represents a creature's environment, no aspect of it will be lost and its neurological infrastructure will be passed on intact to succeeding species. Such successors can indeed only add to that infrastructure, through the random process of genetic recombination and mutation that continues to affect it. The infrastructure seldom, if ever, erodes or deteriorates.

Granted, a particular piece of sensory equipment may be lost if a species moves to a new niche. The ancestors of the oilbirds that now inhabit caves in Venezuela lost their vision, but this was replaced by a type of sonar based on sounds produced by the birds' beaks. Early primates lost a large part of their sense of smell when they took to the trees and no longer had fixed territories that could be scent-marked, but this loss was counterbalanced by an immense improvement in vision. In other words, while particular senses may deteriorate or even disappear, the PRS, as a whole, will either remain at a similar level or actually improve.

Thus, given freedom from catastrophe and sufficient time to work in, normal evolutionary processes inevitably bring about the progressive development of representational systems. Even catastrophe need not be fatal to that development. In the opinion of some experts, among the vast populations of dinosaurs that became extinct some sixty-five million years ago, there were 'advanced' species whose brain-to-body ratio was more favorable than that of other varieties. If no catastrophe had eliminated them, then fifty million years ago there might already have been three-toed lizardlike creatures sitting around wondering how language could have evolved out of dinosaur communication. If, five million years ago, some catastrophe had wiped out mammals, then, tens of millions of years in the future, some species as yet unknown and unimaginable might again have been poised on the brink of the Rubicon of language.

For, given the bias of evolution toward more comprehensive PRSs, this stage of readiness for language was certain, sooner or later, to be reached. Then nothing was needed beyond the selective pressures that would encourage development of an SRS and the modality through which such a system could be expressed. Five million years ago, among the remote ancestors of our species, these conditions were falling into place.

5

The Fossils of Language

Anyone who examines the literature on the origins of language will be struck by a remarkable fact. While this literature includes contributions from anthropologists, ethologists, paleontologists, philosophers, and members of other assorted disciplines, hardly any of it is written by professional linguists. It would be strange indeed if physicists were to say, "We will concern ourselves only with matter as it is now or as it has been in the recent past; the origins of the universe are of their nature unknowable and we shall not even try to explore them." Why linguists have tacitly accepted just such a self-denying ordinance should be a topic of some interest to sociologists of science—it will not be explored here.

One can, however, hardly avoid remarking on the oddity that arises when a school of thought devoted to the proposition that language is a biological adaptation unique to our species repeatedly insists that the origins of language are unknowable and (inspired perhaps by Aesop's fox) that they are not worth knowing anyway. Such, however, is Chomsky's position: language is produced by a 'language organ', which is just as much a physiological organ as, for instance, the human heart is, and since the origins of organs such as the heart cannot be of any great interest, the same must be true of language. A work from the same school, by Eric Lenneberg, was actually entitled *The Biological Foundations of Language*. It was devoted to showing that language must have biological foundations of some kind, yet it insisted that one could not know what those foundations were.

The only coherent argument for this neglect of language origins is what has been described as 'fossilism': the belief that the reconstruction of human development is possible only through scrutiny of the fossil record, and therefore, since language leaves no bones, there is simply no relevant evidence. But one will search in vain for any other field wherein it has been decided, by fiat, that only one type of evidence is admissible. Certainly no such claim can legitimately be made even in paleontology itself, given the immense contributions in recent years from comparative studies of the molecular structure of living species.

It should be apparent that no event happens in the world without leaving traces of itself, subtle and indirect though these may be. Often the only possible evidence for a past event appears in the ripples spreading out from it that can still be discerned in the contemporary world. The origins of the universe, for instance, cannot be observed directly, but can be deduced from currently observable phenomena such as background radiation and the red shift of receding galaxies. It therefore seems only reasonable to suppose that there may exist contemporary phenomena—living linguistic fossils, so to speak—that would give us some insight into the processes through which language emerged.

THE 'LANGUAGE' OF APES

Although estimates of the time still vary between twenty and five million years ago, and although there are almost as many family trees as there are logical possibilities, it is generally agreed that the ancestors of our species branched off from other primates and that our closest living relatives include the chimpanzee, the gorilla, and (perhaps more remotely) the orangutan. If, as was surmised at the end of chapter 4, advanced mammals in general have reached a stage at which a substantial part of the infrastructure of language already exists, then the common ancestor of apes and humans shared that infrastructure, and contemporary apes would be expected to possess it too.

Attempts to teach languagelike systems to apes have been motivated in part by a desire to show that the gulf between our species and others, assumed for so long without any serious questioning, was simply an artifact of our own analysis. Initial results of such experiments gave renewed hope to naive continuists that a bridge between primate communication and human language might actually be forged. However, it soon appeared that the learning capacities of apes were limited—in rather interesting ways.

Apes quickly learned associations between arbitrary elements (whether these were manual signs, figures on a board, or keys on a computer) and concepts. That they associated these elements with concepts, and not with the particular objects that were presented to them, is quite clear from a variety of evidence. For instance, they never made certain kinds of mistakes that one might have expected them to make. They might, for instance, have treated all elements as if they referred directly to individual objects, as proper names do, rather than to categories. Suppose you taught an ape a sign for 'banana', and then the ape ate the banana you had been using in the lesson. What would prevent the ape from assuming that *banana* was the name for that particular banana, so that the next banana it met would need a new name? Such behavior is best explained by assuming that the ape has some concept of 'banana' embracing all members of the class.

But, in that case, what prevented a true proper name such as *Roger* from being generalized to include all members of the class male/human, as human infants often generalize *daddy?* Apparently this never happened. Without ever having been taught it explicitly, apes seem to have grasped immediately the distinction in human language between proper and common nouns. But they could hardly have done this unless, in their models of reality, they could already distinguish between representations of classes and representations of the significant individuals with whom they interacted on a regular basis.

However, the apes had still done no more than form paired associations between symbols and the exemplars (whether various or unique) of particular classes. There are at least two further dimensions in the human use of words. Words can be used in the absence of their referents, and they can be seen as holding particular places in a hierarchical classification system (as, for instance, *dog* holds a subordinate place with regard to *mammal* and is in turn a superordinate term for *spaniel, setter, terrier,* and so on). Early work on apes gave no indication that either dimension had been mastered. But recent work by Sue Savage-Rumbaugh and her associates—with the chimpanzees Sherman and Austin—suggests that apes can be trained in both, although the training required is complex and involves the acquisition of behavior patterns that are uncommon among apes in the wild.

Under natural conditions, chimpanzees do not normally share food, although cases involving the sharing of meat have been reported. It was only after Sherman and Austin had been taught routinely to share food of all types that they could be induced to ask one another for particular kinds of food, even when those foods were not physically present. It was only after they had learned to detach symbols from their referents that they could be taught to classify symbols under abstract headings such as 'tool' or 'foodstuff'.

However, there are still striking differences between ape vocabularies and human vocabularies. The most obvious is sheer size. No ape has so far succeeded in acquiring more than a few hundred elements, as opposed to the many thousands of words that are found in the vocabularies of the average human. But a less obvious fact is perhaps even more significant. In chapter 3, we saw that a full half of the words used in normal conversation are grammatical items (articles, auxiliaries, prepositions, and the like). With trivial exceptions (such as an *if/then* element used by David Premack in his work with chimpanzee Sarah), the vocabularies of apes are strictly limited to lexical items.

Although this is seldom, if ever, explicitly discussed in the literature, the absence of grammatical items from ape 'language' may reflect nothing more than a failure to teach such items. Given the fact that grammatical items cannot be defined ostensively, researchers may simply have been daunted by the difficulties of teaching them, or, not being linguists, may have failed to grasp the significance of the role of grammatical items in sentence formation. For linguists, in the same way they surrendered the study of language origins, have tacitly surrendered the field of ape research to nonlinguists.

Subsequent to Herbert Terrace's study of chimpanzee Nim, it has been accepted by most researchers that apes cannot produce genuine sentences. One would be surer of this if a sustained effort had been made to teach apes grammatical items, for syntax depends crucially on these items. It is to be hoped that someone will soon make such an effort, if only to demonstrate it *is* impossible. Until then, one cannot entirely close off the possibility, unlikely as it may be, that apes could acquire language in its fullest sense.

Certainly, however, no evidence produced to date gives any support to the idea that apes could acquire syntax. Regularity of serial ordering is sometimes claimed as evidence of syntax, but that regularity is far from complete, and even if it were, it would not constitute convincing evidence. Syntax is characterized not by invariant ordering but by a variety of possible orders, each having its own function; it is precisely the fact that the structure of syntax is hierarchical that makes it possible to vary the linear ordering of constituents.

Nor would it be enough to argue that an ape's ability to distinguish *Roger tickle Lucy* from *Lucy tickle Roger* is evidence of syntax. For syntax involves the capacity not merely to use different orders for different meanings, but to use the same order (*Lucy tickled Roger, Lucy was tickled by Roger*) for different meanings, and different orders (*It was Lucy that Roger tickled, It was Roger that tickled Lucy*) for the same meaning. However, to construct such sentences requires the use of grammatical items, and, as noted above, apes do not as yet have these at their disposal.

A fairer test would be the capacity to embed one sentence within another. This does not require any great complexity. *You know he's here, I want you to go, Tell them what to do,* and *Do those who drink drive?* are all sentences of no more than five words, each of which contains two complete clauses. Moreover, not all of them obligatorily require grammatical items (young children frequently render the second as *I want you go*).

But no ape utterances of this kind have been recorded. The longest utterance recorded from an ape (a sixteen-sign string by Herbert Terrace's chimp Nim) has no discernible structure at all: *give orange me give eat orange me eat orange give me eat orange give me you.* Note that in addition to (or perhaps because of) the absence of any discernible grammatical structure, this utterance lacks one of the most fundamental characteristics of human language: that one should be able automatically and unambiguously to reconstruct from it 'who did what to whom'. For instance, in the sequence *give me eat orange,* is *me* the object of *give* or the subject of *eat* or both? There is no way of knowing.

The question posed by the original ape researchers was, can a nonhuman species acquire a language? The answers to this question depended, as many were quick to point out, on how language was defined. If it was defined as the conveyance of information by means of arbitrary (that is, noniconic) elements, then apes could certainly produce languagelike behavior. If it was defined as the deployment of all the structural resources of human language, they equally certainly could not. The fact that behaviors quite similar to the apes' could be produced by sea lions, not usually regarded as the most 'intelligent' of mammals, or even by African grey parrots, tended to suggest that apes might still be far from human attainment. The same fact tends to support either McPhail's null hypothesis (that nonhuman species do not differ in intelligence per se) or the position set forth at the close of chapter 4, that quite a wide range of species may share the neural infrastructure for a very primitive level of language.

Researchers might have contributed more to an understanding of language if they had asked not whether apes could acquire language but, rather, what ape experiments might suggest to us about how language originally developed. Clearly we have to assume one of two possible scenarios for that development. Either language as we know it sprang fullblown into the world, with all of the complexities described in chapter 3, or it emerged originally in a much more primitive form.

The first of these scenarios is inherently less likely. Evolution does not normally, if indeed ever, involve leaps of this magnitude. The case for the second scenario would be strengthened if we could find, in our own species, forms of language, or something resembling language, that also lack some of the defining characteristics of language. It would not be enough merely to show examples of language *use* by humans that violate the normal grammatical structure of human language, for such examples could arise from a variety of causes. One would have to show that there exists a distinct linguistic code, with its own consistent properties, and that those properties are similar to the properties found in ape utterances.

The 'Language' of Under-Twos

Let's begin by comparing two samples of utterances without immediately divulging their sources. Since we are only concerned with analyzing the samples as formal objects, the utterances of interlocutors are omitted:

1.   Toothbrush there, me toothbrush.
      Sleep toothbrush.
      (Sees picture of tomato.) Red me eat.
      Berry, give me, eat berry.
      Come . . . there.
      Give eat there, Mary, me eat.
      Give me berry.
      Afraid, hug,
      Mary afraid, hug.
      Play.
      Pull, jump.
      Tired. Sleep. Brush teeth. Hug.
2.   Rock? (Rocks chair.)
      Rock.
      Chair.
      Chair.
      Chair.
      House?
      Chair.
      Get up. (Asked if wants to get up.)
      Get.
      Please? (Asked if wants juice.)
      Please. (Given juice.)
      Thank-you.
      Thank-you.
      Apple. (It is apple juice.)
      Fan.
      Fan.

T.V.
T.V.
T.V. (Father mentions name of dog.)
Puppy.
Switch.

Both samples are characterized by a high percentage of isolated one-word utterances; the second sample is limited almost entirely to such utterances. Neither contains any grammatical items and, indeed, there is no overt evidence that they have structure of any kind. Where utterances do contain more than one word, the result is often ambiguous. Does *Red me eat* mean 'I [want to] eat [the] red [object]', or is it two comments, '[The tomato is] red' and 'I [want to] eat [it]'? What, if anything, is the connection in *sleep toothbrush*, other than the fact that both are associated with bedtime?

In many cases there are null elements. All verbs entail that someone perform the actions to which they refer, while some additionally require that a Patient be named. Here, however, verbs like *hug*, *rock*, and *sleep* are found unaccompanied by any noun phrase. In full-blown language, such empty slots can always be interpreted on the basis of formal criteria, but here one can only guess or infer from context who participates, or is requested to participate, in the actions.

Of the two samples, (2) may well seem the more primitive. Yet, in fact, (1) was produced by a signing ape, while (2) was produced by a lively and well-developed twenty-one-month-old child.

In dealing with such data, we often apply a kind of double standard, based on our knowledge of the species concerned. We know that the ape will not progress beyond the level of (1). We also know that, within a couple of years or so, the child will produce utterances that may differ, if they differ at all, only in minor grammatical details from the utterances produced by adults. It is natural then to see in the utterances of the child some kind of foreshadowing of adult speech, however indistinct. Thus sequences such as *rock . . . chair* have been treated as embryos of verb +object constructions, and for children at a slightly later stage, where pairs of words are regularly conjoined, grammars have been written using the same categories and formalisms as grammars of adult languages.

The use of identical categories for child and adult grammars has been defended on the grounds that there is no principled basis for assuming that the child employs different types of grammar at different acquisitional stages. Indeed, if that assumption were made, there would be no

111

constraint on the hypothetical structures and processes that could be proposed for any given stage, and baseless speculations could range unchecked. The only alternative, it is claimed, is to suppose that the child employs basically the same grammar from the very beginning of the acquisition process.

This is a perfectly valid argument. It has no force, however, against the proposal that children, from about age two onwards, do indeed use a single grammar, but that younger children have no grammar at all, because what they are learning is not really language.

Suppose that the neural infrastructure underlying formal syntax crucially involves aspects of the brain that do not develop until after birth and are not completed until the child is approximately two years of age. It would then follow that, at the time a child gains enough vocal control to imitate the utterances of elders (a time that may vary from age twelve months to eighteen months in normal children), that child is still incapable of syntactic language. Such a child is, however, surrounded by mature speakers who insist on addressing the child and expect speech in return. What is to be done?

Obviously, children will seek to understand the utterances addressed to them by associating those utterances with objects in the environment. To do this, they need no language ability whatsoever, merely a rather primitive level of vocal control (many infant utterances are quite incomprehensible) and a power to form associations (which they share with many other species). In addition, they will attempt to use utterances in what seem to them to be appropriate circumstances. But again, no special powers are needed—the young of all social mammals learn by doing as their elders do in a variety of situations.

It is true, as has often been pointed out, that imitation plays only a very minor role in the acquisition of language. But then, according to the present account, children under two are not acquiring language—and the ways in which their speech differs from that of adults can be adequately accounted for, unlike the 'errors' of older children, by the hypothesis of imperfect imitation. The 'errors' of older children fall mainly into two classes: either they are formal overgeneralizations, like *feets* or *goed,* or they consist of sentences like *nobody don't like me* or *I no can see you* with structures that are ungrammatical in English but would not be ungrammatical in some other languages. Utterances of younger children fall into neither of these classes. They can be interpreted as truncated versions of adult utterances, their dimensions determined by the fact that children, when they begin to speak, can only do so at first in isolated words, and later only in pairs of words.

It is true that at the two-word stage, nouns, verbs, and adjectives tend to follow the same order as they do in adult versions of the target language. If (like Japanese) the adult language places verbs after the nouns that are their objects, the infant will normally do the same. If (like Tagalog) the adult language places verbs before the nouns that are their subjects, again the infant will do the same.

This regularity is often regarded as an indication that the child has begun to acquire syntax. In fact many of these noun-verb, verb-noun, or adjective-noun combinations could first have been heard as ready-made combinations in adult speech, and could have been learned in the same way that, at any age, we learn fixed idioms like *kick the bucket, keep tabs on*, and so forth. Other combinations that look novel could have been added to one another on a purely pragmatic basis, without any underlying system. A combination of these two strategies would still produce utterances a majority of which seemed to follow the same linear order as adult utterances. But even an almost complete regularity of ordering would not demonstrate syntax. It would at most indicate that children had acquired word classes and perhaps notions like 'object of'.

Many people would regard word classes and 'objects' as being part of syntax, but at the level at which under-two-year-olds acquire them (if indeed they do) they are not. The lexicons of under-twos do not include words (like *absence, anticipate,* or *ambivalent*) that would require formal rather than meaningful criteria to be assigned to their appropriate class. Rather they include concrete objects (*bed, toy, mommy*), physical actions (*run, play, eat*), and perceptible attributes (*big, red, tall*), so that all that is required of the child is to pair word-classes with types of readily accessible meaning—an exercise in semantics, not syntax. The establishment of word-classes is indeed a prerequisite for syntax, but not, therefore, a part of it.

As for notions such as 'object', these are vague lay terms that may be convenient for casual use but that should not, properly speaking, figure in a rigorous formal description of syntax. *Toys* in a sequence like *break toys* is a strictly subcategorized argument of *break* that is also its complement. This is not just a fancy way of saying 'object'. It entails, among other things, that some NP that is breakable should occur immediately to the right of *break*. It entails that no adult speaker of English will say, as a complete utterance, just *break* (unless of course he is a boxing referee!) or *I break*. But the same under-two who says *break toys* is just as likely to say *baby break* or just *break*. Clearly, whatever terms you use, the relationship between *toys* and *break* is conceived of quite differently by under-twos and over-twos.

Moreover, the capacity to join different word-classes in fairly consistent patterns is just as much a characteristic of apes as it is of under-twos. Beatrice Gardner compiled a table, parts of which are reproduced below as sample 3, showing the similarity between the utterances of children at the two-word stage and the utterances of chimpanzee Washoe:

3. | *Child utterances* | *Washoe's utterances* |
|---|---|
| Big train; Red book | Drink red; Comb black |
| Adam checker; Mommy lunch | Clothes Mrs. G.; You hat |
| Walk street; Go store | Go in; Look out |
| Adam put; Eve read | Roger tickle; You drink |
| Put book; Hit ball | Tickle Washoe; Open blanket |

These five sets of examples express, respectively: the attribution of qualities to objects, the possession of inanimates by animates, the location of actions, the relation of Agents to actions, and the relation of actions to Patients.

The original purpose of these examples was to show that Washoe and the children in question were at comparable stages of development and that therefore Washoe was indeed acquiring human language (even if she might never do so as completely as the children). Most opponents of this claim shared the belief that the acquisition of human language was a single continuous process and that the child utterances in (3) must therefore be early examples of language. They were thus forced to argue that the two sets of examples were 'not really' the same, that there must be some subtle criteria that distinguish one from the other. In fact the two sets are formally identical. But this does not prove that Washoe was acquiring human language, so long as we accept that the children concerned were not acquiring language either.

There is one way in which child utterances like (2) differ from ape utterances like (1), but that difference has nothing to do with language per se. It lies in what apes talk about and what small children talk about. Apes talk only about objects that they want (*toothbrush, berry*) or actions that they want to perform or have performed (*play, hug, give*).

On the other hand, Seth, the utterer of (2), is mainly concerned with what one might call 'categorizing for categorization's sake'. His references to *fan* or *T.V.* were not, so far as could be determined, requests for these things to be switched on or off. They occurred in the context of a conversation between his father and some friends which Seth kept trying to break into and his motivation in uttering them was probably to show the grown-ups that he knew what things were called. (His response—

puppy—to mention the dog's proper name was surely designed to show that he knew what category the animal belonged to.) Again, though this difference is nonlinguistic, it indicates a further prerequisite for language (strong curiosity about the environment) that will be examined in chapter 6.

We may conclude that there are no substantive formal differences between the utterances of trained apes and the utterances of children under two. The evidence of childrens' speech could thus be treated as consistent with the hypothesis that the ontogenetic development of language partially replicates its phylogenetic development. The speech of undertwos would then resemble a stage in the development of the hominid line between remote, speechless ancestors and ancestors with languages much like those of today.

Haeckel's claim that ontogeny repeats phylogeny has had a checkered career in the history of biology, and certainly cannot stand as a general law of development. However, it may have application in limited domains. In particular, no one should be surprised if it applies to evolutionary developments that are quite recent and that occur in a species whose brain growth is only 70 percent complete at birth and is not completed until two or more years afterwards.

However, while the evidence is consistent with a 'replication' hypothesis for childrens' early language, it falls a considerable way short of confirming it. There are other possible explanations for the limitations on children's initial speech. The limitations might simply be due to maturational factors. The child might indeed be operating with a mature grammar, but some unknown factor—functioning rather like a governor on an automobile engine that restricts it to certain speeds—might at first permit only one word at a time, then only two-word combinations. It might then disappear as the brain matured. In order to give further support to the hypothesis, one should be able to show that similar linguistic objects can also be produced by mature individuals under appropriate conditions.

THE 'LANGUAGE' OF GENIE

In 1970, in California, a thirteen-year-old girl subsequently to be known as Genie was found wandering in the streets with her mother. It appeared that the two had escaped from a home where, from about the age of eighteen months, Genie's father had imprisoned her alone in a bedroom and kept her from any exposure to language. On being hospitalized for examination, she was found to be incapable of speech.

'Wolf children', children who had been abandoned and supposedly raised by wild animals, had been found before, but in previous cases the data are, for one reason or another, inadequate to determine the linguistic status of the individuals concerned. In most cases, either the child in question died before reaching maturity, or the possibility that speechlessness resulted from mental deficiency could not be ruled out. But once she had recovered from her ordeal, Genie was found to fall well within the normal range of intelligence. It is further claimed that she suffered no lasting emotional damage. Yet, although immense amounts of skill and effort were applied to her linguistic recovery, she never fully acquired language. After passing through the characteristic pre-two-year-old stages, she remained permanently stuck at the level exemplified by sample 4.

4. Want milk.
   Mike paint.
   Big elephant, long trunk.
   Applesauce buy store.
   At school wash face.
   Tell door lock.
   Very sad, climb mountain.
   I want Curtiss play piano.
   Father take piece wood. Hit. Cry.

At first sight, (4) may seem somewhat more sophisticated than (1) or (2). However, its greater sophistication is not really structural. Apart from one sequence that looks like a noun phrase (*piece wood*) and one complex proposition (*I want Curtiss play piano*), (4) consists of groups of two or three content words, loosely linked by meaning but usually with no grammatical items to disambiguate their structure (here a single preposition, *at*, is the only grammatical item). Only hearing the utterance in context could indicate whether *Mike paint* meant *Mike paints* or *Mike's paint*, for example, or could determine who told who that the door was locked.

Even Genie's apparently more complex utterances may not be what they seem. *Piece wood* is her version of a common expression that could have been learned as a single vocabulary item, rather than being created by the combination of two nouns learned separately. The fact that phrases of this kind are extremely rare in her speech supports this possibility. In the same way, all of Genie's sentences that might seem to contain subordinate clauses have the structure *I want . . .* followed by what would otherwise be an utterance complete in itself, like *Curtiss play piano.* There are no *that*s, no *to*s, no overt markers of subordination. It is as if Genie had simply learned a formula by rote: start with *I want* and then tack on whatever utterance describes the state of affairs that you desire.

One might be tempted to attribute the absence of grammatical items from Genie's speech to a cognitive failure to comprehend the differences in time, referentiality, spatial orientation, and so on that grammatical items express in addition to their purely formal functions. But such a failure is clearly not responsible. The reason Genie fails to mark the times of actions by means of grammatical items is not that she is unaware of time differences, nor even that she has not acquired the appropriate grammatical items. Consider the following conversation:

5.   G: Genie have yellow material at school.
     M: What are you using it for?
     G: Paint. Paint picture. Take home. Ask teacher yellow material. Blue paint. Yellow green paint. Genie have blue material. Teacher said no. Genie use material paint. I want use material at school.
     M: You wanna paint it or are you trying to tell me you *did* paint it?
     G: *Did* paint.

Genie knows what past tense means, knows when it is appropriate to use it, and even knows at least one of the ways of marking it in English. But she cannot incorporate this knowledge into her normal ongoing speech. It can only be elicited in isolation, under direct pressure. This suggests not that she has merely *failed to acquire* a full version of human language, but that she *has* acquired *something other than full human language*—an alternative means of communication that incorporates some features of language but rigorously excludes others. Note too that Genie's failure to progress beyond this level cannot be attributed to lack of opportunity. On the contrary, she was the recipient of many-on-one teaching, just as were Washoe, Nim, and the other experimental apes.

The case of Genie is inexplicable if we assume that language is one and indivisible. If language constitutes a unitary system, and if its acquisition requires exposure to some form of linguistic input within a critical period, then Genie should have failed to acquire any kind of language at all. Alternatively, if there is no critical period for acquisition, she should have acquired language completely. On either assumption, at least two of the following three things are left without explanation: why she acquired anything at all; why her acquisition ceased at a particular point; and why it ceased just where it did, rather than at some earlier or later stage.

If we assume that there exists some primitive type of language—some protolanguage, as we might call it, that is just as much a part of our biological endowment as language is, but that lacks most of the distinguishing formal properties of language—then all three of these things can be readily explained. Genie acquired protolanguage because protolanguage is more robust than language (having formed part of the hominid endowment for much longer) and it does not have a critical period (although it does require at least some form of lexical input—unlike some bird songs, it is not fully innate). Genie's acquisition ceased because the faculties of protolanguage and of language are disjoint, and acquisition of the one in no way entails acquisition of the other. It ceased where it did because she had gone as far as possession of the protolanguage alone would permit her to go—although she might still add a handful of rote-learned and unproductive strategies borrowed from the language of her associates and acquired by general learning mechanisms, rather than through the processes of acquisition normally associated with a first language.

Genie represents the case of an individual who, although mature, still employs a variety of language that, despite its richer content and greater cognitive sophistication, is formally no more developed than that of apes or children under two. Yet one might still argue that no firm conclusions can be reached on the basis of a single individual. Let us therefore grant the force of this argument, and turn to speakers who, although capable of full human language, are forced to revert to protolanguage by the social circumstances in which they find themselves.

PIDGIN 'LANGUAGES'

Suppose that you visit a country whose language is unknown to you and where you have no ready access either to bilingual natives or to speakers of your own language. You struggle to make yourself understood, though at first you can do little more than gape and point. Soon, however, you pick up a handful of words so common and basic that you can readily learn their meanings from their social context: words for *please* and *thank you*, greetings appropriate to the time of day, items of food and drink, and a verb or two of physical action like *go* or *eat*. These, then, are your utterances—words produced singly or in pairs, often so mangled in pronunciation that they are uninterpretable save in the presence of the things they are intended to refer to. As communication, this leaves much to be desired, but it is better than nothing, just as the infant's primitive speech is more useful than wailing or babbling.

It is far from true language, however, and unlike the child, there is no guarantee that you will ever become more fluent in the alien tongue. Yet, since you already have a language that you speak fluently, we regard this kind of behavior, too, as produced by the full human language faculty, but stunted through a lack of knowledge, opportunity, or motivation, just as the language capacity of the infant is stunted by a lack of development. After all, there is always the possibility that you will develop beyond this stage, that you will eventually become a passable or even a fluent speaker of the alien tongue, just as the infant progresses from asyntactic speech to a fully mature syntactic competence.

However, if we need not assume continuity of development for the child, there is no reason to assume it for the adult. If the early speech of children is not language but protolanguage, then the speech of early-stage second-language acquisition could be protolanguage too. This idea would be supported if one could point to whole communities in which speakers never develop beyond this stage, despite the fact that they already speak at least one fully developed language.

During the period from the sixteenth to the nineteenth century, European colonialism disrupted the traditional relations among language communities. It did not merely bring into contact languages that would otherwise have remained isolated from one another. It also took speakers of diverse languages, and, usually under conditions of slavery, conveyed them to tropical coasts and islands (such as Haiti, Jamaica, Belize, Surinam, Mauritius, or Hawaii) where they were obliged to work closely with one another. Under normal circumstances, immigrants to a strange country acquire varying levels of competence in the language of that country, and children of those immigrants born in the new country acquire a native or near-native competence in it. However, in colonial plantation societies this outcome proved impossible to achieve.

In the first place, speakers of the target language were outnumbered by potential learners in a ratio of anything up to thirty to one, the reverse of the case in normal immigrant situations. In consequence there simply were not enough models for immigrants to learn from. In the second place, these were rigidly stratified societies in which contacts between the laboring masses and their masters were minimal. Since most, if not all, speakers of the target language belonged to the master class, the chances of acquiring even a modified version of the target language were reduced (except for a handful selected as personal servants) effectively to zero. Yet these immigrants, who had no common language, were obliged to communicate with one another. As a result, what are called 'pidgin' languages developed.

119

The nature of a pidgin may be illustrated by the following utterances produced by immigrants to Hawaii, which in the period 1880–1930 constituted (apart from the absence of slavery) a classic case of a colonial plantation society.

6.   Ifu laik meiki, mo beta *make* time, mani no kaen *hapai*
     If like make, more better die time, money no can carry
     'If you want to build (a temple), you should do it just before you die—
     you can't take it with you!'
7.   Aena tu macha churen, samawl churen, haus mani pei
     And too much children, small children, house money pay
     'And I had many children, small children, and I had to pay the rent'
8.   *Luna*, hu *hapai? Hapai* awl, *hemo* awl
     Foreman, who carry? Carry all, cut all
     'Who'll carry it, Boss? Everyone will cut it and everyone will carry it'.

The speakers were Japanese (6), Korean (7) and Filipino (8), respectively, while the italicized words are Hawaiian. In their speech there are some grammatical items: conditional *ifu* (although *sapos*, from the lexical item *suppose*, would be more common); negative *no;* conjunction *aena;* auxiliary *kaen;* quantifier *tu macha;* question-word *hu;* and the phrase *mo betta* corresponding very roughly to the auxiliary *should.* However, there are no articles, no prepositions, no complementizers, and no markers of tense or aspect. In other words, one finds only the types of grammatical item that are relatively rich in meaning, and not those whose primary function is structural.

Indeed there is no structure for such items to express. The utterances cited, typical of pidgin speech, consist of short strings of no more than four words each. Each of these strings is, except for the one conditional, an utterance complete in itself and separate from all the others. The order within the strings is quite variable: objects may precede verbs (*mani no kaen hapai, haus mani pei*), verbs may precede subjects (*hapai awl, hemo awl*), or verbs may be missing altogether (*aena tu macha churen*). Not one of the verbs that are present has all of the arguments it subcategorizes for. Yet all the speakers in (6) through (8) had languages of their own (Japanese, Korean, Ilocano) in which they had a full native competence. They were forced to revert to a protolinguistic mode by the impossibility, in early twentieth-century Hawaii, of obtaining adequate access to models of spoken English.

However, it should not be assumed that pidgin languages are limited to colonial situations. Pidgins may arise wherever speakers of unrelated and mutually incomprehensible languages are brought into contact. Since the term has been used to designate any language that does not have native speakers, it should be emphasized that its use here is limited to the kind of speech produced by the first generation of speakers in contact situations.

After the first generation, a pidgin may develop in different ways. If it is the only common language of a community, as it was in many tropical colonies, it will be acquired by locally born children and will then become a fully developed language, called a creole language. If it is used extensively as a second language, as it was in New Guinea, it may not be spoken natively for several generations but it will gradually acquire structure from neighboring developed languages. However, if it is used only sporadically, as Russonorsk was used in trading contacts between Russian and Scandinavian sailors, it may remain at a primitive level for several generations.

9. R: What say? Me no understand.
    N: Expensive, Russian—goodbye.
    R: Nothing. Four half.
    N: Give four, nothing good.
    R: No brother. How me sell cheap? Big expensive flour on Russia this year.
    N: You no true say.
    R: Yes. Big true, me no lie, expensive flour.
    N: If you buy—please four *pud* (measure of 36 lbs). If you no buy— then goodbye.
    R: No, nothing brother, please throw on deck.

Sample 9 is a translation of part of a conversation between two sea captains—one Norwegian, one Russian—who are trying to barter fish for flour. Despite the fact that both speakers are normal adults with a fully developed competence in their own language, the formal structure of this dialogue is hardly more complex than that of the examples from apes, Genie, and Seth at twenty-one months. Apart from two conditionals, one preposition, one demonstrative, and a sentence negator, there are no grammatical items. The longest utterance, *Big expensive flour on Russia this year,* contains no verb. When verbs do appear, they often do so without subcategorized arguments (*give* lacks a Goal, *throw* a Patient) and these can only be supplied by context.

Even where there may seem to be utterances of several clauses, these are not constructed in the way that complex sentences are constructed. Take the Russian speaker's *Big true, me no lie, expensive flour,* which translates directly as 'It's absolutely true, I'm not lying, flour is expensive' (three structurally unconnected clauses), rather than 'I tell you it's absolutely true that flour is expensive' (where the third clause is embedded in the second, and the second in the first, according to the 'Chinese-box' patterns of syntax). As for the only two expressions that might be regarded as full phrases, they are almost identical. Each contains the adjective-noun combination *expensive flour*, and one, in addition, includes the term *big*, which can apparently be added to any kind of expression as an intensifier. One can only conclude that both words and utterances are simply strung together like beads, rather than assembled according to syntactic principles.

The passage is all the more remarkable when we consider that the speakers, like those in (6) through (8), possessed full linguistic competence in other languages. The utterances of Nim, Seth, and Genie were the best that their speakers were capable of at the time (for Nim and Genie, the best that they ever would be capable of). None of the three possessed higher capacities that could have been utilized. For the Russonorsk and Hawaiian Pidgin speakers, this was certainly not so. What is truly amazing is how little of their linguistic knowledge they were able to deploy when they had to communicate across language barriers, and how much their utterances resembled those of beings who entirely lack any true form of language.

PROTOLANGUAGE VERSUS LANGUAGE

The evidence just surveyed gives grounds for supposing that there is a mode of linguistic expression that is quite separate from normal human language and is shared by four classes of speakers: trained apes, children under two, adults who have been deprived of language in their early years, and speakers of pidgin. Since this mode emerged spontaneously in the three human classes; since the second class includes all members of our species in their earliest years; and since the fourth class potentially includes any person at any time, we may regard the mode as a species characteristic. It is a species characteristic just as much as language is, although, unlike language, it may be within the reach of other species given appropriate training.

The examples of this mode differ from examples of language in at least five principled ways. The first way involves differences in the superficial order of constituents. It is not that protolanguage order is varied while language order is rigid, or vice versa. Both language and protolanguage may express the same forms in more than one order. But what these orders signify, and the constraints that govern them, are different in each case.

Whenever order differs in language, there are always reasons that have to do with expressive functions, and the variations are always constrained by general principles. The difference between *It was Bill that saw John* and *It was John that Bill saw* depend on what is presupposed (that someone saw John, in the first case, and that Bill saw someone, in the second). In each case the constituent that is being asserted, *Bill* in the first case and *John* in the second, is emphasized by being placed outside of 'its own' clause. But while protolanguage differences between, say, *house money pay* and *pay house money* may be *intended* to convey differences of emphasis or presupposition, we cannot be sure of this in any given case. Since there is no fixed relation between expressive needs and formal structures (in contrast to the situation in all true languages), such differences may merely reflect the basic word orders of the speakers' native languages (OV versus VO) that have been transferred to the pidgin.

Again, consider an utterance like Genie's *applesauce buy store*, where English would require *buy applesauce*. Granted, it is possible to say *applesauce is bought at the store*, but here the verb *buy* is reduced to the quasi-adjectival participle (*is*) *bought* which does not subcategorize for any VP-internal argument. It is also possible to say *It is applesauce that we buy e at the store*, where *e* represents the place to which *applesauce* is related, but here, as in the previous sentence, *applesauce* has to be governed (by *is* rather than *buy*, in both cases). Moreover principles of sentence structure, such as were discussed in chapter 3, link *applesauce* with *e*.

In Genie's utterance, however, there is nothing to govern *applesauce* (it could only be governed by the main verb if the latter carried an overt marker of agreement, as in *applesauce tasteS good*). Since there are gaps everywhere in protolanguage, there is nothing to link *applesauce* to any particular gap. Our assumption that applesauce is what is or was bought is based on pragmatic probabilities and not on structural criteria.

In other words, what determines surface order in language is the interplay between functional considerations (what is being presupposed or asserted, emphasized or de-emphasized) and a formal structure that sharply constrains possible outputs. In protolanguage, formal structure being absent, functional considerations alone apply. Thus the reason *applesauce* occurs first in Genie's utterance is not because it is 'the subject of the sentence' or because it has been moved there from some other position, but rather because *all* the initial constituents in Genie's utterances are simply topics—that is, the things that happened to be foremost in her mind at the time.

The second major difference between language and protolanguage involves null elements—those points in sentences where we can infer that some constituent is notionally present, but where there is no overt constituent. In language we can state quite explicitly the circumstances under which the appearance of such elements is allowed. These circumstances may vary somewhat from language to language, but they are always principled and predictable.

We know, for instance, that if a null element is not related to some overt constituent in the sentence, it must have arbitrary reference, like impersonal *you*. It follows that one of the *e*s in *Bill is too crazy e to live with e* must refer to 'anyone', since there is only one overt constituent, *Bill*, to which *e* can refer. We know, too, that it is the second and not the first *e* that refers to *Bill*.

Moreover, where there is more than one possible referent, we know which *e* refers to which referent. For instance, we know that in *Bill needs someone e to work for e*, the first *e* refers to 'Bill' and the second to 'someone', even though the *e* in *Bill needs someone e to work for him* refers to 'someone' and not 'Bill'. All of these things we know not from semantics, or pragmatics, or context, for there is no nonsyntactic reason why reference in the last two examples should not be reversed. We know these things because they are consequences again derived from the general principles discussed in chapter 3.

In protolanguage, however, any item may be absent from any position. It is impossible to predict when this will occur, and in order to determine what has been omitted, the hearer can only rely on overall meaning, knowledge of the situation, and sheer common sense.

One might of course claim that, since all speakers of genuine languages sometimes express themselves in this fragmentary manner, there is no real break between protolanguage and language. But we should distinguish here between user and used. The fact that the same individual can exploit two modes does not mean that those two modes are aspects of the same thing. We have seen that protolanguage, like language, forms part of the endowment of our species. When persons who are ill, exhausted, drunk, or merely impatient speak in this fragmentary manner, they are simply using protolanguage rather than language, and indeed there should be nothing surprising in the fact that when we are below par in some way we may fall back on some more primitive mode of functioning.

Closely connected to the nature of null elements is a third difference that involves the subcategorized arguments of verbs. It was noted in chapter 3 that all verbs subcategorize for one, two, or three arguments: *sleep* for one, *take* for two, *give* for three, and so on. All these arguments will be overtly realized unless there are principled means, of the types discussed above in connection with null elements, by which they can be identified and linked to their expected locations or to appropriate refer-ents. For example, *what* can be linked to *e* in *What did you take e?*; *I* to *e* in *I opened the door and e took the box; the person* to *e* in *The person I gave the box to e was Charlie;* and so on. This linking process is deter-mined by syntactic principles, is automatic and unambiguous, and re-quires no knowledge of the current situation, the speaker's intentions, or any other factor.

If we were unaware of the necessity for either overtly expressing oblig-atory arguments or linking their positions with elements that *are* overtly expressed, it would be impossible for us to say, when confronted by an utterance like *give four* or *throw on deck*, whether there was anything 'missing' or not. In fact, we know that the first lacks a Goal, the second a Patient. Often, as in these cases, it is not difficult to determine what was omitted: *you* in the first example, and *it* ('the fish') in the second. But 'often not difficult' is not good enough for language, which requires 'al-ways automatic and almost always infallible.'

The fourth difference between language and protolanguage involves mechanisms for the expansion of utterances. The principles for con-structing phrases, described in chapter 3, permit the recursive addition both of constituents to phrases (so as to form more complex phrases) and of phrases to phrases (so as to form clauses and sentences of increasing complexity). By adding constituents to a phrase we can proceed from *man* to *the man, the tall man, the tall man in the black coat, the very tall young man in the black coat and yellow gloves, the very tall young man in the black coat and yellow gloves that made him look like a mortician,* and so on, ad infinitum. By adding one phrase to another, we can pro-ceed from *John wants books* to *John wants books to study, John wants books to study so that he can get into college, Bill says that Mary thinks that John wants books to study so that he can get into college,* and so on, again ad infinitum.

In protolanguage we may occasionally find what look like expanded phrases: the apparent equivalent of *tall man* (Genie's *blue paint*) and even of *very tall man* (the Russian skipper's *big expensive flour*). No-where, however, do we find anything equivalent to *in the black coat* or *that made him look like a mortician.* This suggests that the few examples found may have been rote-learned, just like individual lexical items or idioms, rather than constructed. If this is the case, then, although they may superficially resemble genuine noun phrases, they provide no evi-dence that any syntactic principles are at work.

This is even more clearly the case with the addition of phrases to phrases to form complex sentences. Apart from very rare stereotyped utterances, like Genie's *I want Curtiss play piano*, which is most likely derived from a rote-learned formula, protolanguage consists of strings of isolated utterances of about the length of a short clause though with none of a clause's structure. The virtual absence of complex phrases and sentences from protolanguage follows as a consequence of the absence of structural positions where complements can be adjoined to heads of phrases. If protolanguage is indeed no more than a linear stringing together of lexical items, then there will indeed be no specific structural positions where complements can be attached.

The fifth difference involves grammatical items. As we have seen, these need not be entirely absent from protolanguage, although they are very seldom found in the speech of children under two and will be present in ape utterances only if the apes are explicitly taught to use them—perhaps not even then. However, even where grammatical items are found in protolanguage, their incidence will be quite low as compared with language, and their distribution will be skewed in a particular way.

Protolanguage will seldom if ever have any kind of inflection—any *-ing*s, *-'s*s, *-ed*s, any number- or person-agreement, and so on. It will seldom if ever have any auxiliary verbs whose function is to express tense, aspect, equation, or class membership, although it may have expressions for possibility or obligation. It will lack complementizers, markers of the finite/nonfinite distinction, and conjunctions, and it will show few prepositions, articles, or demonstrative adjectives, although it may have negators, question-words, and quantifiers. In other words, the stronger the meaning element in a grammatical item, the more likely it is to appear in protolanguage. Conversely, the stronger its structural role, the less likely it is to appear.

The foregoing summary suggests that language and protolanguage are indeed distinct modes, and that the differences between them are both wide and deep. However, these differences must, for the most part, be negatively defined. Rather than saying that protolanguage possesses such-and-such characteristics, we are obliged to say that it lacks the distinguishing features of language. This might seem to leave open the possibility that protolanguage is merely a blanket term for any language variety that does not meet all possible criteria for language, and that therefore it does not constitute a unitary mode and cannot be treated as a species-specific adaptation. Such a possibility, however, can be sharply reduced if we can point to some types of utterance that are clearly ungrammatical (therefore not genuine examples of language) and yet differ in a principled manner from protolanguage.

Language and Aphasia

As has long been known to students of aphasia, victims of strokes or head injuries that have affected Broca's area characteristically produce utterances that are markedly ungrammatical in nature, consisting usually of short, quasi-structureless strings with few or no grammatical items. The similarities to child language and pidgins have not gone unnoticed. Such utterances are often referred to as 'telegraphic speech' or (in the French clinical literature) as 'style petit nègre'. The following examples are quite typical.

10. Lower Falls . . . Maine . . . Paper. Four hundred tons a day! And, ah . . . sulphur machines, and ah . . . wood . . . Two weeks and eight hours . . . workin' . . . workin' . . . workin'. Yes, and ah . . . sulphur. Sulphur and . . . ah wood. Ah . . . handlin'! And ah sick, four years ago.
11. Cinderella . . . poor . . . um 'dopted her . . . scrubbed floor, um, tidy . . . poor, um, 'dopted . . . Si-sisters and mother . . . ball. Ball, prince um, shoe . . . scrubbed and uh washed and uh . . . tidy, uh, sisters and mother, prince, no, prince, yes. Cinderella hooked prince. Um, um shoes, um, twelve o'clock ball, finished.

In (10) a patient responds to an inquiry about his former employment, in (11) another patient attempts to tell the story of Cinderella. But, although both were produced by previously normal adult speakers who had suffered similar types of brain damage, they seem, if anything, less similar to one another than do examples (1) through (9), produced by a wide variety of humans and nonhumans. For instance, (10) contains nothing that could be a verb except for *workin'* and *handlin'*, and these, since they have neither subjects nor objects, and since -*ing* can also signal a nominal or an adjectival, are probably not verbs at all. By contrast, (11) contains almost as many verbs as nouns, and even the past tense forms of the verbs are preserved without exception.

Different as these examples are from one another, they differ even more from the examples previously examined. Although protolanguage may omit occasional verbs, especially those that refer to abstract states like possession or existence, there is never the wholesale omission of verbs found in (11). Moreover, protolanguage is usually more coherent and makes more sense than these examples. Even the ape utterances are easier to follow than (10).

In these respects, aphasic speech seems even less systematic than protolanguage. In other respects, however, it is much closer to language. Although protolanguage lacks inflections, (10) contains nine (five plurals and four -*ings*) and (11) contains ten (seven past tenses and three plurals). Moreover, both aphasic samples contain what one might call 'islands of fluency', short stretches in which the patient's output is almost indistinguishable from normal language: 'four hundred tons a day', 'two weeks and eight hours', and 'four years ago', in (10); 'sisters and mother', 'Cinderella hooked prince', and 'twelve o'clock ball' in (11).

At one time it was widely believed that damage to Broca's area actually injured or destroyed those areas of the brain where syntactic rules or principles were stored. The issue is still quite controversial, but the balance of present evidence suggests that syntactic competence (the stored knowledge that determines how sentences are produced) is unaffected, although performance is disrupted as a result of damage to the units that actually process and produce sentences. Perhaps the most telling evidence in this respect is the capacity of many aphasics to judge the grammaticality of sentences in what is apparently much the same way as normal subjects do, even when they themselves cannot produce or process sentences of the types in question.

Samples (10) and (11) appear to be more consistent with the second approach. Some features of language are preserved almost intact, while others are depressed even below the level of protolanguage. It seems reasonable to conclude that aphasic speech represents a deformed version of language rather than an example of protolanguage, and hence that protolanguage is more than merely a blanket term for any kind of ungrammatical language.

If there indeed exists a more primitive variety of language alongside fully developed human language, then the task of accounting for the origins of language is made much easier. No longer do we have to hypothesize some gargantuan leap from speechlessness to full language, a leap so vast and abrupt that evolutionary theory would be hard put to account for it. We can legitimately assume that the more primitive linguistic faculty evolved first, and that contemporary language represents a development of that original faculty. Granted, this assumption still does not smooth the path, for the gulf between protolanguage and language remains an enormous one. But at least it makes the task possible, especially since the level of representational systems achieved by some social mammals amounts to a stage of readiness, if not for language, at least for some intermediate system such as protolanguage.

To start a protolanguage, all that was necessary was for some kind of label to be attached to a small number of preexisting concepts. The protolanguage examples that have been given indicate that no further mechanism is required in order to progress to short propositional utterances. Once a few concepts of entities and actions had been labeled, yielding a handful of prototypical nouns and verbs, the linking of these in simple propositions was no more than a reconstruction of what the senses perceived.

The question remains, however: if so many species were at a stage of potential readiness for some primitive version of language, how was it that out of all those species only our ancestors attained the goal?

6

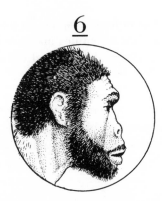

The World of Protolanguage

The one thing we know for certain about the origin of language is that it emerged somewhere between the separation of the hominid line from other primates and the dawn of recorded history. Everything else is speculative to some degree. Yet if evidence from a variety of sources is taken into account, it should be possible to produce a scenario explicit enough to be tested against future discoveries.

It seems not unreasonable to assume that what first emerged was a protolinguistic mode lacking most or all of the formal structural properties that characterize language. Several considerations support such an assumption. First, as suggested in chapter 5, such a mode forms part of human ontogeny and remains accessible to all members of the species throughout life. The case of Genie also suggests that it might be more robust than true language, requiring less in the way of triggering, or at least not requiring triggering to take place within a relatively narrow developmental window. The mode is also accessible, given adequate training, to other primates (and indeed perhaps to a wide range of other species). From this we may conclude that the spontaneous emergence of such a mode, though it would have required factors not present in other species, need not have required anything either particularly novel or particularly elaborate in the way of neural infrastructure.

Moreover, the protolanguage hypothesis is consistent with the duality of language shown in chapters 2 and 3. Language as our species knows it consists of two easily separable components: a maplike representation that uses hierarchically structured categories, and an itinerary-like representation that generates sentences (formally structured propositions) drawn from the contents of this map. There are only three logical possibilities: the lexical component emerged before the syntactic, the syntactic emerged before the lexical, or the two emerged simultaneously.

The syntactic component could only have *evolved* first in the sense that the capacity to construct sentences could in principle have derived from some previously established function. For instance, it is often argued that, since both are located in the left hemisphere and involve some form of serial activity, the capacity to use tools and the capacity to create sentences are closely connected, with the second capacity being perhaps dependent on the first. However, there is no way in which the syntactic component could have *emerged* first, since syntactic principles can only be expressed by and through a lexicon.

Simultaneous emergence is possible but unlikely, unless there already existed some structure and/or function preadapted for syntax. If one assumes that meaningful utterances and formal structures both *evolved* simultaneously, the leap involved is too great to be plausible, unless the two were inextricably connected in some way. But the evidence surveyed in chapter 5 suggests that meaning can be (and is) found quite independently of formal structure. Thus the possiblity of simultaneous emergence seems, also, to depend on finding that syntax simply utilized existing neural structures.

The emergence of the lexical component before the syntactic one requires no such assumptions. There might have been no preadaptation for syntax, leaving the syntactic component to develop at a later date. Alternatively, there might have been a preadaptation which, for one reason or another, did not function as such until after protolanguage had developed.

If the lexical component did not emerge first, then the very existence of protolanguage raises a problem. One might expect, for instance, that if lexicon and syntax had co-evolved, it would be quite difficult for members of our species to detach lexical items from their syntactic matrix and use them in structureless utterances. However, the fact that we can detach and use lexical items separately, at will, and that we may spontaneously revert to this mode when sickness, fatigue, alcohol, or some other cause depresses our normal functioning, suggests that the link between the two components cannot be a particularly tight one. It will accordingly be assumed that the lexical component emerged before the syntactic one, and that protolanguage, though it now coexists with language, emerged before language in some particular species of the hominid line.

But which species? Any account of the origins of language has to face the fact that the structure of the hominid family tree remains controver-

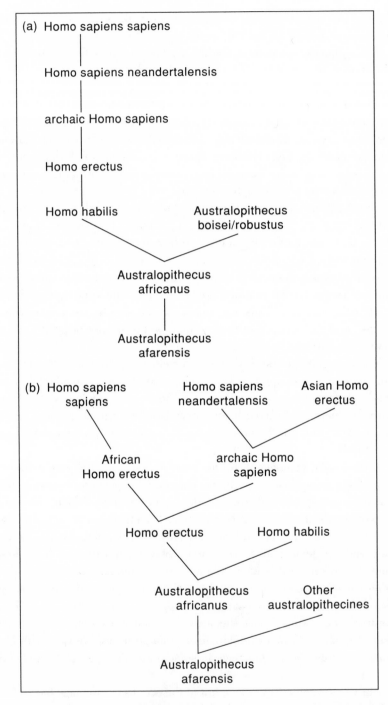

FIG. 6.1. Two models of hominid evolution: a 'straight-line' classical model (a) and an 'adaptive radiation' model

sial. New fossil finds, far from reducing hypotheses, have only served to multiply them, so that hypotheses now range from a 'straight-line' model (from australopithecines through *habilis, erectus,* archaic *sapiens,* and *neandertalensis,* to modern *h. s. sapiens*) to an 'adaptive radiation' model in which there are as many branches as there are species (see figure 6.1). Fortunately the account that follows does not depend in a crucial way on the outcome of these controversies. At one point, it may perhaps affect that outcome, rather than be affected by it.

One means often adopted in attempts to determine the first linguistic species is to examine features of early hominids that are more accessible than language, yet that might plausible be supposed to correlate with language in some way. Three of these (brain features, artifacts, and behavioral patterns) are discussed below.

BRAIN SIZE AND CONFIGURATION

As noted in the introduction, there is no evidence that language ability is a direct result of brain size. Furthermore, it is well known that midgets and microcephalics with brains very much smaller than the human norm may be capable of normal language use. However, when differences in body size are allowed for, the normal human brain is proportionately larger than that of any other species. It can therefore hardly be coincidental that our species is the only one with language. Given that language could be a *cause,* rather than a *result,* of increased brain size, or that there could be a more indirect relation between the two, it seems reasonable to assume a connection of some kind.

Reconstructing even the absolute brain size of extinct species (let alone the relative brain size) is fraught with problems. Fossil skulls are often fragmentary and incomplete. Relatively few are available and these may vary markedly in size, making the norm for a given population difficult to determine. Disputes over species boundaries may make it difficult to decide which species a given fossil should be attributed to. Since the only evidence of body weight consists of skeletons, or in most cases fragments of skeletons, the calculations of brain/body ratios cannot be overly reliable. To make things more complex, there are a variety of ways in which brain/body ratios can be calculated. Two of the most popular are Jerison's enchephalization quotient (EQ) and Hemmer's constant of cephalization (CC), but even these can give different results depending on the reference equation that is chosen for them.

One set of figures derived from calculations of brain/body ratios (from work by Philip Tobias) is illustrated in Table 6.1. These figures would

TABLE 6.1.   Coefficients of Encephalization for Human and Ancestral Species

	Mean Endocranial Capacity (cm)	Estimated Body Mass (kg)	EQ	CC
A. afarensis	413.5	37.1	3.1	36.8
A. africanus	441.2	35.3	3.4	39.7
H. habilis	640.2	48.0	4.0	53.6
H. erectus	951.4	53.0	5.5	77.7
H. sapiens	1350.0	57.0	7.6	108.8

After Tobias, 1987.

EQ = encephalization quotient; CC = constant of cephalization. *Erectus* figures averaged from four subpopulations in source)

suggest an advance from *A. afarensis* (the only australopithecine more or less universally accepted as being on the direct hominid line) to *H. habilis* that is very closely comparable in size to that from *habilis* to *erectus*. The EQ figures represent a gain of 33% by *habilis* over *afarensis* as compared with a gain of 37.5% by *erectus* over *habilis;* the CC figures indicate a gain of 46% by *habilis* over *afarensis* as compared with a gain of 45% by *erectus* over *habilis*. A similar picture of gradual, steady advance is obtained if we take the relation between gross brain size and geological age (Figure 6.2). Both these measures would seem to confirm a picture quite widely accepted in paleoanthropology, one of a gradual, steady increase in brain size over the whole course of hominid evolution, in which no single decisive event serves to accelerate the process.

A moment's thought, however, should suffice to cast doubt on this picture. The data displayed in fig. 6.2, seemingly a clear indication of a 'straight-line' increment in brain size, leave out the factor of body weight. Body weight increased by about 37% between *afarensis* and *habilis*, and by only about 10% between *habilis* and *erectus*. In other words, a large part of the gain of *habilis* over *afarensis* shown in fig. 6.2 can be attributed to the natural consequence of size increase, since each unit of body size increase requires up to 0.75 of a unit increase in brain size simply to take care of the same functions. The gain of *erectus* over *habilis*, however, cannot be accounted for in this way.

The absence of the time dimension in Table 6.1 creates a similarly false impression. The gain of *habilis* over *afarensis* no longer looks like the gain of *erectus* over *habilis* when one takes into account the fact that the values for *afarensis* were drawn from a period between 3.5 and 3.0 Mya (million years ago), whereas the values for *habilis* were taken from between 2.0 and 1.6 Mya, and the values for *erectus* from a period beginning around 1.6 Mya. Granted that the *erectus* period lasted until the quite recent emergence of our own species, the fact that the values for *erectus* used here are valid for early specimens means that the increase in brain size was considerably more rapid in the *habilis-erectus* period than it was in the *afarensis-habilis* period. A more probable interpretation is indicated in figure 6.3, which incorporates all three relevant factors: increase in body mass, increase in brain capacity, and time.

Figure 6.3 divides the time span between *afarensis* and the present into two roughly equal periods of approximately a million and a half years each: in other words, into an *afarensis-habilis* and an *erectus-sapiens*-period. Since *afarensis* is assumed to have existed prior to 3 Mya, an

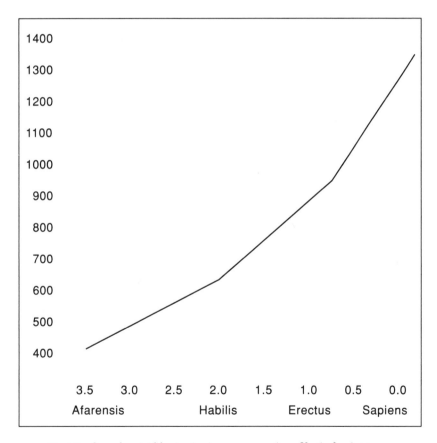

FIG. 6.2. Gross hominid brain size increase over time. Vertical axis = gross endocranial capacity in cubic centimeters; horizontal axis = time in millions of years, 0.0 = present.

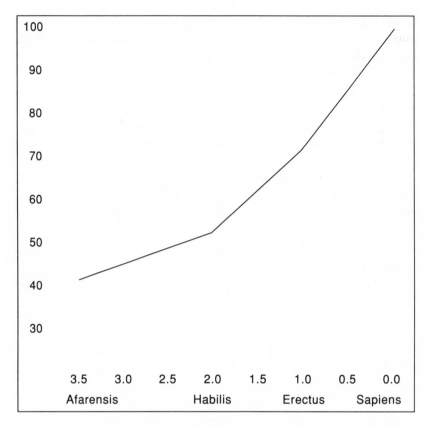

FIG. 6.3. Encephalization quotient increase in real time. Vertical axis=EQ as a percentage of *h.s. sapiens* EQ; horizontal axis = time in millions of years, 0.0=present.

equal division is, if anything, overly generous to the earlier species. Yet in the *afarensis-habilis* period, brain size increased over body mass by a margin of only 25% (55% brain size increase minus 30% body mass increase), whereas in the *erectus-sapiens* period, the margin of increase was 91% (110% brain size increase minus 19% body mass increase).

These figures strongly suggest that whatever accelerated brain growth began with the emergence of *erectus* rather than with the emergence of *habilis*. If we assume that there is a connection of some kind between brain size and language, it is therefore more likely that language emerged with *erectus* than with *habilis*. But since organization is probably more directly relevant to language ability than mere size, knowledge of how hominid brains were structured should, in principle, be able to tell us more.

Unfortunately, the study of hominid brain configurations is even more fraught with practical and conceptual problems than are the more quantitative studies referred to above. Since brains themselves do not fossilize, the only possible procedure is to make and study endocasts (casts of the interior portions of fossilized skulls). These, of course, can give information only about the exterior surface of the brain. From changes in the dimensions of the various brain regions, plus all of the convolutions, bumps, and fissures that may be represented with more or less fidelity in the endocast, it may be possible to make certain inferences about the brain's actual structure.

But even if agreement can be reached on these issues, the assumption that given areas of the brain subserved the same functions in extinct hominids as they do today can, again, be no more than a plausible inference. If it comes to that, we still have only the sketchiest idea of how the 'language areas' (Broca's and Wernicke's) function in our own species. Damage to Broca's area disrupts sentence production and damage to Wernicke's area disrupts the recall of lexical items, but exactly how these areas, and perhaps others, divide up the functions of storage and production, or how they work together, remains mysterious.

It has been claimed that *habilis* is the first of our ancestors to show enlargement of both Broca's and Wernicke's areas, and also that *habilis* was the first species to consistently use the right hand (a fact, if correct, indicative of strong lateralization for serial processes). Thus the possiblity that the protolanguage began with *habilis* cannot be ruled out. However, this possibility depends on *habilis* being the direct ancestor of *erectus*, rather than being on a side branch, as in the more radical 'adaptive radiation' trees.

The present account assumes, for reasons to be considered in more detail in chapter 7, that there were only two stages in the development of language: a type or types of protolanguage similar to that described in chapter 5, and fully developed human language. If *habilis* was on a branch, and if *habilis* had protolanguage, then the common ancestor of *habilis* and *erectus* (presumably some form of australopithecine) should also have had protolanguage, since protolanguage would hardly have developed independently in two lines. On the basis of what we know about australopithecines, this seems unlikely. Moreover, if a side-branch *habilis* had protolanguage, it is puzzling that the species disappeared so rapidly. *Habilis* was only slightly smaller than *erectus*, and (so far as is known) exploited roughly the same resources; if it, too, had protolanguage, it should have been equally well equipped to exploit those resources and to survive.

Although little in the account that follows will depend crucially on this, it seems likelier that *erectus* was the initiator of protolanguage. This decision seems to be confirmed by findings in the areas of artifacts and behavior.

So far as is known, *habilis* was the first of our ancestors to actually manufacture stone tools. The use of tools, or even their manufacture, is of course not unique to hominids. Chimpanzees make sponges by crushing handfuls of leaves, and they make termite-hunting equipment by stripping leaves from twigs or grass blades. Nor is the use of unimproved stones restricted to our line, for chimpanzees use them to open palm nuts, sea otters use them to open shellfish, and so on. But, so far as we know, not even the australopithecines, who were already walking erect, actually chipped pieces of stone to produce sharp cutting instruments.

The tools made by *habilis* were, however, extremely crude. It was not until about 1.6 Mya that *erectus* began to produce bifaced stone hand axes of a symmetrical design. But this innovation was not succeeded by others. The Acheulian hand ax was used fundamentally without change for over a million years, indeed until the time that *erectus* began to break up into the species and/or subspecies sometimes given the cover-term of 'archaic *homo sapiens*'.

In fact, the fossil record almost certainly gives only a partial account of tool manufacture and tool use. It is highly probable that our remote ancestors used a variety of more perishable materials (wood, vines, animal hides and intestines, and so on) to manufacture such things as digging sticks and baskets. But the exact epochs in which the various kinds of nonlithic artifacts emerged must remain conjectural. In the absence of other kinds of evidence, many writers have assumed some kind of connection between the manufacture of stone tools and the emergence of language. But there has been little agreement as to the precise form that this connection took.

Some have claimed that the fine motor control and the routinization of serial actions developed in toolmaking subsequently became the source of language structure. Others have claimed that if hominids had not already possessed language, they would have had neither the foresight to design and make tools nor the capacity to form a cultural tradition of toolmaking. Yet others have claimed that toolmaking and language developed side by side, each helping to improve the other in a kind of beneficent spiral. None of these arguments seems particularly compelling. That toolmaking skills should have given rise to modern syntactic abilities is hard to accept. Syntax is not serially but hierarchically arranged, with structures nesting inside other structures. There is, however, no indication that either toolmaking itself or the knowledge required for it is structured in this way. On the contrary, simple tool production seems to involve what has been termed a 'string-of-beads' activity in which a set of actions is serially chained.

In other words, it is toolmaking and *protolanguage* that share the same processes. There is still, however, no need to suppose that there was any causal connection between the two. Both were processes the infrastructure for which was available to creatures simpler than either *habilis* or *erectus*. If no modified tools survive from earlier species, the possibility that such tools existed but were made of perishable substances is at least as great as the possibility that toolmaking was beyond the capacities of those earlier species. Certainly, if chimpanzees were to become extinct, researchers four million years hence would be unlikely to find any fossil evidence of their tool use.

If all this is so, then the argument that language of some kind was a prerequisite for toolmaking would also seem to have little force. There are, in principle, two ways in which language might aid toolmaking. It might be required for thinking about new tools in terms of their possible functions, or it might be required to instruct neophytes in the making of tools. But neither function would seem to be necessary, at least not where tools as simple as those of *habilis* are concerned.

If language did confer the power to think of new tools and new uses, then the crudity and uniformity of its tools suggest that *habilis* made virtually no use of such power. As for instruction, there is no evidence that language need be involved. Even within our own species, modern hunter-gatherers often carry out instruction in the making of artifacts and in hunting techniques without any use of language. The elder performs the activities, the neophyte watches closely and imitates.

Finally, the argument that toolmaking and language co-evolved in some kind of mutual feedback process comes up against the undisputed and massive facts of tool development. Whether or not hominid species conformed to the punctuated-equilibrium model of evolution, their tools certainly did. The tools of *habilis* were consistently crude and rudimentary throughout the life of the species. The original *erectus* tool kit constituted a massive advance, but after that it showed no significant improvement, or even change, over a period of approximately a million years. Thus there cannot have been any kind of ongoing feedback process whereby a gradually developing language brought about an improvement in toolmaking techniques, and/or vice versa.

In sum, then, tools have little if anything to tell us about how either language or protolanguage began. If we assumed any connection at all between tools and language, we would be led to conclude that it was *erectus* rather than *habilis* that developed a protolanguage. The reasoning is as follows.

If we assume that *habilis* developed protolanguage, then the greater technological skills of *erectus* could have been caused by the development either of language itself or some mode intermediate between protolanguage and language. It is difficult to believe that *erectus* developed language, for we would then have to believe that a species with capacities comparable to ours remained at a primitive level for its entire lifetime, one that lasted perhaps as long as one and a half million years. Yet we have no evidence for any linguistic mode intermediate between protolanguage and true language, and indeed considerations that will be taken into account in chapter 7 suggest that any such mode may be an evolutionary impossibility. Therefore it is likelier (if far from certain) that *habilis* was speechless and that only *erectus* developed protolanguage.

BEHAVIOR

Between *habilis* and *erectus* there are some gross behavioral differences. *Habilis* was limited in distribution to sub-Saharan Africa, whereas *erectus*, originating in the same area, spread as far as Java and China in the East and Europe in the West. This spread suggests that *erectus* was a more flexible creature, capable of exploiting a much wider range of environments. A protolanguage might have given just such flexibility, although it should be noted that leopards, wolves, and other predators underwent a similar dispersion around the same time.

It is not clear whether *habilis* ever developed a home base. Such a base is characteristic of our species; even hunter-gatherers and nomadic pastoralists do not wander aimlessly, but return habitually to seasonal bases. Apes, on the other hand, roam constantly, sleep where night finds them, and then wander on again to some other point in their habitual range. The as yet unanswered question is at what point fixed bases developed. *Erectus* certainly had them, both in caves and in constructed temporary shelters like that found at Terra Amata on the Mediterranean coast near Nice.

But perhaps the strongest evidence for the superior capacities of *erectus* is that of fire. There is no evidence that *habilis* either made or utilized fire. *Erectus* may not have made it, for even within the last century or so, Tasmanians and Andaman Islanders were obliged to carry fire about with them. However, *erectus* certainly used it, possibly in hunting (to drive animals into swamps) and certainly at home bases, whether for cooking, protection from other species, or both. It is hard to imagine fire, which all other species fear and flee from, being tamed and handled by a species with no kind of secondary representational system.

Recall the discussion, in chapter 1, of the difference between the vervet warning calls for pythons and the human word *python*. It is impossible to utter the first without creating alarm, for the cry is a direct reaction to the presence of the thing. But unless a special kind of intonation is given to it, the utterance of the word *python* causes no alarm at all. What the word summons to mind is merely the concept, not the thing itself. In other words, a language, even a protolanguage, uncouples stimulus and response, allowing its owner to look objectively at things that under other circumstances might arouse emotions too violent to control. It is like the magic mirror in which Perseus fixated the Gorgon's head that would otherwise have turned him to stone.

Thus a creature equipped with a protolanguage could have thought about, and discussed with its neighbors, the possibility of using fire, long before making any attempt to use it. Thinking and talking about things deprives them of their mystery and their capacity to arouse fear. Sooner or later, one of the group grits its teeth and, still trembling, picks up a blackened, smoldering branch—and nothing happens! The secondary representational system is vindicated, the unthinkable not only can be thought but performed.

Arguments such as these, though falling far short of proof, increase the likelihood that protolanguage did not develop until *erectus* emerged. This would give protolanguage a time depth of around a million and a half years, enough for the mode to become firmly established in the hominid line and therefore for it to be less vulnerable than true language to genetic accident or inadequate triggering. However, short of science fiction developments like time travel or the reconstruction of species from fossil DNA, it is unlikely that we will ever know the date of the earliest linguistic utterance. It may be more instructive to ask not when the earliest forms of language appeared, but exactly how and for what reasons.

THE VOCAL CHANNEL

As noted earlier, for any kind of language to emerge there were two prerequisites: motivation for its development and a channel through which it could be expressed. Let us begin by examining the second of these.

If, as was just now suggested, our early ancestors 'talked' or 'communicated' about fire, how exactly could they have done this? Apes cannot be taught to speak, and indeed it was the failure of attempts to do this that caused investigators to turn to some kind of sign language. It has been suggested that the earliest forms of language did not use the vocal channel at all, but took the form of manual signs. However, this suggestion merely complicates linguistic history without adding any explanatory dimension. The two major questions in language phylogeny—how elements acquired reference, and how syntax developed—cannot be answered by it. Moreover, it would seem to make predictions (for instance, that spontaneous signing should occur in infants prior to spontaneous vocalization) that are easily falsified.

In consequence it will be assumed that protolanguage used the vocal channel from the very beginning. There were at least two obstacles to the use of this channel by earlier species. One was the degree of cortical control over vocalizations, the other the structure of the vocal tract. The first is perhaps of lesser importance. Cortical control is required if vocalizations are to be voluntary, but it is not needed for the giving of alarm calls. Indeed, for alarm calls cortical control might be dysfunctional—if a creature takes time to ponder whether to call or not, the delay could be fatal.

However, cortical control is essential for linguistic utterances, since these may be required to provide information, and the giving of information must be a deliberate, intended action. Control of vocalizations is indeed more strongly established in humans than in apes, but the difference now seems to be scalar rather than absolute. It is perhaps impossible to determine at what stage hominids achieved a degree of cortical control adequate to support voluntary utterance. It seems likely though that this threshold was crossed well in advance of articulate speech, probably by the time of *Australopithicus afarensis*.

Afarensis was much smaller and lighter than our species, at a time when predators were often larger than they are today. Moreover, it operated in areas where the possibilities of escape up a convenient tree were limited or nonexistent. But, if the performance of modern apes is anything to go by, it descended from a line in which certain vocalizations (alarm calls on the appearance of predators, food barks on the discovery of food) are quite automatic and impossible to suppress: recall Jane Goodall's telling anecdote of the ape that discovered a supply of bananas and, although anxious to keep them to itself, inadvertently gave away their location by its unsupressible food barks.

Noise at the wrong time must have been far more deleterious to *afarensis* than to any ape species. Alarm calls always have some kind of trade-off factor—the majority of the group may be saved, but the caller itself is put at greater risk than would have been the case if it had silently run for cover. In areas without trees to escape up, that factor tilts against the call-using species. It tilts still further if (as will be suggested shortly) hominoids foraged individually or in small groups; in the first case an involuntary alarm call would be suicidal, in the second fewer individuals would be saved by the potential self-sacrifice of the caller. Moreover, a food bark appropriate in the case of nuts or bananas that can neither hear nor run away would make opportunistic stalking of birds, small mammals, or lizards an almost impossible task.

Thus any *afarensis* specimens whose neural equipment allowed them to voluntarily inhibit vocalization would have been favored by evolution. However, motor control, like neural mechanisms in general, characteristically works in terms of opponent pairs. It would therefore have been impossible to develop a capacity for voluntary silence without simultaneously developing increased control over voluntary vocalization. It seems likely that by the time of *habilis* the latter had been achieved.

In all probability, however, the actual capacity of *habilis* for vocal communication was less developed than the capacity for controlling it. Here, again, the disappearance of the softer parts of hominids means that the relevant organs can only be hypothetically reconstructed from fossil remains, so no conclusion can be more than provisional. The human vocal tract seems to have developed gradually out of the primate supralaryngeal tract, which is primarily adapted for eating, drinking, and breathing, and only secondarily employed, in some species, for vocal calls. This change may have been linked to other changes entailed by a predominantly upright mode of locomotion. Certainly walking upright would have changed the normal orientation of the tract from roughly horizontal to vertical.

However, these developments did not come without cost. As often happens in evolution, a trade-off was involved. In the higher mammals generally, the larynx is positioned high in the neck, leaving a reduced supralaryngeal portion for the production of sounds, but enabling its owner to breathe and swallow at the same time. So far as can be judged from fossil remains, this typical mammalian feature was shared by all primates up to and including australopithecines. It served as a safety device, the loss of which was part of the price we paid for articulate speech. That such a price could be paid is a warning against panselectionism, the belief that every evolutionary change must be, in and of itself, adaptive. For as a result of this particular change, humans cannot simultaneously breathe and drink, and not infrequently they choke to death on food that gets lodged in their windpipes.

The lowering of the larnyx seems to have been related to a change in the degree of basocranial flexion. The bases of the ape and early hominid skulls are fairly level, whereas the human skull is tilted so that it comes lower in the rear than in the front. Presumably this could have brought about the lowering of the larnyx as a side effect. But, although a tendency in that direction can be observed in the skulls of earlier hominid species, it became marked only as our own species emerged, and can perhaps be regarded as merely forming part of the general restructuring of the hominid skull that accompanied that emergence.

If this is so, then no species prior to ours was really equipped for articulate speech. It would then follow that if linguistic output required a fully perfected vocal tract, no species prior to ours could have developed even protolanguage. But there is no reason to suppose that protolanguage had to wait for a perfected vocal tract. Indeed, if it had done so, the earlier development of the tract would have been entirely dysfunctional, with no compensatory advantage.

A reverse scenario is much more convincing. Once speech, however crude, had emerged, it would give an adaptive advantage to those individuals whose vocal tracts were capable of improved articulation. Indeed, the fact that the vocal tract seems to have begun a gradual development from the time of *habilis* argues that selective pressures favored it. Since speech was the sole benefit such changes conferred, surely speech of some kind was already present.

The counterargument is that the partially developed tract possessed by pre-*sapiens* species could not have produced anything like the wide array of speech sounds that characterizes language today. But there is no reason to suppose that archaic speech—protolanguage speech—used modern speech sounds, and good reason to suppose the contrary.

In contemporary languages there is an inventory of sounds, each of which is in itself completely meaningless. These sounds can be combined in different ways to form different words, just as words can be combined in different ways to form sentences. Despite obvious differences, there are commonalities between phonology and syntax which suggest that the evolution of the two may have been linked.

We have seen evidence for a presyntactic stage in language acquisition. There is also evidence for a prephonological stage. Children just beginning to speak seem to treat words not as conjunctions of clearly delineated sounds, but rather as indissoluble units, continuous modulations of sound. Evidence for this is that they can often pronounce, in the context of particular words, sounds that a few months later they are unable to make in *any* word—even the words that they used to pronounce correctly.

It may well be that early in the phylogenetic development of speech, meaningful symbols were treated as unanalyzable wholes. They might have sounded to us more like grunts or gurgles than articulate speech, but provided that they could be distinguished from one another by their hearers, they would serve their purpose. Certainly they would be better than no speech at all. It is true that one could hardly amass a very large vocabulary in this way, but there is no reason to suppose that the original vocabulary was very large. Moreover, as that vocabulary grew, it would, in its turn, exert a selective pressure. Those hominids who could reliably articulate and comprehend the greatest number of words would function more efficiently than others, would occupy leadership roles in their groups, and would become more desirable as mates, thereby leaving more progeny than the less adept.

Thus the relatively slow development of the vocal tract would not have prevented *erectus* from speaking, provided that all the other necessary prerequisites for protolanguage were in place. The chief of these was motivation, and to this we now turn.

MOTIVATION AND EVOLUTION

It may seem strange, even contradictory, to argue on the one hand that language is primarily a representational system and on the other that language could come into existence only as a communicational device. In reality there is no contradiction. Language provides a secondary representational system (SRS), and an SRS is already latent in any creature whose primary system is well developed enough to analyze the world into a sufficiently wide range of categories—as experiments with chimpanzees, dolphins, sea lions, and parrots have shown.

In this sense and to this extent, our remote ancestors should have had protolanguage before they even uttered the first recognizable word. But language in such a latent form is as unuseable as ore in the ground, even for thinking with. The internal function of a word (or a manual sign, in sign language) is to replace the complexities of a concept—all the leafiness, branchiness, trunk- and root-possession that clutters up our concept of 'tree'—with a smooth, bland counter that can be manipulated, along with other such counters, either in thought or in speech. (How this

145

works will be treated in the latter part of this chapter.) In other words, a latent SRS might exist, but it could not be used, even internally, until it had been fitted out with a set of concrete units that could be handled more easily than raw concepts, just as a handful of gold coins could be handled more easily than the bales of cloth that they represented. The form those units took was unimportant (they could have been manual just as well as vocal) but they had to be physically expressed.

You might say that physical expression was not necessary, that individuals with a latent SRS could have invented purely mental labels for the categories it contained, and thus could have enjoyed all the benefits of thought even without the existence of a public language. In principle they could have done so, but what could ever have motivated an evolutionary creature to do this? No creature could have foreseen those benefits. Indeed, no benefits could have existed until a vocabulary of some size had been amassed. There is precious little advantage to be gained from mentally manipulating a mere handful of symbols.

There is, however, an advantage in being able to exchange a mere handful of words. You can then warn of danger or pass on information about food sources—actions that might help preserve the lives of individuals or even whole groups. Thus while there was no immediate motivation for developing a private language, there was immediate motivation for developing a small working vocabulary for communal use. Communication may not be language, or even protolanguage, but it was perhaps the only means by which either could have bootstrapped its way up from mere latency to the status of a useable representational system.

There remains the question of why, among a range of other creatures that might have developed some form of language, only an ancestor of ours did so.

The answer suggests itself if we regard language as simply one form of evolutionary adaptation. Evolutionary adaptations normally occur as a result of changes in the environment. Such changes may take many forms. They may be climatic, or they may involve the spread of other species—potential prey or potential predators—from other areas. Alternatively, an existing prey species may acquire some new defense: a grub may begin to produce poisonous secretions, a favored food plant may develop spines. If the gene pool of one's own species, with or without the help of mutation, produces individuals equipped to exploit this new situation, an adaptation takes place.

An adaptation may precede or follow a behavioral change. For instance, if a species begins to become aquatic, foraging more and more in shallow coastal waters, any variation or mutation that enables it to go for longer periods without breathing, or that streamlines its shape, or that adds fatty tissue that will help maintain its temperature level, will be favored and will tend to increase over time. More rarely, perhaps, a structural change will precede a behavioral one, as when certain Hawaiian treecreepers with beaks shorter and more blunt than those of related species began to dig into the bark of trees instead of merely probing their cracks, and were thus able to exploit a rich and hitherto untapped source of food.

But whether they precede or follow behavioral changes, the adaptations that are favored will be those that provide immediate and specific advantages to the creatures concerned. Moreover, they cannot occur simply because they would be advantageous. There has to be some existing function that can be adapted, or extended, or modified in some way: the necessary neural infrastructure has to be in place. If these conditions are not met, the creature may fail to adapt and may become extinct, as have an overwhelming majority of species since evolution began.

These considerations apply to every adaptation, and language is no exception. We have then to ask what developments would bring a species to a level of absolute readiness for language? And, to what set of environmental circumstances would language constitute the best response (in the sense that improved breath control, streamlining, and so on constitute the best response to an aquatic environment)? We tend to think of language as something that is self-evidently advantageous, forgetting that all contemporary species but our own get along perfectly well without it—forgetting too that the payoff has to be immediate if an adaptation is to flourish.

For example, language increases problem-solving abilities, and one might think that since problem-solving abilities are universally useful, any species would be benefited by language. But language could not have been used for problem solving until it had become firmly established and quite well developed. What would drive it to become so? Only some benefit that, however slight, was actively life-lengthening and could be derived from the most minimal move in the direction of language.

READINESS FOR LANGUAGE

An as yet undetermined number of species may have a latent SRS and may, under intensive training and in laboratory conditions, exhibit some form of protolinguistic behavior, but it is by no means clear that they are all equally ready for such behavior. We have no way of knowing, in each case, just how many changes, structural and behavioral, they would have

147

to undergo before they reached a level at which protolanguage could spontaneously emerge. We may therefore imagine that parrots and sea lions are somewhat further from such a level than dolphins or apes, but this may merely reflect human prejudice.

However, there were certain developments in the primate line that might seem to increase readiness. Most important of these, perhaps, was stereoscopic vision. Most mammals have eyes set on either side of a rather elongated head, giving them a wide visual field but rather poor depth perception and object definition. But an arboreal existence puts a premium on both of these last two capacities. If you are on a branch and want to jump to another branch, you need to know within rather fine limits just how far away the second branch is and whether it is thick enough to support your weight. Thus evolution favored animals whose muzzles were more and more retracted, permitting the left and right visual fields to overlap.

Although some birds had developed keen vision, primates were perhaps the first terrestrial creatures to enjoy this advantage. The benefits of keen vision, as it turned out, were more extensive than might at first be supposed. For the ancestors of the primates, smell and hearing were the master senses. It seems possible, however, that by their very nature, the senses of smell and hearing are more restricted than the sense of sight. Eyes have a relatively large surface area, so that even without movement, their receptor cells yield a three-dimensional, almost 180-degree image of the environment. Ears and nostrils are narrow tubes with receptor cells usually located deep within them. Although we cannot know how smell-dominant or hearing-dominant creatures perceive the world, it is hard to imagine that they perceive the aural or olfactory equivalent of complete landscapes. It is true that sound, for bats, dolphins, and blind humans, can provide a very accurate indication of where things are. Yet there is surely a limit on the number of things a creature can smell or hear *simultaneously,* whereas there is virtually no limit to the number of objects a creature with efficient vision can see at one time.

In other words, primate senses may be able to provide not necessarily more information than canid senses, but more *simultaneous* information. Given an identical quantity of information, more apparatus is required to process it simultaneously than would be needed if processing were serial. Thus, reliance on sight should increase the relative size of brain areas devoted to the analysis of sensory data. But it is precisely those areas that generate a creature's PRS, the system of categories into which its experience is divided. The result of better vision and better vision processing should, therefore, have been an increase in the number of

PRS categories and hence an ampler and more useful model of reality. This in turn brought its possessor still closer to a state of language readiness.

This increment in visual processing is one of the main reasons the brains of primates tend to be proportionately larger than those of other mammals, and also why the brains of australopithecines were larger than those of other primates. For what was originally an adaptation for rain forests turned out to be a preadaptation for life on the savannas.

In rain forests, the distances over which vision can operate are too short, and the environment too undifferentiated, for vision's full benefits to be reaped. But the resolution and depth perception necessary to achieve absolute accuracy in a twenty- or thirty-foot leap should still be pretty accurate over two or three kilometers. The capacity to gauge exactly the thickness of a branch just out of reach translates into the capacity to recognize the different species long before they can recognize you. In the savannas, sight came into its own.

Another inheritance from arboreal ancestors was that of prehensile hands. First developed for grasping branches, they were and are used by apes for a variety of other purposes—in particular for feeding, since no primate feeds directly with its mouth. When our remote ancestors adopted a bipedal gait, those hands were freed from their role in locomotion and made available for tactile exploration of objects; for groping, probing, and throwing; and ultimately for the manufacture and use of tools. All of these activities would also have enriched the network of neural connections. In particular, they would have increased the number of cross-modal connections, ensuring linkage between the visual, auditory, and tactile aspects of things, and thereby giving concepts a more unitary nature. (Some creatures may well have distinct concepts of, say, 'auditory tiger' and 'visual tiger', which might not even trigger the same behavioral responses.)

But some parts of the arboreal inheritance had to be quickly abandoned. In the forests, apes subsist primarily on tropical fruits and nuts, normally found year-round in such abundance that day-ranges may be less than a kilometer. There is no such abundant source of any kind of food in the savanna except perhaps grass, and even grass will be greatly reduced in the dry season. Moreover, due to higher temperatures and the absence of shade, an animal's water requirement is much higher in the savanna, and sources of water are, in general, much more widely scattered. For these reasons, newly terrestrial species may have to change their diet and also substantially increase the size of their range.

It is not clear how recently our remote ancestors forsook the forest.

The present status of our nearest relatives, the chimpanzees, gorillas, and orangutans, is not necessarily revealing. It is suspected, for example, that orangutans were once terrestrial and returned to the trees because of competition from our own species. The ancestor that we have in common with the great apes could have been a species already terrestrial for a long period; the climatic changes that reduced African forests, and thus increased the number of terrestrial species, began as long as 15.0 Mya. Alternatively, our ancestors could have been arboreal until the split, or even after it.

But whether their terrestrial history was long or short, they were obliged to become wide-ranging omnivores. This too would have served to increase their neural processing mechanisms and thus their overall brain size. For the larger the range and the more diverse the foods consumed, the greater the demands on memory, on cognitive mapping of the range space, and on internal representations of edible entities and their environments. A consequence of this is that among living species, those that have varied food sources and wide ranges tend to have brains proportionately larger than the brains of species that utilize a single source (e.g., herbivores) and/or a restricted range.

In a savanna environment, all of these factors (primate vision, hand development, foraging patterns) would have united to increase those areas of the brain devoted to the processing of sensory information, and would thereby have increased language readiness. Under such circumstances, the quite modest advantage in EQ that australopithecines had over modern apes is hardly surprising. What is more noteworthy is that the advantages of superior brains, hands, and vision were essential to hominid survival. For in most other respects, early hominids were inferior to the competition.

For an omnivore that eats with its hands, grass is ruled out as a food source. Leaves remain a possibility, as they are for apes, but their availability is limited on savannas, and the low-grade nourishment they supply would hardly repay the energy lost in rushing from source to source. This effectively limits the diet to: fruits, nuts, and large seeds; tubers; edible fungi; freshwater fish and crustaceans; birds' eggs; wild honey; small mammals, ground-nesting birds, lizards, frogs, and so forth; the young of larger animals; and the carcasses of animals of any size killed by predators or dead from natural causes. Many of these sources were seasonal in nature, and relatively few of them would be concentrated in any area. These facts entailed that our remote ancestors should have wide and continually shifting ranges.

A further problem was competition from other hunters and scavengers. During the Pliocene and early Pleistocene periods (roughly 5.0 Mya to 0.7 Mya) there existed no fewer than eight genera of predators competing directly with hominids, including four that are now extinct. All of these had a longer evolutionary history of terrestrial predation and were better equipped than hominids in terms of both speed and offensive weaponry (teeth, claws, and musculature adapted for seizing and tearing prey). Hominids were also potential prey for many of their competitors; again, their relative weakness and their relative slowness over short distances made them vulnerable. If they were to survive and compete effectively, early hominids would have to exploit their few advantages to the full.

What were those advantages? Vision has already been mentioned. Bipedalism was another. A variety of reasons have been proposed to explain why our ancestors adopted this pattern, but one thing is certain. Once bipedalism was adopted, it brought at least two novel methods of hunting within reach. Most predators do not pursue over long distances (canids are an exception), and no other predator pursues over long periods of time. In other words, there was a niche available for a creature that could either run down animals over distances of a mile or so, or track them over periods of many hours or even days.

We cannot know whether either method was adopted by our early ancestors. The second is still used today by some hunter-gatherers, while George Schaller, author of a classic study of lions, personally showed that the first is still within the powers even of contemporary Western academics. Tracking over long periods requires not so much speed or stamina as cognitive skills (the ability to interpret natural signs such as animal droppings, footprints, broken twigs, and so forth) and capacities such as that of pursuing a goal for long periods without being distracted from it.

These skills and capacities are not shared by contemporary apes, but they entered the hominid line at some point. However, the question of whether they helped to develop readiness for language or were impossible without the representations afforded by language, cannot, at this stage, be answered wtih any degree of confidence. Since the maintenance of purpose even in the visual absence of prey seems dubious in the absence of an SRS, the answer may well prove negative.

A third advantage of early hominids was the capacity to use stones as instruments. It is reasonable to assume that, since both chimpanzees and later hominids share this capacity, it developed in their common ancestor. Useful in the forests for cracking open hard-shelled nuts, it would have served equally well in the savannas for cracking large bones and extracting the marrow from them. In other words, it would have given hominids immediate access to a food source that, though not exactly plentiful, could not be utilized by any other species. From such a source, food could be extracted at leisure, after predators and scavengers alike had deserted the scene of a kill.

It is even possible that the first shaped tools came into existence accidentally, as a direct result of marrow extraction. If a stone lay immediately beneath the bone (and the use of larger stones as anvils does not seem implausible), then hammer-stones would sometimes have cracked, and occasionally the break would have yielded stones with a relatively sharp cutting edge.

Indeed, it is not beyond the bounds of possibility that all pre-*erectus* stone 'tools' were produced in this quasi-accidental fashion. But, however cutting tools were invented, they could have opened up a further untapped food source. Carcasses of animals like the rhinoceros that have very thick, leathery skins cannot be utilized by other scavengers until the outer skin has begun to decay, a process that even in the tropics might take several days. A creature that could cut through the skin, rapidly butcher at least parts of the interior, and carry them off before other animals could (quite literally) get wind of the discovery would thereby have carved out for itself an almost unassailable niche. But again, of course, we can only surmise how, and how far, and at what stage of hominid development such a niche might have been exploited.

Although no one can say precisely how our early ancestors subsisted, the foregoing considerations suggest that they very likely did so in an opportunistic manner, switching rapidly from one food source to another as the seasons changed and as chance prompted them. Sandwiched as they were in the food chain between species they could eat and species that could eat them, they had to exploit to the full whatever versatility they already had, simply in order to survive. Under such circumstances, the hominid that could spot the most opportunities and foresee the most dangers would survive longest and contribute a larger share of seed to future generations.

Thus an evolutionary premium was placed on curiosity and observation. Recall, from chapter 5, that the main difference between the content of ape utterances and the content of child utterances is that while apes' utterances are concerned only with the creature's wants, children's utterances show an intense interest in recognizing and categorizing objects in the immediate environment. Chimpanzees have few enemies or competitors and abundant food sources, so they have little motivation to be curious about their surroundings. Early hominids had many enemies and competitors and exploited sparse and widely scattered food sources. For them, curiosity about their surroundings may have been simply a matter of life or death, and thus a quality that would have been selected for over a period of perhaps millions of years.

Immediate Motivation

Thus at some point in the hominid line, most likely at either the beginning or the end of the *habilis* period, our remote ancestors had reached a state of readiness for language: they had a highly developed sensorium, rich cross-modal connections, and a diverse and copious PRS. Owing to their relative vulnerability, they had a constant need for more and better information. Thanks to their developing mental faculties, they were able to take advantage of such information. Here perhaps lies the key to the breakthrough.

It is perhaps no accident that the only other species known to transmit information that is both objective and variable is a social creature that forages as an individual or in small groups, utilizes widely scattered and seasonally variable food sources, and benefits by transmitting information about those sources to conspecifics. The information conveyed by the dances of honeybees is objective, in that it expresses not the dancer's current mood but facts about the environment. Moreover, it is variable, in that food sources differing in distance, direction, and quantity can be indicated. For a species that pursues highly varied and often seasonal food sources over large and probably shifting ranges, nothing could be of more value than some means of transmitting and receiving information about these sources.

Note that the precise set of problems that faced our remote ancestors is faced by few, if any, other creatures. Nonsocial creatures subsist (or fail to subsist) on what they can find for themselves, and therefore they do not need to communicate about food sources. Social creatures are usually either herbivorous or carnivorous. Of the exceptions to this, few, if any, vary their feeding habits as much as contemporary hunter-gatherers do and as our remote ancestors may have done. Since grass and foliage tend to be concentrated in particular areas, social herbivores tend to move in herds. Food sources for carnivores are much more dispersed, but social carnivores, such as wild dogs, hyenas, and wolves, have evolved systems of cooperative hunting. Such strategies enable a pack of canids to hunt much larger animals, so that a single kill may feed the entire pack. It is at least questionable whether any pre-Neanderthal hominid habitually hunted animals several times larger than himself, and extremely unlikely that the skills and weaponry of 2 Mya would have been adequate for this.

Primates, too, generally travel in troops. These troops may disperse over small areas of forest, but it is unusual for any member to be out of sight or hearing of the others. When a rich food source is discovered, loud cries are enough to bring other members of the troop. Thus for primates in general, as for other advanced mammals, there would be little to be gained from a device for exchanging information about alternative food sources.

The situation for early hominids was rather different. No one, of course, knows whether they foraged in bands, in small groups, or individually. Foraging in bands is not the most efficient way of exploiting a wide and fluctuating range, except for things like seeds and berries that are dense where they occur and whose locations are predictable. Game of any kind, or carcasses suitable for scavenging, do not occur predictably. A higher proportion of these can be foraged if the band splits up into smaller groups and any find too large for a small group to consume is then reported to the band as a whole.

But how is the reporting to be done? Not by yelping or bellowing, since most of the band might be out of earshot. But neither would it be very efficient simply to find other group members and, by tugging or gesturing, to try to convey to them that you knew of something to their advantage. Perhaps they too had made discoveries of their own. Perhaps they would be reluctant to accompany you without knowing how far away your discovery was and whether it was worth the effort that would be expended to get there. Precisely the kind of information that bees transmit—which way, how far, and how much—would come in handy here. But how to transmit it?

The bee's means of communication is built-in and was developed over millions of years. For an advanced mammal, especially for a species that could already conceptualize the various species, along with things such as size differences, distances, and directions, no such solution was possible or, ultimately, even desirable. Moreover, this particular mammal had developed a fair degree of cortical control over the vocal channel, certainly enough to vocalize freely and at will. All that was now needed was to put these two capacities together.

Whatever brought them about, the first uses of protolanguage were surely cases of trial and error, error perhaps being more common than success. That would not have mattered. A single success, a single occasion on which the whole group *did* pay attention to the mouthings of the lucky foragers and *did* find the otherwise irrecoverable food source, would have been remembered, although not necessarily for long. The beginnings of protolanguage may have been found and lost and found again countless times before becoming firmly established. As long as the selective pressure was maintained—a need for information richer and more accurate and more swiftly delivered than that available to competitors—protolanguage would go on struggling to be born.

Most speculations about language birth have focused in on this first truly referential use of sound, sometimes to the exclusion of all else. In the framework of the present account this step may seem less important. It was, after all, only a stage, albeit a crucial one, in the long march from the earliest internal representations to the thousands of complex languages that exist today. It was perhaps inevitable that a species with a rich enough PRS, an acute need for information, and control of an output channel would eventually stumble on protolanguage.

'Stumble' is probably the appropriate word. Given that a linguistic act of communication has to be intentional on the part of the actor, how (especially in the absence of an overt referent) would others have recognized it as such? Or, if they had recognized it, how could they have determined what *kind* of communication was being undertaken? Some accounts have leaned heavily on the transmutation of existing calls, calls like those of the vervet alarm system. These may not be true words, but they are associations between an arbitrary element and something in the external world, that might somehow be bleached of their warning function. The problem again is one of comprehension. How would the addressee have known that the addressor was giving factual information rather than warning? It may well have been easier to transmit information by using sounds that were quite unconnected with alarm calls.

Also, call-continuity hypotheses fail to take account of the fact that, while alarm calls necessarily have to do with predator species, information on food sources would deal mostly with prey species. Hominids might have had alarm calls for lions or leopards or snakes, but they would have been unlikely to have any kind of call for gazelles, dead hippopotamuses, or bees' nests. On balance, then, it seems likely that the first referential units of protolanguage evolved as something quite distinct from the preexisting call system.

The chance that such units were originally imitations of animal sounds has been discounted on the grounds that in contemporary languages there are very few onomatopoeic words, while the vast majority of words are quite arbitrary in structure and vary unpredictably from language to language. This argument is implicitly based on the notion that language evolved in a single continuous development—a notion parallel to that which sees the child's earliest utterances as steps in a single process of 'language learning'. If language and protolanguage are discrete yet partially overlapping entities, such arguments no longer go through. Moreover, the differences here have to do not merely with language versus protolanguage, but with two different species. There is no way we can know what *erectus* words would have been like, except that they would have been whatever worked.

The dawn-of-language scenario may, from one viewpoint, be regarded as no more than an exaggerated form of what was encountered by immigrants to areas where pidgin languages formed—where anything worked as long as it was understood. The freestyle flavor of this was well expressed by Rachel Kupepe, who witnessed it in Hawaii: "So we use the Hawaiian and Chinese together in one sentence, see? And they ask me if that's a Hawaiian word, I said no, maybe that's a Japanese word we put in, to make a sentence with a Hawaiian word. And the Chinese the same way too, in order to make a sentence for them to understand you." In just the same way, hominids may have at various times used alarm calls, animal imitations, expressive grunts (with or without accompanying gesticulations), chance associations formed through infant babbling, or any of a variety of other possible forms of protoword, in order to get their point across.

What form of signal was first used is relatively unimportant. Whatever was used and worked would have established the principle that signs could function in the absence of their referents. Regardless of their origins, once referential items had been established, they could be passed on to children as part of the general socialization program found in all social mammals. In this way they would have begun to form the store of such units that would eventually revolutionize the inner as well as the outer landscape of our ancestors' lives.

BENEFITS OF THE PROTOLANGUAGE

The immediate, practical benefits that hominids would have gained from communicating with one another in even the simplest form of protolanguage are obvious enough. What is perhaps less obvious is the way in which that protolanguage would have remodeled their internal world.

Consider the relationship that exists between words and concepts. Give any normal individual of our species a word, say *leopard,* and ask what its referent is and does. You will be told something like 'a leopard is a mammal; it has spots, eats meat, runs fast, lives in Africa' and so on. Conversely, if you show that person a picture of a leopard, from any angle, with any degree of occlusion, and ask what it is, you will be told 'a leopard'. Such capacities seem so basic to our species that they are among the first to be tested if any kind of mental abnormality is suspected.

We may therefore not notice that the first capacity is of a very different order from the second. Something analogous to the second could probably be done by a pigeon. You could train a pigeon to recognize leopards, and thereafter reward it every time it pressed the leopard button in response to a leopard picture. For an analog of the first task, however, you would first have to train it to press a 'mammals' button, then a 'lives-in-Africa' button, then a 'spotted' button, then a 'fast-running' button, then a 'carnivorous' button, and so on. Once it could reliably and appropriately assign these and other categories (to other things as well as leopards, of course), you would somehow have to train the pigeon so that, whenever you showed it a picture of a leopard, the pigeon would press all the buttons of all the categories that the leopard belonged to. Then you would somehow have to fix things so that *when you merely pressed the leopard button*, the pigeon would press all of the appropriate category buttons.

Although we are continually being surprised by the things other creatures can do, it seems safe to predict that no pigeon, and probably no nonhuman primate, could pass this test (although a 'language'-trained chimpanzee might conceivably succeed at a very simple version of it). And yet any creature with experience of leopards should somehow 'know' that a leopard is a mammal (not a fish or a reptile), that it eats meat, that it runs fast, and that it has spots. But such a creature would have nothing with which to tie together all these different aspects of its concept of 'leopard'.

It is hard to imagine how a creature without language would think, but one may suspect that a world without any kind of language would in some ways resemble a world without money—a world in which actual commodities, rather than metal or paper symbols for the value of these, would have to be exchanged. How slow and cumbersome the simplest sale would be, and how impossible the more complex ones! Or imagine trying to use a library which had no indexing system: no cards, no terminals, and no numbering on the spines of books. Even if the books themselves were arranged in some logical order, you would be lucky to find the ones you wanted, and to research any issue that covered more than one or two topic areas would, even if possible, be prohibitively expensive in terms of time.

True language functions in a way that combines aspects of indexing in a library and coins in a monetary system. Like a file index, it gives rapid and immediate access to any part of a store of knowledge. Like coins, its units can be manipulated freely and easily in an infinite number of situations to achieve an infinite number of results.

It is questionable whether a mere protolanguage would have conferred all of these advantages. The 'coin' function is likely to have been acquired before the 'index' function, for it does not depend on the number of units acquired. A handful of words can be manipulated so as to yield a range of elementary propositions. But it is conceivable that the 'index' function was not achieved until the emergence of our own species, depending as it does on a hierarchical, binary branching system or organization (evinced in the 'predicability tree' illustrated in chapter 3) closely resembling that of syntax.

Thus the *erectus* lexicon would have resembled a miser's shoebox full of coins rather than a numismatist's ranked and ordered collection. Such a lexicon would still have provided great conceptual advantages, particularly in the realm of learning. As shown in chapter 4, the course of development followed by animate creatures led from a state in which all responses were innately determined to an ever-increasing reliance on responses that had, wholly or in part, to be learned from experience. But to say that a creature 'learns from experience' is too vague, for it might mean any of at least three things.

It might mean, for example, something like the following: A creature is pursued by a predator, and its only line of escape is through a creek. It swims the creek, and the predator fails to follow, since its dislike of water exceeds its hunger. Subsequently, if pursued by the same predator, the creature will head for water, if water is available. Let us call this type of learning *experiential learning*.

But it might also mean the following: Suppose that another creature has never itself escaped from a predator by crossing water, but that it has seen one of its fellows do this. So, the first time it is pursued by that predator, it escapes by swimming. Let us call this *observational learning*.

But now suppose that a third creature has observed this predator from afar on several occasions but has never used water as an escape route nor seen any other creature do that. However, it has happened to observe that the predator will take a long walk around the arm of a lake when a short swim would have taken it where it wanted to go. Instead of having to wait for an actual attack on itself or another, this creature is able to construct a kind of propositional machine: 'Predator avoids water. Suppose predator chases me. I cross water. Predator does not cross water. I escape'. Thus despite the absence of any direct example, the first time the creature is pursued by that predator, it escapes by swimming. Let us call this *constructional learning*.

The advantages of constructional learning over the other types of learning are obvious. Experiential learning and observational learning require events external to the creature, chance occurrences over which it can have no control: that is, these forms of learning have to await the appearance of such events. But constructional learning requires only that the creature put together bits of information that it already knows. In other words, constructional learning need not wait on external events; it relies rather on internal events, events within the creature's mind that it can make happen whenever it is motivated to do so. In the other two types, the environment is the teacher. In constructional learning, the environment provides only the raw data. *The creature itself is both learner and teacher.* For the benefits of constructional learning to be maximized, data gathering must be maximized. As we have seen, hominids were conditioned, both by their visual powers and their ecology, to be constant observers.

Practically all creatures are capable of experiential learning in some form or other. The range of observational learning may be smaller, but it is certainly present among the primates. One example is that of the Japanese macaques who quickly adopted the custom, acquired by one of them perhaps through experiential learning, of shifting grit from grain by throwing the mixture into water. But observational learning may well be present among many other species. For instance, birds of the tit family that began throughout Britain to peck through the foil or cardboard tops of milk bottles are unlikely to have acquired the habit through experiential learning by each individual bird.

But is a creature without language capable of constructional learning? Many experiments designed to test the intelligence of apes, in which they have, for example, to stack boxes in a pyramid or fetch water to extinguish a candle in order to get at otherwise inaccessible food, suggest that some degree of constructional learning may be accessible to them. Still more revealing, perhaps, are experiments by David Premack involving spatial inference. In one of these, an ape saw an orange and a banana placed in different containers, and then (without actually seeing the experimenter remove it) saw the experimenter eating a banana; af-

159

ter that the ape was allowed to look for food. In this test, chimpanzees headed unerringly for the 'orange' container, just as three- to four-year-old children do (younger ones usually fail this test). Premack concluded from his experiments that apes must have available to them some kind of abstract, prelinguistic code.

However, it does not seem necessary to draw such a conclusion, unless by 'abstract code' we mean no more than those representational processes discussed in chapter 4, which vary considerably among species with regard both to type and degree of development. What characterizes both Premack's experiments and the earlier ones is that the elements necessary to solve the problem correctly all had to be physically present. Also, Premack's experiments depended on the capacity to construct maps of physical space, a capacity which, as we have seen, is widely distributed among even invertebrates. On more abstract tests involving same-different relations, naive apes failed totally, even after extensive training at the task, while apes that had been exposed to 'linguistic' training again performed at the level of young children.

What this suggests (subject, of course, to much further empirical investigation) is roughly as follows: Constructional learning is possible for at least some nonhuman species, provided that all the elements involved are physically present in the immediate environment—not necessarily perceptible to the senses in all phases of the experiment, but perceptible in at least some phases. When these conditions are not fulfilled, when it is necessary to make inferences about absent individuals or about classes, some form of representation beyond those available to nonhumans is required.

Constructional learning supported by language enables us to draw inferences about classes and absent individuals. It is this that has given our species its dominance over nature, for the capacity to make such inferences allows us, among other things, to alter our behavior, if only within as yet ill-defined limits. Other species may modify their behavior, but the alterations are usually quite small, or else they take a very long time. Only a species with language is capable of behavioral change that is simultaneously both rapid and radical.

It is only with some kind of linguistic system, whether protolanguage or language—in other words, with an SRS—that any creature can construct things as abstract as models of new behaviors in its mind, and can then try them out, so to speak, to see if they work at least within the model of the world that the SRS creates. If they do work within the SRS-model, then the assumption is that they will work in the world. Of course they do not always work in the world, because the SRS-model is not the world, or even a model of the world (it is in fact a model of a model of the world, the primary model being that created by the PRS). But they work often enough to give a constructionally learning species a decisive advantage over all others.

For example, it took evolution countless millions of years to produce the ant lion, a creature that digs a hole, hides in the bottom, and grabs any prey that falls into the hole. It took constructional learning only a tiny handful of those years to produce a hominid that could dig a hole in a game trail, place sharpened stakes in the bottom of it, cover the hole with brush, and wait for any prey that falls into it to get impaled on the stakes. Moreover, the ant lion is limited to that one behavior, while the hominid has a potentially infinite stock of new behaviors.

Constructional learning can also account for the rapid increase in brain size that now took place within the hominid line. As noted earlier in this chapter, in the *afarensis-habilis* period brain-size increase exceeded body-mass increase by a factor of only 25%, while in the *erectus-sapiens* period the equivalent figure was 91%. Recall, too, that the added contents could not merely have been 'spare neurons' but must have had specific functions to perform. Given that the neural infrastructure required for protolanguage per se may have been little if any greater than that available to chimpanzees, it is unlikely that most of this increment was devoted specifically to linguistic functions, although, as time passed, there would have to be space for lexicon storage and richer connections between that storage and the various components involved in speech and hearing.

What surely accounted for the bulk of the increase was a continuous feedback process. Constructional learning constantly generated new information, new information had to be stored in the memory, and a copious memory store meant a larger bank of data to serve as the input for constructional learning, which in turn generated information that required more storage space. These processes provided all that was necessary for a purely autocatalytic increase in brain size. In this sense, and in this sense only, does the claim that 'the brain got bigger so as to process more data' have any validity. If the data involved were gathered by ordinary sensory (rather than linguistic) processes, then any species at any time could have undergone equally spectacular brain growth— though in actuality not one ever did.

But there was a limit on what *erectus* could do, even with constructional learning. If there had been no limit, *erectus*, in its million or more years of existence, would surely have achieved at least a part of what we have achieved. Moreover, that limit had nothing to do with brain size.

Toward the latter end of that million years, many *erectus* individuals had brain sizes that fell within the normal human range, and Neanderthals had brain sizes rather larger than ours. In all probability, the limit lay in the nature of protolanguage.

That nature had, of course, not one but two major defects. In addition to lacking syntactic structure, it must have been severely limited by the status of the vocal tract, which in *erectus* was still far from fully developed. It is possible that *erectus* developed fully syntactic language but that its inability to articulate clearly was what held the species back. However, that possibility would leave several things unexplained.

One is why, if *erectus* had syntactic capacity comparable with ours, that capacity was not expressed via sign, as it is among members of our own species whom deafness deprives of an adequate vocal channel. If this had happened, then *erectus* would have been our cognitive equal, contrary to what the fossil record suggests.

Another problem lies in the relation between phonology and syntax. Many linguists believe that whatever force organized the structure of sentences also organized the structure of sound systems. This suggests that phonology and syntax developed together. But the sound systems we know today could hardly have existed prior to the emergence of our own species. Therefore, syntax too could only have emerged with us.

The third problem is the most crucial. What gave our own species its ascendancy was not so much the power to communicate as the power to think, to imagine, and to plan, using our language-constructed model of reality as an arena in which to rehearse possible future actions. This power could have flourished in the absence of any adequate means of expression. If *erectus* had it, again, why is there nothing in the fossil record to suggest it?

It seems likely that syntax did not exist prior to our own species. Thinking of the kind that humans do is at best extremely difficult in the absence of syntax, since it depends crucially on the existence of structures like: x happened because y happened; whenever x happens, y happens; unless x happens, y will not happen; if x happens, either y or z will happen; although x happened, y did not happen; x thinks, believes, says, hopes, expects, fears, knows that y will or will not happen; x does y in order to z; x wants the y that z-ed, not the a that b-ed; and so on.

In protolanguage, these structures are not available. As we saw in chapter 5, complex sentences of any kind are impossible in protolanguage because there is no way in which one clause can be inserted into another. Even if this could be done, there would be no way of telling where clause 1 stopped and clause 2 started. But this is not the only reason propositions in protolanguage have to be short and simple. Another is that, without any reliable way of determining 'who did what to whom', ambiguities will quickly accumulate until they are too numerous to process. This would present almost as much of a problem for coherent thought as it would for speech.

Yet another weakness of protolanguage lies in its lack of grammatical items. Without a system of verbal auxiliaries or verbal inflections, there is no automatic and umambiguous mode of expressing time reference. Without a range of prepositions, or other units that do the work of prepositions, there is no way of indicating the directionality of actions and processes or the location of states and entities. A language that cannot map onto its model a matrix of space and time may not be irrevocably tethered to the here and now, but it leaves the here and now at the peril of endemic and swiftly accumulating misunderstandings. This limitation, plus the inability to produce more than simple propositions, would surely account for the relative lack of originality and inventiveness found in the artifacts of *erectus*, as compared with those of our own species.

Before such weaknesses could be overcome, before our ancestors could begin to think in a human way, protolanguage had to be transformed into true language through the emergence of grammatical items and syntactic structures. The chapter that follows will try to determine, as far as is possible, how such a transformation might have come about.

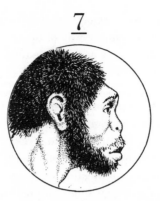

7

From Protolanguage to Language

No matter what set of assumptions we adopt with regard to post-*erectus* developments, any attempt to describe how language might have developed from protolanguage will still face serious problems. For such an attempt must be accountable, not merely to the linguistic facts, but to the facts of human evolution, insofar as these are known. The same is true, of course, of any attempt to describe the emergence of protolanguage. However, for the period of *afarensis*, *habilis*, and early *erectus*, the evolutionary data is much more sparse than for the period of late *erectus*, *neandertalensis*, and *sapiens*, hence the constraints on possible analyses are much stronger in the latter case.

While there are no clear criteria for choosing among a number of possible family trees for early hominids (see figure 6.1 and the discussion thereof), all of the relations that might have existed among our more immediate ancestors can, if we abstract away from disagreements over specific evolutionary mechanisms and other details, be reduced for practical purposes to just two.

In one view, *erectus*, after spreading through most of the Old World, developed into three (or more) populations not yet distinct enough to be regarded as subspecies: one in Africa, one in East Asia, and one in Europe and Asia Minor, of which perhaps only the latter, the neanderthals, were clearly distinguishable in physique both from earlier *erectus* populations and from the other two regional groups. But in all of these *erectus* populations, the same evolutionary forces were at work, causing each group individually (aided perhaps by a limited gene flow between groups) to develop to the level of present-day *Homo sapiens*. If this view is correct, then there is no need to devise elaborate scenarios to account for the contemporary absence of *erectus* and Neanderthal populations. These are simply our ancestors, who evolved into us.

In an alternative view, *sapiens* is a distinct species originating from an event, presumably a mutation of some kind, that affected a single female living in Africa at a time (according to some accounts) between 140 and 290 Kya (thousand years ago). The descendents of this female began, not later than around 70 Kya, to radiate from their original habitat and by 30 Kya had spread throughout the Old World and perhaps (although this is still controversial) throughout the New World too. In the meantime the original *erectus* and neanderthal populations of these areas had disappeared. Perhaps they disappeared simply as a result of interbreeding with the more dominant *sapiens* strain, perhaps they were outdone in competition, or perhaps, as some darker scenarios have suggested, they were victims of genocide.

The first, 'gradualist' view seemed to be supported, at least until recently, by the bulk of the fossil evidence. The second, 'catastrophic' view is supported by genetic evidence, in particular the study of mitrochondrial DNA in living populations, and by some recent paleontological evidence from South and East Africa. Whichever view is chosen has obvious simplications for the development of language.

If the 'gradualist' view is correct, then we might expect language, too, to have developed gradually over the course of the last million-and-a-half years. There are several problems with this. First of all, there is no evidence that language developed gradually. Such evidence might consist, for example, of some linguistic mode(s) intermediate between protolanguage and true language. But there is no evidence that any such mode exists. On the contrary, there is evidence, from at least two areas, that protolanguage can change into true language without any intervening stage, as well as evidence (to be surveyed later in this chapter) that there can be no plausible intermediate stage between the two.

GRADUALISM AND CHILD LANGUAGE

Recall the output of Seth at age twenty-one months, that was discussed in chapter 5:

1. Rock? (Rocks chair).
    Chair.
    Chair.
    Chair.
    House?
    Chair.

Get up. (Asked if wants to get up.)
Get.
Please? (Asked if wants juice.)
Please. (Given juice.)
Thank-you.
Thank-you.
Apple. (It is apple juice.)
Fan.
Fan.
T.V.
T.V.
T.V. (Father mentions name of dog.)
Puppy.
Switch.

Six months later, Seth's output was characterized by sentences like the following (not part of a dialogue—these examples are selected from sentences produced at that age).

2.   I want to put the squeaky shoes some more, Daddy.
      Let's get a piece of rock and make it go ding.
      Where'd the ball go? Where's the ball?
      There's Geoffrey. There's ya cookie monster. There's the nother cookie
         monster.
      I saw Robert, and saw Kevin, and saw Luanna.
      I did go in the kitchen throw it, Dad.
      Didja sit down tray a give me a little pudding?
      Was a good job I throw a diaper a rubbish.
      I want to play catch. I'm gonna throw it to you.

In contrast to (1), (2) is characterized by inflected forms (*saw, was, shoes*), noninflected forms for tense and mood (*'d, did, gonna*), prepositions (*in, to, of*), infinitive markers (*to*), articles (*a, the*), pronouns (*I, it, you, me*), quantifiers (*some more*), determiners (*nother*), conjunctions (*and*), and expletive locatives (*there*). Note that at least one pronoun, the first singular, incorporates a suppletive case distinction (*I, me*). The ratio of grammatical to lexical items is slightly better than fifty-fifty, substantially the same as in adult speech. While some of these fall into the 'more meaningful' range of grammatical items (*some more, there, I*), at least as many fall into the 'more structural' range (*of, a, to, the, and,* and *did*).

On a higher level of structure, we find a variety of noun phrases (*the squeaky shoes, the nother cookie monster, a little pudding*) including postmodified ones (*a piece of rock*). On a still higher level, there are both conjoined clauses (in the first and fifth examples) and embedded clauses (*I want TO PLAY CATCH*), which include causatives (*make IT GO DING*) and moved-subject clauses (*was a good job I THROW A DIAPER A RUBBISH*). This last sentence is a good example of the relatively trivial differences that still divide Seth's syntax from adult syntax. *I throw a diaper a rubbish* is of course the notional subject of *was a good job*. This would normally be extraposed, because of its length, just as Seth extraposes it. 'That I threw the diaper in the rubbish was a good job' sounds far more stilted and awkward than 'It was a good job (that) I threw the diaper in the rubbish'. All Seth has failed to learn is that when a subject clause is extraposed, the 'dummy' subject *it* has to be inserted.

As for other diagnostic features of true language, all the internal arguments of verbs are supplied (*give ME (Goal) A LITTLE PUDDING (Patient)*), and sometimes even optional ones as well (*throw IT (subcategorized Patient) to YOU (optional Goal)*). Apart from the nonreferential *it* noted above, the only 'missing' forms are subjects in the fifth sentence (*I saw Robert, and e saw Kevin, and e saw Luanna*)—and the referents of these are predictably determined by regular syntactic process, not by the mixture of semantic and contextual criteria required to determine referents of 'missing' forms in protolanguage.

It is true that Seth sometimes leaves out, mixes up, or misuses grammatical items. Sometimes, too, his grammatical sentences are not exactly what an adult would have said. The fifth example, for instance, would almost certainly have been rendered as *I saw Robert, Kevin, and Luanna*. It is also true that, between twenty-one months and twenty-seven months, Seth, like any other child, produced many sentences that were intermediate between (1) and (2). However, none of the above entails that there is a *linguistic mode* intermediate between (1) and (2), or even that the onset of the properties of (2) described in the two preceding paragraphs was a gradual one.

Those properties of (2) are precisely four out of the five properties that, in chapter 5, were shown to distinguish language from protolanguage: use of grammatical items, systematic expansion of structure in phrases and clauses, obligatory expression of subcategorized arguments, and automatic identification of null elements. These properties appear, not one by one, but as a cluster. The fifth, the relating of varied orders to varied functions, is not yet clearly apparent. For instance *where'd* and *where's* in the third example may not be what they would be in adult language (contracted forms of *where is* and *where did*, showing clear inversion of subject and auxiliary) but may have been acquired as single units. In this case, Seth would not yet have related two different possible orders of constituents in English to the difference between questions and statements.

It has often been noted that children around Seth's age or even older tend to stick to a single rigid configuration of constituents and have problems with sentence types (such as questions or passives) that do not show this configuration. But this should not surprise us. Means for the expansion of structure, subcategorization-frames of verbs, and principles that govern identification of null elements are constant across languages. The possibilities of order change, however, though constrained by general principles, are highly language-specific. For instance, English marks the question-statement distinction by switching subject and auxiliary, but some languages mark it by switching subject and main verb, while others do not mark it by movement at all.

There are no functional rules that state 'functional distinction X *must* be marked in all languages'. Still less are there rules that stipulate *how* a given functional distinction shall be formally marked. In other words, each language has its own idiosyncratic mapping of function onto structure, and this should not surprise us, if syntax and functional considerations are handled by independent modules in the brain. It seems reasonable to suppose, then, that children are rather conservative about changing the basic word order of their language, normally needing rich, positive evidence before they will do this. Note, however, that this kind of rigidity is at least as remote from the unprincipled, topic-driven variability of order in protolanguage as it is from the principled variability found in true language.

In general, phenomena found around the onset of true-language acquisition in ontogeny can be accounted for in much the same way as were the examples of speech from Broca's aphasics discussed in chapter 5. Although the two sets of phenomena show formal differences (as is surely to be expected from the differences between normal children and brain-damaged adults), both represent mixtures of protolanguage and true language. As we saw, aphasic speech seldom consists of pure protolanguage. The speaker is usually able to recover chunks of true language, but has to link them and eke them out with protolanguage. Child speech, in the few months between protolanguage and the acquisition of a full (if not yet adult) language, must also, from time to time, fall back on protolanguage, but for a different reason. Even if the principles of universal grammar are freely available, the individual requires an adequate lexicon (in particular, one that is rich enough in grammatical items) in order to instantiate those principles. But such a lexicon takes time to acquire, so that a few months inevitably elapse between the emergence of syntactic capacity and the deployment of fully developed structures based on that capacity.

GRADUALISM AND THE PIDGIN/CREOLE INTERFACE

The second area where protolanguage gives place to true language without any intermediate stage is in the transition from pidgin to creole language. A creole language has been defined as a nativized pidgin. It is what results when a pidgin, created by adults, is learned by the children of those adults. However, the gulf between a pidgin and its associated creole, in terms of formal structure, is immense. A pidgin, as we saw in chapter 5, is structureless, whereas a creole exhibits the same type of structure as any other natural human language. Recall the following examples cited in chapter 5, from pidgin speakers in Hawaii:

3.   Ifu laik meiki, mo beta *make* time, mani no kaen *hapai*
     If like make, more better die time, money no can carry
     'If you want to build (a temple), you should do it just before you die—
     you can't take it with you!'
4.   Aena tu macha churen, samawl churen, haus mani pei
     And too much children, small children, house money pay
     'And I had many children, small children, and I had to pay the rent'
5.   *Luna,* hu *hapai? Hapai* awl, *hemo* awl
     Foreman, who carry? Carry all, cut all
     'Who'll carry it, Boss? Everyone will cut it and everyone will carry it'.

Here, again, we found the typical characteristics of protolanguage: 'guesswork' identification of null elements, variant orders unrelated to function, the absence of structural mechanisms for expansion, and random absence of subcategorized arguments. Some grammatical items are present, but only at the 'meaningful' end of the range. Even with these, the ratio of grammatical to lexical items is only around 1:2.

However, the children of pidgin-speakers in Hawaii (and elsewhere) produced sentences that met all the criteria for true language. Among these is the unambiguous identification of null elements through principle rather than through context. For instance, in (6a) *e* refers to the matrix subject *they,* whereas in (6b) it refers to the matrix object *one carpenter.*

6a.   They wen go up there early in the morning e go plant
      'They went up there early in the morning in order to plant (crops).'

169

b. I gotta go hire one carpenter e go fix the form
'I have to hire a carpenter to fix the form.'

These facts do not have to be worked out from context or meaning, they follow automatically from the fact that the Patient argument (who or what is affected by the action of the verb) happens to be a subject in (6a), while it happens to be an object in (6b). It is the matrix argument with a Patient role that controls the empty category when this is the subject of a complement clause, as is the case in both sentences of (6).

Similarly, these speakers show variations in order that are clearly related to function:

7a. Some guys they get different belief
'Some guys have different beliefs.'
b. They get different belief, some guys
c. Different belief some guys they get
d. Different belief they get, some guys
e. *Some guys, different belief they get
f. *They get, some guys, different belief

The utterances in (7) show a high degree of variability in word order, but that variability is far from random, arising as it does from the intersection of two regular and legitimate processes: 'fronting', or left-movement, of emphasized elements (*different belief*) and 'extraposition', or right-movement, of elements that may require to be de-emphasized (*some guys*). The intersection of these two processes gives the four possibilities illustrated in (7a through d): (a) neither procrss, (b) extraposition only, (c) fronting only, and (d) fronting plus extraposition. That the process is systematic is shown by the fact that other types of movement (7e and f) give rise to sentences that, in contrast to those of (7a through d) are quite ungrammatical in the creole.

Again, devices for expansion are freely available. One clause can be made an adjunct of another, as in (6), or relative clauses can be employed, as in (8).

8a. [The guy gon' lay the vinyl] been quote me price
'The guy *who* was going to lay the vinyl had quoted me a price.'
b. You see [the island get coconut]?
'Can you see the island *that* has coconuts on it?'

Note, however, that in Hawaiian Creole, as distinct from English, no overt marker of relativization, like *who* or *that*, is required, even if the head noun of the relative clause is the subject of that clause. Indeed, although Hawaiian Creole uses a vocabulary the forms of which (if not always the meanings) mostly come from English, its grammar is not that of English, nor could it have been derived from mere exposure to English, as the structure of examples (6) through (8) illustrates.

With regard to the remaining two criteria for language, all subcategorized arguments are in place or can be linked to their appropriate places by regular process, and there is a fifty-fifty proportion of grammatical to lexical items. It should be noted however that some of these grammatical items are formed from English lexical items, for example *go* in the subordinate clauses of (6*a* and *b*) conveys no sense of motion but has been downgraded to a purely formal marker of nonfinite verbs, like English *to*. If we consider, as we should, the function of grammatical items rather than their form, (6) through (8) contain a markedly higher percentage of 'nonmeaningful' grammatical items than do (3) through (5).

Once again, then, all five properties of language occur as a cluster. There is no linguistic mode intermediate between (3) through (5) and (6) through (8) that has some of the five properties but not others, or that has properties not found in either. What happened in Hawaii was a jump from protolanguage to language in a single generation. Moreover, the grammar of the language that resulted bore the closest resemblance not to grammars of the languages of Hawaii's immigrants; nor to that of Hawaiian, the indigenous language; nor to that of English, the politically dominant language; but rather to the grammars of other creole languages that had come into existence in other parts of the world. This fact argues that creole languages form an unusually direct expression of a species-specific biological characteristic, a capacity to recreate language in the absence of any specific model from which the properties of language could be 'learned' in the ways we normally learn things.

GRADUALISM AND PHYLOGENY

The preceding two sections showed cases where the transition from protolanguage to language was abrupt, occurring in the space of a few months in individuals, in a single generation where whole communities are concerned. There is no indication of an intermediate phase in either case. Moreover, no situation is known where any other type of transition occurs.

These facts do not, of course, furnish conclusive evidence that the original transition from protolanguage to language took place in a similar way. First of all, evolutionary abruptness is not the same as everyday abruptness. An evolutionary change may be considered abrupt if it takes

171

place in a few thousand years as opposed to a few hundred thousand. Second, while the existence of some distinct transitional mode in the contemporary world would have increased the probability that some similar mode existed in the past, the absence of such a mode tells us merely that, in principle, it is possible to do without one. However, that absence, when taken in conjunction with other types of evidence, suggests that any 'intermediate stage' hypothesis should fall under Occam's razor.

Perhaps the most forceful evidence in this respect is the fossil record. One of the few undisputed facts about that record is that, until almost the end of the *erectus* period, there was relatively little development in the species's tool kit; in particular, very few new types of artifact were developed. Only with the emergence of our own species did there appear bladed tools, cave paintings, stone figurines, moon calendars, and a rich variety of other artifacts. This sudden enrichment of the paleontological record did not coincide with any dramatic enlargement of the human brain. In fact, the average human brain is smaller than the average Neanderthal brain. Nor did it appear to coincide with any change in the mode of subsistence similar in scale to the agricultural revolution of around 10 Kya, which might have led to such an enrichment.

It would seem that these dramatic changes could have arisen only as a result of some qualitative change in capacity. We have seen that the success of any species is determined to a large extent by the degree to which it can internally represent its environment, and we have seen that language constitutes a system of representation far more powerful than that provided by the sense organs and their processors. As the agent of constructional learning, language was what enabled a primate species to alter its behavior more rapidly than any previous species. Instead of waiting to learn from observation or experience, that species could now *learn at any time.* For a PRS can represent only what is happening or has happened, while an SRS can additionally represent what has not yet happened, but might conceivably happen.

Since so much turns on this point, it is worth looking a little more closely at why a change in the numbers, kinds, and qualities of artifacts should be so closely linked to a change in language. To understand this, it is essential to understand the nature of behavioral change. In other species, changes in behavior and changes in morphology are generally linked. Most often, a new behavior or a new environment renders adaptive certain existing variations in the size, shape, or structure of a creature, and these characteristics are then further developed. More rarely, perhaps, an accidental change in morphology opens up a new environment or renders possible a new behavior. Very occasionally, a species may support a behavioral change by the use of extrasomatic devices. For instance, when chimpanzees began to exploit palm-oil nuts, they did not have to wait until they developed jaws and teeth massive enough to crack them—they smashed them open with stones.

This means that an artifact can take the place of a change in morphology. Thus, if any species is to behave like ours, it needs, in addition to an SRS, the purely physical capacity to manufacture a wide range of artifacts—something that our remote ancestors already had in the form of prehensile hands with a powerful grip. It may well be that, without some such morphological advantage, even a species with language might not succeed in radically restructuring its behavior. It may even be that the complex reasoning processes we can now deploy in language could not have arisen had they not been derived in some fashion from equally complex technological processes that we mastered first. These and many similar issues will not be pursued here. For our purposes, it is enough to note the interdependence of language and technology in radical behavioral change.

Since the power to conceive logically precedes the power to create, we may therefore assume that a radical improvement in conceptual power (such as might result from the development of protolanguage into language) logically preceded a radical improvement in artifacts, rather than vice versa. Certainly all the technological advances of recorded history have had not one iota of effect on the structure of language. Nor has anyone suggested that some radical difference between the hand of *erectus* and the hand of *sapiens* was what caused artifacts to improve and diversify.

It might seem illogical to argue that protolanguage was not necessary for early tool development and then to argue that language was necessary for later tool development. But such an objection ignores the vast differences both between pre-*sapiens* and *sapiens* artifacts and between protolanguage and language. Early artifacts were required for doing simple, practical tasks like chopping up carcasses. Later artifacts were used in a wider range of ways, including for ornamental and symbolic purposes— purposes that were neither practical nor strictly necessary. Limited as it was to the here and now, the protolanguage neither conferred sufficient constructional power for its possessor to conceive of radically novel functions and purposes, nor offered the resources required to explain such functions and purposes to others. But without that power and those resources, later artifacts could not have been brought into existence.

Given the assumption that language had to immediately precede or accompany advanced artifacts, the argument from the fossil record works in two distinct but parallel ways. The suddenness of its enrichment at the *erectus-sapiens* interface suggests that some wholly new element had emerged. The relative absence of development during the million-year-plus *erectus* period suggests that this new element's emergence was sudden, rather than gradual.

If *erectus* had developed something intermediate between protolanguage and language, one would expect to find, at some time in the *erectus* period, an improvement in tool quality, followed perhaps by a further plateau. Alternatively, if true language had developed gradually during the *erectus* period, one might expect to find an equally gradual improvement in tool quality. Since neither expectation is fulfilled, it seems not unreasonable to conclude that protolanguage persisted substantially unchanged until it gave place quite abruptly to language.

But this conclusion carries consequences for the path of human evolution. If language emerged suddenly, the most likely causative factor would have been some change in the internal organization of the brain that had resulted from a single genetic mutation. But at the time at which language emerged, the hominid population consisted of at least three major groups (those of Africa, East Asia, and Europe) between which there could have been relatively little, if any, gene flow. The odds against the same genetic change occurring almost simultaneously in three distinct populations are more than astronomical. Hardly less imposing are the odds against such a change originating in one population and spreading by normal mechanisms of inheritance throughout that population and throughout the other two in anything less than a million years.

It seems, therefore, more likely that the development that gave us language took place in a single individual at a not very remote period and that the progeny of this individual spread throughout the then-inhabited world and superceded previous hominid populations in all parts of it. This is essentially the 'catastrophic' version of human origins discussed at the beginning of this chapter. However, that version cannot be accepted without first considering the problems that it, too, raises.

CATASTROPHISM AND PHYLOGENY

From a purely evolutionary viewpoint, the 'catastrophic' emergence of *sapiens* raises two main problems. The first concerns the fossil record in East Asia; it has been claimed that several marked morphological traits of East Asian *erectus* specimens are found also in East Asian *sapiens* specimens. From this it is argued that the former are the direct ancestors of the latter. This debate must be left for professional paleoanthropologists to resolve. However, it does not seem implausible that such traits could have been perpetuated by interbreeding between the resident *erectus* population and invaders from the west.

This suggestion also bears on the second problem, which concerns the fate of preexisting populations generally. Arguments can be mounted against a 'competition' scenario, an 'interbreeding' scenario, and a 'genocide' scenario. However, none of these arguments seems particularly compelling.

For instance, one argument against interbreeding is that if our forefathers had emerged from Africa as a distinct species, interbreeding between them and other hominids would have been impossible. But at what stage in the development of a new species do crosses with other species begin to be infertile? Obviously this cannot happen immediately, or the individual in whom a critical mutation occurred would be unable to produce progeny, rendering speciation impossible. Obviously it must happen eventually, or species crosses would be everywhere. But until it can be determined how long a full separation between species may take, this argument against the interbreeding of our species with previous populations, whether *erectus* or Neanderthal, cannot be sustained.

In any case, arguments against a particular scenario do not rule out the possibility of a combined one. It seems quite possible that our species sometimes slaughtered its predecessors, sometimes mated with them, and sometimes merely pushed them out of their current niche into a more hostile environment where they failed to survive. We may leave these issues, too, to be resolved by professionals in the field, and turn instead to a problem that involves language.

If what seems to be the most convincing current hypothesis is correct, our species originated around 214 ± 75 Kya. There are two possibilities. Either this figure is simply wrong, or there is a gap of 100–250 Ky between the point of species (and presumably language) origin and the appearance of novel artifacts. At first sight such a gap may seem hard to account for within the framework proposed here, which leans heavily on the role of language as an agent of technological advance.

However, it may well be that language is a necessary prerequisite for radical technological progress but not a sufficient one. After all, there have existed into our own times human communities, such as the Australian aborigines and the Bushmen of the Kalahari, that have not developed for themselves or even borrowed from others any of the technological

175

advances of the last ten millennia. Yet these groups fully share all of our cognitive and linguistic resources. This suggests that language is not some irresistible Juggernaut that drives its possessor remorselessly on to progress—rather it is the great enabler.

The perils of fossilism—of assuming that only fossil evidence counts—should also be borne in mind. Not every technological improvement leaves an imperishable record. If our species originated, as has been claimed, in tropical Africa, and if it did not begin to move out of that environment until 70 Kya, then there were many substances easier to work than stone that it could have used: fire-hardened wood for spears, bamboo tubes for blowpipes, interwoven strips of bamboo or bark for carrying baskets, lianas for snares or for nets into which fish or small game could be driven, and so on. These and many other innovative ways of exploiting nature, such as modern Pygmies' use of vegetable poisons to stun fish, could have been developed without leaving any lasting traces in the environment. Moreover, if any symbolic objects had been made, they would most likely have been made out of wood, rather than stone, as are most of the carvings of tropical peoples to this day.

However, all that presumably changed when our species moved into subglacial Europe. For tens of thousands of years this area had been occupied by the Neanderthals, who had adapted both physically and culturally to its harsh conditions. Physically, their bodies had grown squat and sturdy to diminish heat loss, and their massive jaws and teeth were adapted to a diet largely, if not exclusively, composed of meat. Culturally they had taken over caves from cave bears and developed weapons and techniques suitable for the hunting and slaughtering of large mammals—their main, and in some places perhaps their only, source of food.

If two species with no linguistic differential, one equipped as Neanderthals were and the other equipped as humans were, had competed for the former's terrain, the latter would surely have had little hope of conquering it. Our ancestors, with a gracile physique highly vulnerable to cold, and a culture dependent on the foods and materials of tropical or subtropical climates, could not have replaced Neanderthals unless they had had some subtle advantage. That advantage cannot have been 'intelligence,' if intelligence is a function of brain size, since Neanderthals had bigger brains. It can only have been some feature of brain *organization*, and the most plausible candidate for such a feature is language, given the greater representational and computational power that language brought.

That power, then, produced a range of artifacts much richer and more varied than those of the Neanderthals, rich enough for our forefathers to adapt even better than their competitors to the rigors of ice-age Europe. However, it seems that it still took the combination of a new habitat and fierce competition to stimulate the cultural-technological capacities that could potentially be derived from the possession of language. If this is so, a catastrophic account of human evolution remains compatible with a catastrophic account of language emergence, despite the time lag between that emergence and the efflorescence of artifacts.

Indeed, if a date of around 200 Kya is confirmed for both catastrophic events, it will serve to remind us that language could not, in and of itself, have obliged our ancestors immediately to change their behavior. It could only have made future changes possible. Since the representational power it afforded was so great, those changes might ultimately seem all but limitless in their extent. Perhaps, ultimately, such a degree of change was an inevitable consequence of language. But the pace of change itself would be governed not by language but by catalytic events in the environment. It is, after all, just such events that throughout evolution have determined changes in the behavior of species.

THE IMPLAUSIBILITY OF AN INTERLANGUAGE

So far, this chapter has suggested that a direct transition from protolanguage to true language is possible, at least in principle, since such a transition can be seen in all individuals of our species as well as in certain historical communities. It has also been suggested that the fossil record argues against the existence of an 'interlanguage'—any distinct linguistic mode between protolanguage and language—and against the gradual development of language itself. It remains to be demonstrated that, on purely linguistic grounds, these last two possibilities are equally unlikely.

The immense gulf that seems to lie between protolanguage and true language has caused one scholar from the field of ape research (David Premack) to suggest the possibility of some kind of interlanguage that might serve to bridge that gulf. Premack has proposed two possible interlanguages. In the first of these, words that referred to the addresser and addressee would have a fixed order, but words that referred to other entities would 'drift freely in the sentence'.

This proposal seems to reflect a common lay assumption that what is most difficult about (yet characteristic of) language is its reliance on fixed serial ordering. In fact, fixed serial ordering is neither a problem nor a characteristic of language. Serial orders of varying kinds simply fall out from the ordering of abstract constituents (V/V-Comp, and so on) within a hierarchical structure, plus the various movement possibilities implicit in such structures. Thus, there is no reason to believe that a system that ordered some constituents but not others would be any easier to acquire than a natural language.

Indeed, for a species such as ours, it might well be harder. One of the most significant developments in the linguistics of the 1970s was the realization that all linguistic processes and principles apply across the board, without exception, and that they are constrained only by other processes and principles whose requirements conflict with theirs. Since it would seem more economical to apply a principle automatically than to figure out whether or not it should apply in a given instance, it is hard to believe that it would have been easier for a species ancestral to ours to acquire Premack's first 'language' than to acquire true language.

Premack's second 'language' would map thematic roles directly onto surface ordering. Subjects would always be Agents, direct objects would always be Patients, indirect objects would always be Goals, and so on. This might work if every sentence obligatorily expressed every thematic role. However, if an Agent were unexpressed, as is often the case (*the milk boiled, the house burned down, the plate cracked*), an empty space would presumably have to be left before the verb (_____ *boiled the milk,* _____ *burned down the house,* _____*cracked the plate*). Problems would immediately arise when one sentence was embedded as the complement of another. Without grammatical items, it would be impossible to determine whether *John tell Bill boil milk* meant 'John told Bill to boil the milk' or 'John told Bill that the milk was boiling'. These ambiguities would multiply, of course, every time an embedding or a conjunction took place.

On the other hand, the mechanisms available to true language, even without grammatical items, could adequately distinguish between *John tell Bill boil milk* ('John told Bill to boil the milk') and *John tell Bill milk boil* ('John told Bill that the milk was boiling'). Once again it would seem that Premack's proposed interlanguage is not really less complex than natural language, and the interlanguage would certainly be more difficult to process on account of the ambiguities described.

Another problem with accepting Premack's (or any similar) 'languages' as possible interlanguages in human evolution is that they involve the acquisition of properties that are in direct conflict with the principles of human language. Provisions for fixed serial ordering and for a fixed mapping from thematic roles to syntax both fall into this class. This means that properties would have had to be acquired for the interlanguage and then discarded when true language arrived. In other words, any such 'language' would have been a detour from the path to true language rather than merely a way station along that path. In contrast, moving from protolanguage directly to language does not require that anything should be 'unlearned.'

If human languages were acquired in the way that computer languages are acquired, that is, by conscious and deliberate learning, such a 'detour' on the road to language might be harder to rule out. But there is every reason to believe that languages are not acquired in this way. If human languages can be acquired only through the unfolding of biologically determined characteristics, a shift from one set of principles to another becomes highly implausible, even more so than a simple jump from protolanguage to language. Such a process would imply that one type of processing mechanism in the brain grew and flourished for a time but was then replaced by another. Although such possibilities cannot be completely discounted, there would seem little point in adopting them if a more convincing alternative exists.

If, so far, no one has succeeded in proposing a plausible 'interlanguage', what about the possibility that the properties of true language, instead of appearing simultaneously, were acquired one by one? Several reasons make this seem unlikely. First, the properties are interdependent. For instance, there is a clear connection between the need to identify null elements and the obligatory expression of subcategorized arguments. Both assume that every unit of language has its place, a place defined not by linear ordering as in the Premack 'languages' but by each unit's hierarchical (vertical) relations with other units. Both entail that although a unit may not have to be overtly expressed it has to be identifiable both in terms of its grammatical function and in terms of its reference; this is usually established via some element of the sentence that *is* overtly expressed.

In turn, both of these properties depend on the existence of a principled and recursive structure. Such a structure ensures that there will always be a place where appropriate constituents can be inserted in a sentence but, at the same time, narrowly determines what places will be available for what constituents. Without such a structure, it would be impossible to determine which was 'the right place' for a constituent to be in, and thus impossible to determine (or at least impossible to determine automatically and unambiguously, without taking context and common sense into account) whether a given constituent, such as a sub-categorized argument, was present or not.

A fourth property depends on the preceding three. We know that the order of constituents may be variable, dependent on functional considerations such as differences between sentence types (e.g. statement, question) or emphasis on particular constituents. We also know that, at the same time, all constituents must be identifiable and all arguments (somehow) represented. For these two facts to be compatible, all 'moved' elements must be relatable to their original positions. Thus the existence of variable ordering is impossible unless there somehow exists a single basic ordering of constituents in their original positions, from which all permissible variants can be derived by regular processes. Finally, the fifth property, the existence of grammatical items, makes little sense unless there is a regular and productive structural system within which such items can discharge the various purely formal functions imposed by that system.

Thus it should hardly surprise us that, wherever protolanguage gives place to something more complex, this 'something' should immediately exhibit all of the central, distinguishing properties of language. But there remains at least a theoretical possibility that, while all these properties may have emerged together, they emerged first in an immature form, and only gradually expanded to their present dimensions.

Such a possibility might be interpreted in at least two different ways. It could mean, for instance, that when the properties began to emerge, they affected some items but not others—only some subcategorized arguments had to be expressed, only some null elements had to be identified, and so on. This is implausible, for reasons discussed above. If learning is involved, it may be easier to perfect a skill in a small domain and then to extend it, but if a biological development is involved, it may be expected to apply across the board from its first emergence.

The size of the board across which a biological development applies is, however, another matter. Another way to interpret the 'gradual expansion' possibility would be to say that all the properties of true language emerged simultaneously and in a fully developed form, but that, initially, there was little for them to work on. Syntax is, to a large extent, a projection of the lexicon, wherein all the subcategorization frames of verbs and all the grammatical items (among much else) are stored. If the initial lexicon was drastically limited, then not all of the structures implicit in syntactic principles could immediately be realized. To take an extreme example, if there were no verbs of reporting, and no 'psychological' or 'intentional' verbs, then biclausal structures of the type *he said/ thought/believed/ hoped that X had happened/would happen* would still be impossible to construct, even though the hominid concerned had all the necessary structural principles at hand.

This last kind of 'gradualness' is probably the only kind that could have played a part in the original development of language. In the sections that follow, a hypothetical series of steps that could have led from protolanguage to language will be outlined.

Protolanguage Development: Grammatical Items

It should be emphasized that the account given here can only be conjectural. Although some inferences may be drawn from child language and from pidgin and creole languages, nothing definite can be concluded from these. However, a conjectural account is not only better than none, it is a prerequisite, in any field of study, for the more firmly based hypotheses that one hopes will follow it. Even if conjectures prove wrong, they serve a purpose in calling forth and sharpening their own antitheses.

It seems reasonable to suppose that protolanguage showed some degree of development during its lifetime. Starting perhaps from the understanding of a single truly referential item, it would have expanded at least to include words for all the significant entities with which *erectus* interacted and for the activities that this interaction involved. But would any other type of element have developed?

Even a rudimentary protolanguage could hardly have functioned if it had only had terms for entities and behaviors, that is, only referential items, whose referents could be identified by pointing at them (if they were entities) or by performing them (if they were behaviors). Quite early on, a handful of terms had to be developed that did not refer directly, but either referred indirectly or performed some communicative function that required an abstract element for its expression.

One such early function of language would have been to negate information believed to be incorrect. In contemporary languages this function is usually performed by some particle to which negative meaning has been arbitrarily assigned. This is not necessarily the same particle that is used to answer questions negatively, witness English *no* versus *not* or French *non* versus *ne...pas*. But in creole languages the form for the two functions is often the same and often (although by no means always) taken from the source language question-answering negator (e.g., *no*) rather than from the source language sentence negator (e.g., *not*). The same is true of infant speech. Children typically learn *no* as a question-answerer, then transfer it to negative statements. At the two-word stage, a child may use utterances like *no sock* to mean 'I don't want my socks put on.' This suggests that a negative question-answerer is more primitive than a sentence negator, and it shows that once one has been obtained the other can be straightforwardly derived from it.

Certainly a protolanguage could hardly have managed without questions, since any but the simplest of communicative codes needs to be able to solicit information as well as provide it. In pidgins, as in creoles, 'yes-no' questions require only a change in intonation. However, to solicit more complex information, any language requires 'wh'-questions: questions with equivalents of *what, who, where,* and so on. Again, findings in pidgins and creoles are instructive. If question-forms from a source language are not adopted, the alternative is always to take a single 'wh-word', usually *who* or its equivalent, but sometimes *what* or *where,* and add to it the appropriate referential item. Thus *who* may be rendered by the equivalent of *who-man* or *who-person, what* by the equivalent of *who-thing, where* by the equivalent of *who-place* or *who-side,* and so on.

Much work on creole languages has assumed that these duplex question words (far from unknown in noncreole languages, incidentally) were innovations by creole speakers. This seems unlikely, however, insofar as a pidgin could not do without question words. Unfortunately, Hawaiian Pidgin, which might have decisively resolved this issue, succeeded in adopting all of the English question words except *why,* which it rendered as *wassamatta* (from 'what's the matter'). Still, this single example, though somewhat idiosyncratic, suggests that pidgins *can* innovate complex question words. The advantage from an origins-of-language perspective is that if duplex question words are adopted, only one nonreferential item would have to be coined, rather than several.

There are still problems with question words. For instance, *thing,* in *who-thing* and similar combinations, is a highly abstract term of great generality (think what you would do if asked to define *thing* ostensively). *Place* is similarly abstract, and it is hardly surprising that many pidgins preferred *side,* which is a little more concrete. Whether *erectus* ever reached a sufficient level of abstraction to produce words like *thing* or even *side* must remain an open question. If such a level was not reached, question words would have been hard to frame, and the protolanguage would not have made a very effective instrument for soliciting information.

Pronouns would have been extremely useful, but it is at least questionable whether they existed in protolanguage. Sound linguistic sense may underlie the Hollywood convention by which characters in Tarzantype movies consistently refer to themselves by their proper names. Given that 'language-trained' apes consistently distinguish between proper and common nouns, and that dolphins identify themselves by unique signature-whistles, distinct in mode from their other utterances, it seems reasonable to suppose that members of *erectus* bands had personal names. In language, we assume that if a proper name is repeated within a sentence, it refers to two people: either *John thought that John was kind* is a mistake, or the second *John* refers to someone different from the first. But if, in the protolanguage, no sentence contained more than one clause, the repetition of proper names need not have become unduly irksome.

A class of nonreferential items with a slightly better chance of originating in the protolanguage is that of verbal auxiliaries such as *can* and *must*. These clearly fall at the 'more meaningful' end of the grammatical item continuum in contemporary language, and they occur freely in pidgins, although they do not normally emerge in child language until the two-word stage is past. Although one cannot argue from need, expressions such as *can?* (to determine capacity and/or willingness) and *must* (to enforce cooperation through moral pressure) would certainly have been useful for *erectus* in a variety of situations.

Equivalents of *can* and *must* have, in some languages, properties of full verbs, and they are everywhere more verblike than the particles or inflections that express tense, mood, and aspect. The latter (absent alike from pidgins and early child language) are unlikely candidates for the protolanguage, and yet it is hard to imagine that the protolanguage lacked any means for the expression of relative time at least.

Pidgins usually have two expressions that mean, respectively, 'earlier/completed' and 'later' (*pau* and *baimbai* in Hawaiian Pidgin, *pinis* and *bai* in Melanesian Pidgin). Reflexes of what were probably expressions meaning 'earlier/completed' in their antecedent pidgins (*don* in English creoles, *fin* in French creoles, *kaba* in Portuguese creoles) are found in almost all creoles and are all, like the Hawaiian and Melanesian examples, derived from verbs with the meaning 'finish.' It is possible that similar expressions existed in the original protolanguage, representing an analysis of time more primitive than the tense analysis of true language.

If a protolanguage needed nonreferential expressions to orient its users in time, it probably had an even higher requirement for orientation in space. In a great many creole languages one finds a single particle of direction/location, with a wide range of meanings ('on/in/at/to/from'), which, like 'wh'-question words, was presumably inherited from antecedent pidgins. In creoles, these particles are disambiguated by accompanying lexical items. For instance, 'walk to X' may be rendered as *walk go particle X* while 'walk from X' is rendered as *walk come particle X*. Similarly 'lie on X' might be rendered as *lie top particle X* and 'lie under X' as *lie bottom particle X*. In each case a single identical particle would be used, and its meaning disambiguated by a verb (as in the first two examples) or a noun (as in the second two) that already existed with its own specific meaning. It is not entirely clear whether this procedure is limited to creoles (its systematic use certainly is) or whether it, too, arose in the pidgin stage.

Certainly, information about the sites of food sources would have been vital to hominids whose survival might depend on knowing exactly in which direction a source lay, whether it was above or below or between describable landmarks, how long it would take to walk to the spot, and other information of this kind. Note that the means suggested here, the coupling of a single nonreferential item with referential ones that related to common actions (*go, come*) or body parts (*head, bottom, side*), closely parallels the means hypothesized for the formation of duplex question words.

Quantifiers, too, may date from the original protolanguage. Even bees can indicate to one another the relative richness of a food source. It seems unlikely that members of an *erectus* band would have been unable to tell their fellows whether *many* or *few* fruits were to be found in the new valley they had stumbled on, or whether there was *much* or *little* meat left on the carcass they had just seen. Quantifiers would also have been vital in another function that language made available: that of planning the day's activities.

Again, we cannot know whether members of an *erectus* band planned their day's activities. Yet it seems improbable that the members of any social group with protolanguage would have risen in the mornings and gone off on their respective missions without even telling others of their intentions. On the contrary, for a species that utilized scattered and extremely varied food sources, it would have been of the greatest advantage to make sure that their limited resources were employed to the best advantage. Alternative sources could have been discussed and compared, and decisions reached by the older and wiser heads. Should *all* members of the group be assigned to some single opportunity that was of its nature short-lived (the scavenging of an immense but rapidly decaying carcass, the collection of fish stranded by the recession of a flash flood)? Or should only *some* be assigned to that task while *a few* made sure of alternative types of nourishment?

Excessive speculation about such issues is pointless. However, they suggest that over the million or more years for which, if this account is correct, protolanguage existed, there could have accumulated quite a large stock of items which, in a developed language, would constitute the 'more meaningful' end of the continuum of grammatical items.

For, while it is inconceivable that a protolanguage without any formal structure should have invented 'pure' grammatical items such as agreement-markers, or purely functional phrasal heads like *of* in *a box of bricks*, it is almost as unlikely that grammatical items were a complete innovation arriving only at or after the emergence of true language. It is unlikely that the protolanguage of *erectus* would lack *all* nonreferential items, and it is equally unlikely that a systematic structure could come into existence before there were *any* of the grammatical items which that structure required. The chicken-and-egg problem posed by grammatical items—how could a protolanguage have had them, how could a language be born with them?—can be neatly resolved if some of those items originally came into existence for their semantic value, and only later acquired structural functions.

It seems likely, then, that protolanguage did develop a set of protogrammatical items, that is, meaningful if somewhat abstract units that may have included some or all of the following: negators, question words, pronouns, relative-time markers, quantifiers, modal auxiliaries, and particles indicating location. But this may not have been the only contribution that protolanguage made to true language.

Protolanguage Development: Thematic Roles

In chapter 3 it was noted that verbs could be divided into three classes (*sleep*, *take*, and *give*, for example) which were differentiated by the number of arguments they took (one, two, and three, respectively). It was further noted that these arguments were specified for their thematic roles: Agent, Patient, Goal, and so on. Both the number of the arguments and the nature of the roles are determined by the meanings of these verbs. Indeed, this area is one of the few that never give us any unpleasant surprises when we learn a foreign language. If we find a verb that means 'sleep' we know immediately that it will have one obligatory argument, if we find one that means 'give' we know it will have three, and so on, while the thematic roles selected for each of those arguments will somehow automatically be known to us.

This universality of thematic structure suggests a deep-rooted ancestry, perhaps one lying outside of language altogether, in the analysis of nature made by the PRS. It may be tempting to place the origins of thematic structure further back still, in the real world, and to say that, if there is an act of giving, that act logically includes, as its minimal par-

185

ticipants, someone who gives (Agent), something that is given (Patient), and someone to whom that thing is given (Goal). However, to adopt such a position neglects the fact that acts of giving have no separate existence in nature, but occur as part of an unbroken pattern of behavior that we happen to segment in a particular way (perhaps because, for a food-sharing species, giving was an act of special significance). Things being otherwise, we could easily have carved experience into longer sequences of behavior ('transact' or 'interact') or series of smaller ones ('take *X*, carry *X*, put in hand of *Y*').

Similarly, numbers and types of role cannot be determined by objective facts. For instance, we can be reasonably sure that early hominids, in common with other social mammals, never slept alone, and probably a majority of our own species do not sleep alone. It would be perfectly possible, then, for *sleep* to subcategorize for a Comitative argument, so that in *I slept with X, with X* would represent an obligatory prepositional phrase. One who did sleep alone would then have to say *I slept with no one for eight hours* instead of just *I slept for eight hours,* which is not noticeably more bizarre than saying things like *the trunk of the tree* or *I have a headache.* In other words, although numbers and types of roles may seem to reflect reality directly, they are really just as arbitrary as anything else in language.

Moreover, the roles that we do choose are certainly not given by nature, but constitute high-order abstractions. Even to conceive of the role of Agent it is necessary to generalize over a wide range of superficially dissimilar actions: picking a fruit, killing a prey animal, carrying food to others, eating it, striking another hominid, ordering someone to do something, and so on (as opposed to sleeping, walking, being attacked by a predator, dropping a hand-ax, falling down a cliff, and so on). Each of the Agent roles shares with others the sense of deliberate, voluntary action necessarily involving some entity distinct from whatever suffers the action, and showing some form of dominance over the latter (the Patient). Given the power to abstract it, the role of Agent may well have seemed, to a species seeking to understand and control its environment, both the most important and the most desirable of roles. It is for this reason, perhaps, that language sees the world predominantly from an Agent's viewpoint, and gives Agent the highest rank among roles (see figure 3.6).

It is worth noting that all the thematic roles would have played a part in the everyday experiences of a species that engaged in extractive foraging and that shared food. One hominid (Agent) procures food (Patient) which was obtained at a particular Location and Time with the help of a

186

hand-ax or other Instrument and gives this food to another (Goal), who perhaps takes it merely so as to pass it on to a child (Beneficiary). It is not necessary to suppose that thematic roles originated in foraging and foodsharing procedures, but the daily experience of hominids over countless millennia would surely have reinforced the tendency to analyze actions and events in these terms rather than in others.

It seems highly possible, then, that thematic roles, and perhaps even some notion of a hierarchic ranking of roles (at least as far as the supremacy of Agent was concerned) may have preceded the emergence of true language. It is unlikely, however, that these roles would have been systematically expressed. For such a systematic expression, as compared with the lack of it, forms one of the dividing lines between true language and protolanguage. Pidgin speakers, small children, and experimental apes alike say *give me* or *give orange* at least as often as they say *give me orange*.

Thus there are two major ways in which developments in the protolanguage period could have facilitated the emergence of true language. Those developments could have created a number of potential grammatical items and could have refined, although without systematically expressing, the range of thematic roles that language would eventually utilize. Both developments involved factors essential for syntax. However, the story of protolanguage enrichment would be incomplete if some consequences of the use of protolanguage were not briefly touched on.

So far we have considered only the information-bearing function of protolanguage, which was arguably though not necessarily its first function. But once protolanguage had come into existence, it certainly could not have been limited to that function. How many of the functions of language it fulfilled can only remain conjectural, but in a social species we can be pretty certain that it had social uses. It seems difficult to believe, for example, that an individual equipped with protolanguage would continue, as other primates do, to express its feelings about other members of its group exclusively through gestures, grunts, and facial expressions. It is more plausible that some ways of verbally expressing 'I am angry with you/like you/hate you/love you' came into existence. Moreover, if hominid societies were like other primate societies, a constant jockeying for position went on, with each animal trying to form alliances that would enhance its rank. Language would surely have come to play a role in these political maneuverings.

In such beginnings we can perhaps see the germs of a capacity to make reference to internal states of the individual. Although such overtly intentional activites as 'thinking that', 'doubting that', 'believing that', 'hoping that', and 'knowing that' may have had to await the emergence of complex sentences, the function of language as mirror (or author?) of internal states could have been decisively launched at this stage. But these areas will be explored further in the next chapter, so let us for now return to the more formal aspects of bringing language into existence.

SOME PROBLEMS FOR THE EMERGENCE OF LANGUAGE

Even with thematic roles and some grammatical items in place, one may still feel that the distance between protolanguage and language was immense, too vast to be spanned in a single leap. Language seems to have so much that is missing from protolanguage: infinitely recursive processes; the binding of anaphors and the traces of moved constituents; government, 'proper' as well as ordinary; case assignment; the processes by which null elements are identified; constraints on movement; adjunction, conjunction, and the embedding of constituents; not to mention a host of technical concepts such as 'scope', 'valence', 'c-command', 'm-command', 'bijection', 'subjacency', 'strong and weak crossover', 'promotion', 'chomage', 'quantifier-float', 'extraposition', 'exceptional case marking', 'preposition stranding', 'chains', 'parasitic gaps', and many more that, doubtless to the reader's relief, will not be discussed here.

From where can all these principles and processes have sprung? The mere fact that they have all, at one time or another, been proposed as concepts indispensible for the proper understanding of language argues that language is itself an immensely complex, multifaceted, and essentially mysterious thing.

This is not necessarily the case, however. It should be borne in mind that the structure of language was, to all intents and purposes, a new field as recently as the 1950s, since only taxonomic studies of syntax had been conducted until then. When a field of study is confronted for the first time, there is no way it can be grasped in its entirety. The only way to begin is by applying hunches to bits of empirical data and seeing where they lead you. Early generative grammarians had the hunch that the best way to proceed was by compiling transformational rules (rules that would explain how to turn one kind of sentence into another kind of sentence). The ultimate result would be a long list of rules that, if correctly stated and properly ordered with respect to one another, would 'generate' (produce, when applied, all the grammatical and none of the ungrammatical sentences in) an entire language.

It turned out that this wasn't the best way to account for language, but a better way emerged only because the original line of research was taken to the limit. Work in at least the last decade and a half has produced a grammar that is not merely simpler and more elegant than its immediate predecessors, but differs strikingly from them in its overall conception. A very sketchy and informal version of this grammar was provided in chapter 3. In essence, a few modular theorems now interact with one another and with the properties of lexical and grammatical items. But, although the consequences of these interactions can now be worked out deductively, the proposed modules themselves were arrived at by inductive processes.

Grammars consisting of long lists of rules were of course difficult, if not impossible, to explain in evolutionary terms, quite apart from the many other problems, conceptual as well as practical, that they raised. How and why would each of these rules have come into existence, and what kind of genetic mechanisms would have ensured their intergenerational transmission? Perhaps this kind of embarrassment was what deterred nativists from pursuing their biologism to its logical conclusion, thereby giving rise to the paradoxical stance observed at the beginning of chapter 5. But is the newer grammar any more explicable in evolutionary terms?

At first sight the answer might seem to be negative. The current model contains theorems to account for the following:

a. Hierarchical structure (X-bar theory)
b. The reference of items that lack independent reference (binding)
c. The reference of null subjects of subordinate clauses (control)
d. How far items can be moved (bounding)
e. The distribution of thematic roles (theta theory)
f. Conditions for government
g. Conditions for case-assignment
h. Movement processes

Each of these components contains its own principle(s), from which, it is hoped, all the phenomena that have given rise to the concepts listed in the first paragraph of this section (and many others) can be deductively derived. But we still have to explain how *a* through *h* arose—eight quasi-independent entities that are required simply for syntax, itself only one component (albeit arguably the most crucial) of human language.

Not surprisingly, attempts have been made to collapse two or more components into one. The most obvious candidates are *b* and *c*, while *b*, *c* and *d* might be collapsed into a single 'locality theory'. Also closely allied are f and g. But even if such efforts prove successful, an evolutionary account is still problematic for the reasons that follow.

The evidence surveyed above indicates that language could not have developed gradually out of protolanguage, and it suggests that no intermediate form exists. If this is so, then syntax must have emerged in one piece, at one time—the most likely cause being some kind of mutation that affected the organization of the brain. Since mutations are due to chance, and beneficial ones are rare, it is implausible to hypothesize more than one such mutation.

Several factors suggest, indeed, that just such a single mutation gave rise to our species. It is here that problems arise. For our species is distinguished from all others not merely by syntacticized language but also by changes in the features and dimensions of the skull and by our typical supralaryngeal tract.

The problem, bluntly stated, is: How could any single genetic event, whether a point mutation or a reshuffling of chromosomes, occasion so many and such diverse changes? The problem would be bad enough if only a single principle were required to set syntax in motion. If seven or eight were required, the situation would be still worse.

THE CRUCIAL MUTATION

Let us consider the minimum a mutation would have had to do in order to provide syntactic structure as we know it. Would it have been sufficient merely to routinize and automatize the production of protolanguage? In ontogeny, such processes play a vital role. Compare, for example, the hesitant, slow, and clumsy movements of a child using a spoon for the first time with the smooth and efficient movements of that same child some months later. But while these two sets of movements are still essentially of the same type, a fully routinized and automated protolanguage would still not constitute language. It might be argued that greater facility in processing the protolanguage could have made possible the production and comprehension of longer utterances, but there is no reason to suppose that it would have given those utterances the properties that distinguish language from protolanguage.

This can be illustrated by the output of a handful of individuals who have developed protolanguage beyond what are, today at least, its normal limits. These are the inventors of makeshift, idiosyncratic languages: children, almost always twins, who for one reason or another are more than usually involved with each other. In most cases these languages develop in parallel to normal acquisition, yet there seems to be no transfer of syntactic structure. The two examples typical of the genre that are given below were produced by a German and a Danish child (both twins) respectively:

9. da   kjob hoto krei loch ich du mach
    there snow horse more hole I you make
    'Over there in the snow you and I made a horse with holes in it'
10. nina   enaj una   enaj hana math enaj
    rabbit no young-one no   get food no
    'We shall not fetch food for the young rabbits'

How the translations were arrived at is not stated.

As (9) and (10) suggest, twin languages exhibit most of the features found in the protolanguage examples of chapter 5. Like the protolanguage examples, they lack any systematic word order and are limited to single propositions. They differ only in that they try to include more information in their propositions and contain more grammatical items (*there, no, more*). But these items, like similar items in pidgins, are at the 'more meaningful' end of the grammatical-item continuum and do not serve any formal, structural purposes. Moreover, the attempt to lengthen utterances makes them, if anything, less comprehensible than those of other protolanguage varieties. Although it is claimed that parents and others sometimes learn them, it is no accident that twin languages are produced only by siblings who have more than normal levels of intimacy, shared psychological characteristics, and common experience.

Thus a mere automatization of protolanguage was not enough to yield language. What had to happen was something that would impose on language the three-tiered structure of the phrase (X, X', and X", see figure 3.4) and the recursive insertion of phrases within phrases. If one could show what that 'something' was, and how it could have yielded (alone or in concert with preexisting capacities) all the principles and properties included in (a) through (h), then the task of showing how a single genetic incident could have changed protolanguage into language would be considerably lightened.

This chapter has already suggested that an analysis of experience into actions and events (with a strictly limited number of stereotyped participants) arose from factors present at least at the protolanguage stage, if not before. This analysis constituted the foundations of a theory of thematic roles (see (e) above). We saw in chapter 3 that the core of syntax lay in the mapping of thematic roles onto the output of X-bar theory, assuming of course that a third element was present. That element was a lexicon rich in properties that could, in principle, flesh out the skeleton

191

formed by the other two components in a variety of ways. If the properties of the remaining theorems can be derived deductively from these three components, then the crucial mutation that gave rise to language could simply have been whatever yielded a fusion of the three.

To attempt such a derivation here would involve technical discussion inappropriate for a general work on language. Suffice it to say that the attempt is at least conceivable. But how, even in principle, could a mutation have given birth to recursive, hierarchical structures?

Consider a tree such as that illustrated in figure 7.1. We normally draw (and think of) syntactic trees from the top down, but they can be equally well constructed from the bottom up, in the series of steps *a* through *f* that the figure illustrates. What has been constructed is in fact

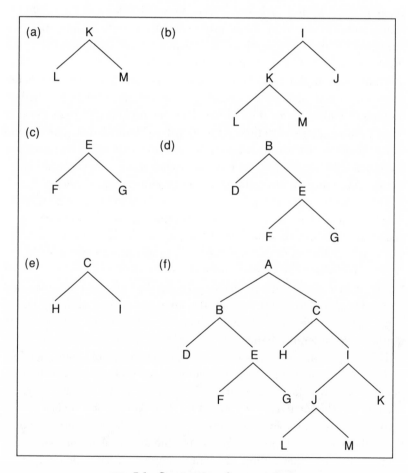

FIG. 7.1. Construction of syntactic trees

one of the basic forms of a sentence, with A equivalent to I", B to the subject NP, I to the verb phrase, and H to the inflectional head of the sentence.

The process itself, at least conceptually, strongly resembles the process by which those parts of the brain that process visual data fit together bits of information about lines and angles and surfaces and colors ultimately derived from individual receptor cells. It does not surprise us that a smooth surface or a crooked edge should show up, in our visual field, at the exact point at which our fingers can confirm its presence, rather than elsewhere. Perhaps it should no more surprise us that our processing mechanisms for verbal information are able, just as automatically, to put each word 'in the right place'.

The two tasks are not fully commensurate, of course. Visual processing reconstructs an already-existing scene that may differ from moment to moment, whereas verbal processing creates novel sentences from a template that does not change. But these differences may lie more in the nature of the material than in what happens to it. For instance, the visual field resembles what is before your eyes because each piece of information it contains comes labeled, so to speak, by a particular receptor whose position on the retina is known. If the information comes from the upper right area of the retina, the brain is not going to show it in the lower left of the visual scene. In just the same way, verbal processing could assemble sentences if (among other things) their component parts came from fixed and known locations. The 'view' to be reassembled in each sentence would be determined by the action, event, or state described, along with its monad, dyad, or triad of obligatory (subcategorized) participants and any incidental information.

In other words, the recursive production of complex systems may be no more than what the nervous system naturally does, given appropriate synaptic connections. However, in order to produce anything as specific as syntax, the right things would have to be connected in the right way. Those 'right things' would include, minimally, the area where an appropriately partitioned lexicon was stored, and the area devoted to analysis of actions and events where thematic roles were selected and assigned.

What is being proposed, then, is a model in which syntax is not localized but implicit in the wiring diagram of the brain, while elements in the lexicon are localized in terms of grammatical as well as semantic classes. To what extent does the little we so far know about brain function support such a model? One of the consequences of this design would be the absence of any central 'storehouse of syntactic principles'. If 'syntactic knowledge' exists only in the way the brain is hard-wired, it might

193

be relatively easy to interfere with the production of sentences, but difficult, if not impossible, for any but the most drastic of traumas to destroy the brain's syntactic capacity.

At one time many believed that Broca's area represented some kind of storehouse of syntactic knowledge. As noted in chapter 5, much recent research suggests that that is where the speech production of sentences is carried out. Since the ability to distinguish grammatical from ungrammatical sentences persists in quite severe cases of Broca's aphasia, even when the patient is unable to produce any of the sentences he or she has judged grammatical, it does look as though syntax is somehow diffuse and hard to extirpate.

The same is not true, however, of the lexicon. Patients suffering from Wernicke's aphasia, Alzheimer's disease, and other conditions exhibit to varying degrees the complete loss of particular lexical items. This suggests that storage of lexical items is extremely localized. Primary localization might well be by meaning, but there may also be localization by grammatical class, so that nouns, verbs, prepositions, and so on would be stored in separate locations or at least in relatively separate neural networks. Indeed, the patterns found in aphasia seem to be consistent with the hypothesis of a nonlocalized syntax, which is based on an actual mode of neural processing (rather than on, say, information stored in the form of rules or principles), and which is employed for the automatic sorting of lexical items whose points of origin are fully identifiable to the processing mechanism. Note that this localization and parcellation of lexical storage could be a relatively recent development. In the phylogeny of brain development it is not uncommon for cells with similar functions to appear first in different regions of the brain and then to migrate towards some common site. Let us suppose that such a process continued during the lifetime of *erectus*. This would have provided late *erectus* and *neandertalensis* with more efficient storage and recovery of lexical items, but still would not have substantially changed the nature of protolanguage. The upper limit then may have been one of comprehension rather than production. Perhaps words could be strung together endlessly along the lines of speech samples 9 and 10, but such strings could seldom be unambiguously understood.

If that was the case, what was needed was not greater connectivity but some kind of governor, some mechanism(s) that would inhibit the proliferation of word salad. Two such potential mechanisms already existed, and perhaps all that was necessary was to link them to each other and to the automatic assembling of words.

Perhaps the most basic mechanism was the template of the phrase itself. Elsewhere it has been suggested that verbs and nouns form the most basic categories of language and that nouns may have preceded verbs in evolution. Suppose, then, that the noun phrase served as the prototype for all phrases. What noun phrases do as wholes is describe individuated entities: *a large book with a dark red cover, this friend of Mary's, three things that you told me about.* But at the heart (or head!) of each phrase is an abstract category: *book, friend, things.* Thus the three layers of X-bar structure represent, respectively, (*a*) a generic class, X; (*b*) the properties peculiar to particular members of that class (*large, with a dark red cover, of Mary's*), and (*c*) the specification of the complete individual in terms of abstract relations such as quantity, proximity, familiarity, and so on (*a, this, three*).

As a conceptual analysis applied to some of the other types of phrase this might seem far-fetched at first. But consider even prepositional phrases. Their heads (e.g., *to, at, of*) express generic relations like direction, location, and possession. Their complements express particular examples of those relations: *to the station, at home, of great significance.* Their specifiers, where present, particularize the individual expression in terms of abstract relations such as quantity, duration, probability, and so on (*ALMOST to the station, STILL at home, PERHAPS of great significance*).

Phrases, then, are simply machines for going from class to individual. As such, they serve to locate exactly what we are talking or thinking about in terms of the overall model of reality constituted by our SRS—in other words, they link the itinerary to the map. At the same time, and on a purely formal level, their three-layered structure constitutes a template that provides uniform structure for all linguistic material. This template may have originated with noun phrases, and subsequently extended, quite automatically, to units of all types regardless of their content.

The other mechanism was a tacit and automatic analysis of all that happened in the world into clusters consisting of a single verb and all the arguments of that verb. Given the overall recursive nature of the phrase, these clusters could now be instantiated simply by inserting a verb and its arguments into an automatically generated phrase matrix. Thus, a verb and its arguments, instead of being merely strung together as in protolanguage, now formed parts of a single cohesive unit.

These units, roughly equivalent to clauses, would then impose a series of boundaries on the stream of speech, thereby enabling the hearer to know where one unit of utterance ended and the next began—a result

195

that could never have been achieved in the undisciplined protolanguage. Within each unit, arguments and verbs would be assembled according to something like the following algorithm: build the internal arguments of a verb (that is, the nonsubject arguments) into phrases; join them into a phrase with the verb as its head; build an external argument (the clause subject) along the same lines; and then insert the external argument and the verb phrase under the nonhead nodes in a superphrase.

Our understanding of language is still far from complete. And our understanding of how major areas of the brain not devoted to sensory or motor activity function and interact with one another is perhaps even more limited. Given these facts, the foregoing proposals are unavoidably incomplete; they are vague even where they try to be explicit, and speculative in the extreme—perhaps even entirely misguided. But they do at least provide some kind of framework, sketchy though it may be, within which, or against which, future inquiry might be conducted. If that framework holds up, even in modified form, it would suggest that a single genetic event might indeed have been enough to turn protolanguage into syntacticized language.

Such an event could have consisted simply in the linking (or the dramatic strengthening of preexisting links between) those areas of the brain where the lexicon was stored and those areas where the structure of actions and events was analyzed. These linkages would then have inhibited the random chaining of words and facilitated their rapid and automatic organization into the structural units described.

There remains, however, the question raised earlier of how the same mutation could have simultaneously introduced syntax, an improved vocal tract, and a modified skull. It can hardly be coincidental that each of these three changes somehow involves the human head. Could one of them have entailed the others? If so, which?

Of the two more visible changes, those necessary to alter the vocal tract do not seem extensive enough to have caused skull changes like the disappearance of brow ridges and occipital buns. On the other hand, changes in the dimensions of the skull do seem adequate to have modified the vocal tract, in particular by changes in the lower part of the skull (the degree of flexion in the basicranium). The question would then seem to be, which is the likeliest—that a change in skull shape should have modified the brain, or that a change in the brain should have modified the shape of the skull?

A change in skull dimensions could have brought into juxtaposition areas of the brain that had previously been separated from one another. However, such a development is by no means a necessary prerequisite for the linking of brain areas, nor do there seem to be parallel cases in other species. Conversely, changes in the brain are known to have brought about changes in the skull. To take a rather obvious example, at earlier stages of hominid development the skull had to enlarge considerably to accommodate an expanded brain. However, the emergence of our species does not seem to have been attended by any conspicuous enlargement, and whatever alterations in the brain's hard-wiring may have been required to initiate syntax, it seems unlikely that there should have resulted from them a change in the shape of the brain sufficient to cause such marked alterations in skull dimensions. Perhaps some additional factor could be found that would underlie all three changes. But at present there are no obvious candidates.

Indeed, a fully satisfactory answer to the questions raised here is unlikely to be forthcoming until brains and their organization and mode of development are better understood. However, we do seem to be approaching a stage at which the boundary conditions imposed by neurology, genetics, evolutionary biology, paleoanthropology, and linguistics will radically reduce the area of the search space. If this is so, then it may be possible, within measurable time, finally to resolve just what it is in the workings of the human brain that makes us, and us alone, capable of language. We need have no fear that such a discovery would exhaust the scientific interest of language, since the mere fact of possessing it raises, for our species, problems far more intractable—problems that will be reviewed, though surely not resolved, in the two final chapters of this book.

8

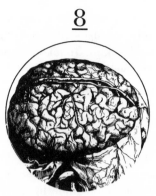

Mind, Consciousness, and Knowledge

The evidence surveyed in previous chapters strongly suggests that language as we know it developed through a long series of evolutionary events. Because such mechanisms were adaptive, creatures continued to build up representations of significant (to them) environmental features in terms of configurations of nerve cells activated by those features. The process of building was slow and erratic, but, thanks to the conservatism of neural systems which continually incorporated older structures into newer ones, it became, short of the severest catastrophe, irreversible. Eventually, in social species, these representational systems began to interact with (much more rudimentary) communicative systems that had almost as long an evolutionary history.

The interaction between these systems, fully realized only among hominids (although realizable at a low level, given adequate training, in a variety of species), produced a second representational system in which elements of the primary system, rather than objects in the external world, were directly represented. The age of models of models had arrived. But note the crucial difference that develops as soon as a species has not one but two representational systems working in tandem, as illustrated in figure 8.1(b).

All other species are limited to the configuration shown in Figure 8.1a. Information flows from the external world to the senses and from the senses to the PRS. This configuration by no means precludes the possibility of some kind of 'thinking' that may go on strictly within the PRS. It is likely, for instance, that the problem solving performed by apes is done in this way. The trigger seems to be (and to have to be) some sensory input to the PRS. An ape is shown food but access to it is made difficult, so that a ladder or box (already in view somewhere) must be

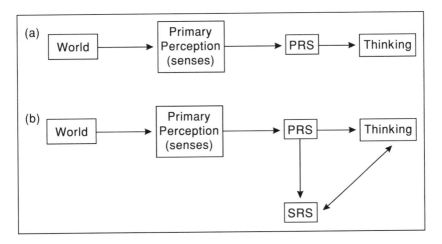

FIG. 8.1. Interaction between representational systems; primary representational system alone (a), secondary representational system added (b)

moved, or a flame must be extinguished (again by means of some currently visible agency), or several moves of this kind must be chained together in order to obtain the food. However, one seldom hears of apes solving unposed problems, or setting themselves problems, as humans do.

Our species, on the other hand, has the configuration shown in figure 8.1*b*. A sense impression is no longer the only means by which thought processes can be initiated. Thinking can be triggered by linguistic input from the SRS, and can in turn generate further entries in the SRS. This is precisely why constructional learning, and the rapid pace of behavioral change that constructional learning permits, is found in our species alone. In other species, thinking has to await an external trigger and it may well be severely hampered by the fuzziness and intractability of prelinguistic concepts. In ours, an internal trigger can cause thinking to commence at any time; lexical items, like well-worn coins, stand in place of concepts and allow us to manipulate them freely.

It may now be possible to clarify the relation between language and thought. Is human thought possible without language? Or are the two inextricably intertwined? The question has been complicated by people who (like Einstein) claimed to think mainly, if not exclusively, in images without words. Though the evidence for this is introspective, there seems no reason to doubt that such claims are genuine, as far as they go. But they do not go very far, for only the surface levels of thought, on which the results of long series of computations are expressed, are accessible to

199

introspection. This has become apparent through recent work on artificial intelligence (AI), where attempts to make machines that will replicate human thought processes have shown that a vast iceberg of inference-drawing and irrelevance-excluding activities (of which the thinker is entirely unaware) underlies conscious levels of thought.

Thus it is quite conceivable that thought processes conducted entirely in linguistic terms could, before arriving at conscious levels, be translated into imagery. Alternatively, images could simply take the place of words, but they would still have to be organized by syntactic mechanisms. In either case, if the elements of thought, whatever they might be, were not arranged in some type of formal structure in which their relations to one another were lawful and predictable, but instead they were just allowed to swirl around as they pleased, then no serious thought process could be carried through. Thus, either some mysterious, additional way of structuring thought is available, or syntax discharges that function.

If the nature of our thinking is determined by the possession of two distinct representational systems, the question naturally arises whether other phenomena peculiar (or so we suppose) to our species derive from the same cause. Considerations of parsimony and the nature of evolution both suggest that at least some of them should. Parsimony rejects alternative explanations when these are superfluous, while evolution is held in check by the difficulty of remodeling existing structures, and the impossibility of pure *ab ovo* innovation. In this chapter, some reasons will be provided for thinking that three of the phenomena supposedly unique to humans (mind, consciousness, and our search for knowledge) may derive directly from the possession of a language-based SRS with a syntactic processing unit.

MIND AND MACHINE

The concept of something known as 'mind' and regarded as somehow problematic goes back to the dawn of recorded thought. On the one hand, there were rocks, trees, and animals—things that could be seen, smelled, and grasped in the hand. On the other, there were thoughts, ideas, wishes, fears, and desires—things that could not be apprehended by any sense, and yet seemed as real as (some philosophers might argue, more real than) things known through the senses. Were there two parallel realities, one physical, and one not? Was one set of phenomena unreal? Did one set merely reflect the other? If so, which was the real and which the reflection?

Over the centuries, almost every possible answer to these questions has been espoused by someone. No solution seems to have worked, least of all the solution of claiming that there was no problem. In this, the mind-body problem rather resembles language origins. In both cases we have been told that the issues were insoluble, or illusory, or not worth thinking about. But, despite every effort to get rid of them, they obstinately kept coming back. Unfashionable though these issues might be, people somehow could not rid themselves of the need to resolve them.

Curiously enough, in spite of these similarities, few seem to have suspected that the mind-body problem and the problem of language origins might turn out to be related. A more common reaction has been to get rid of mind through some form of reductionism. One way of doing this, which has been very popular in recent years, is to think about building a machine that could perform any mental operation that humans can perform. Then one could point to such a machine and challenge the skeptic to declare whether it was conscious or not. This challenge could not be met, one argument goes, because we do not have direct access even to the minds of other members of our own species, and therefore cannot *know* that any mind other than our own is conscious. Thus the skeptic could not deny the consciousness of the machine except on the same grounds on which others could deny the skeptic's own consciousness. Yet, since we had built the machine ourselves, we would know that there was nothing in it but mechanical stuff.

Such reasoning is widespread, not so much in the AI community itself, which tends to take a more purely pragmatic approach to the issues involved, but among philosophers such as Daniel Dennett and Paul Churchland who hope that research in AI will clarify some long-standing philosophical problems. There is, however, something odd about their reasoning. They tend to begin by talking about consciousness, and may even admit, at this stage, that consciousness, if it means anything at all, means what it feels like to be a particular kind of being. Then, as the argument develops, they talk less and less about consciousness itself and more and more about mental processes, about how one perceives, or categorizes, or draws inferences.

This is hardly surprising. There is a lot to be said about perceiving and categorizing and drawing inferences, and these are things that machines can do, and can be seen to be doing, even though they may not yet do some of them quite as well as, or even in the same way that, we do them. There is relatively little to be said about what it feels like to be a human being or a particular person, except that . . . well, that's just what it feels like. So by imperceptible stages the argument slides into accepting the capacity to perform complex computational processes, rather than the capacity to have subjective experiences, as evidence for the possession of a conscious mind.

It may be helpful to return to some of the humble organisms discussed in chapter 4, the first creatures to react variably to stimuli. Practically everyone would agree that it is premature here to talk about mind. After all, what is the difference between a flatworm that responds to changes in light intensity and a thermostat that responds to changes in temperature? Both, one is tempted to say, are merely machines. In fact, however, there is already an essential difference.

The difference is that the actions of a thermostat (in a refrigerator, say) have no consequences for the thermostat. Having done what it was built to do, the thermostat rests passively until there is another significant change in temperature—significant because it has a potential effect on the refrigerator that contains it, not because of any effect on the thermostat itself. But what the flatworm responds to always has some effect on the flatworm. It moves towards food because food is needed to sustain it, or it moves away from a touch because the touch might signal some organism capable of damaging it. The flatworm, like any other animate creature, interacts directly with its environment for its own benefit in ways that may change both creature and environment. The thermostat does not.

Of course you might object that the right level of comparison is not between a flatworm and a thermostat but rather between a flatworm and a refrigerator (of which the thermostat could be construed as a primitive sense organ) or between a thermostat and a flatworm's light-sensitive cells. For instance, if a thermostat, unlike a flatworm, doesn't undergo habituation, that is because habituating to temperature changes would be damaging to the purposes of a refrigerator. And if it is objected that the refrigerator has no purposes of its own, you might respond that according to some biologists, we have no purposes of our own either—if the refrigerator is merely a carrier of food for humans, we are merely carriers of genes. In other words you could establish a simple analogy: just as genes impose purposes on humans, so humans impose those same purposes on machines.

There is however a significant difference. Even if we grant the most extreme version of the 'selfish gene' hypothesis, genes are something that are inside us, while we are not inside our machines. This gives the purposes of genes and us an identity that is not shared by the purposes of us and machines.

The relevance of this can be shown by a simple thought-experiment. Even if they do not already exist, it is doubtless possible to create robots that would behave in many ways like autonomous organisms. They might, for instance, recoil from a strong light or rush, plug in prosthesis, towards the nearest power outlet—perhaps even overturn and break other machines competing with them for the same energy source. However, from time to time, organisms, at least human organisms, commit suicide. Could our quasi-autonomous, survival-seeking machine commit suicide? Of course: its human owner could program it under particular circumstances to stand there with its plug dangling until it ran out of power, or to dive into a pond and short-circuit itself.

But then our equation (human:machine = gene:human) no longer stands. It would be bizarre, for instance, to claim that all and only those people programmed by their genes to commit suicide do commit suicide, and impossible to claim that such action suits the purposes of the genes concerned. Yet all and only all machines programmed to self-destruct would self-destruct.

Let us assume that living organisms have their own purposes, but that machines don't—in other words that, as stated in chapter 4, '[animate creatures] are continually acting in their own interests to maximize their chances of survival, whereas [inanimates] aren't'. (Inanimates, of course, include robots and computers, even supercomputers.) Note that this in no way assumes that organisms in general have *conscious* purposes or pursue any deliberate, reasoned-out policy. On the contrary, it is based on no more than the observation that creatures try to eat and not to be eaten (as opposed to trying the reverse, or attempting to do just one of the two things, or being indifferent to both); that this behavior tends to prolong their lives; and that, to the best of our knowledge, nothing that is not within them makes them do this.

Several factors support the view that autonomy is a large part of what determines that humans have minds and consciousness, while machines don't have them and probably never will. First, there is the feeling of autonomy that consciousness gives. Even if that feeling were an illusion, one would still have to explain why consciousness should give just that particular illusion and no other (why doesn't it give us the feeling that our behavior is wholly determined by the environment, for instance, or subject to pure chance?).

Then there is what is sometimes referred to as 'the frame problem'. Briefly, there is a number of things—perhaps literally an infinite number—that we seem to know or assume about the world without ever having consciously learned them: things as basic as knowing that the same thing can't be in two places at once, or that water seeks its own level; or things as absurdly obvious as that dialing a phone number doesn't change the number, or that you can't eat a pickup truck.

We do not merely know these things. A great deal of our everyday behavior rests on them, so that we have to know instantly which of them is relevant to which situation. Yet, because they were never consciously acquired, we take them for granted—until we program a machine to try to replicate some of our behaviors and find that, since it does not know these things we take for granted, the machine makes bizarre errors. How did we acquire such knowledge, how do we know when it is relevant, and how could we instantiate it in a machine?

The real root of the frame problem lies in treating humans and machines as organisms that are both engaged in producing an objective analysis of reality. This viewpoint is not limited to workers in AI. In chapter 2, we saw that many psychologists concerned with category perception take a similar view of humans. Now, *we* may manufacture objects aimed at producing an objective analysis of reality, but evolution manufactures creatures aimed at maximizing their life-chances. We may choose to assume that relevant information is information relevant to a particular task. But for evolved creatures, relevant information is information relevant to a particular type of organism.

For instance, just because we are the kind of creatures we are, we know that we can't eat pickup trucks, bales of hay, plankton, and a variety of other things. We know we are of a particular size and strength, so we can pick up bricks and bales of hay but not pickup trucks (despite their name!) or fallen redwoods. We know we have thin skins and thinnish skulls, so we avoid spiked railings, chain saws, falling rocks, and flying plates. We know that our survival may depend on split-second reactions, so infallible strategies that could take minutes or hours to develop are not even rejected—we just don't think of them.

How do we know all this? Because from the beginning of the evolution of animate life forms, 'knowledge' of this kind has been steadily accumulating, locked into the genetic codes of species and instantiated in each species's PRS. Our brains have been fine-tuned by hundreds of millions of years of evolution to analyze the world in terms of the needs, wants, and avoidances of highly specified living organisms (even if, proud as the fly on the chariot wheel, many of us adopt the flattering assumption that we somehow 'learn' much or most of all this). It is this kind of knowledge, variable between species, invariant within species, plus the sense of ourselves as creatures with purposes, that enables us to achieve the core of consciousness, a sense of feeling 'what it is like' to be some particular kind of creature. But machines have *tabula rasa* brains and no autonomy, so there is nothing for them to *be*. It makes sense to ask "What is it like to be a bat?", even if the question is, as Thomas Nagel correctly concluded, quite unanswerable. A bat would have some sense of what it was like to be a bat. But it makes no sense to ask, "What is it like to be a robot?"

We can now see what makes the frame problem so intractable. We can even distinguish between what makes it difficult and what makes it impossible. The difficulty lies in furnishing a robot with all that eons of evolution have given us. The impossibility lies in teaching a robot what is relevant and what isn't, when there is no autonomous entity there for things to be relevant or irrelevant to.

But deciding that machines are unlikely candidates for minds still doesn't tell us what a mind is, who has one, or where they come from. Of these questions, the third is perhaps the easiest to answer. Minds come from the coupling of growing representational capacities with growing creature autonomy that was catalogued in chapter 4.

Where, in this ongoing process, mind can be said to begin is a definitional issue rather than a substantive one. Once a creature can take, from both outside and inside sources, information that is both factual (memory, learning) and nonfactual (desires, emotional states), can integrate all those sources of information, and can base its own decisions on the outcome of that process, then it would seem reasonable to begin speaking of mind. But mind is perhaps better conceived of as a continuum reaching from the simplest internal representations to our own complex and sophisticated models. That continuum can, of course, be divided at any one of a number of points: at the first melding of external with internal information, at the first emotion, at the birth of secondary representation, and so on. The decision where to divide it is quite arbitrary and therefore uninteresting.

MIND AND LANGUAGE

Let us suppose, however, that we adopt the most restrictive definition of mind: that is, a mind like the only one that we can know directly, that of our own species. As suggested above, there is good reason to suppose that a mind of this nature can be made possible only by the existence of both an SRS and a syntactic module. The SRS can directly trigger the PRS (something that in other creatures can be done only by sensory information). Moreover, it can set it to work in any direction, at any time (unlike sensory information, which is limited to what the environment can provide at a given time and place). A syntax is required, in addition, in order to automatically organize concepts into propositional structures.

But even if the human mind does derive from the possession of language, this does not tell us the precise relation that exists between language and mind. There are at least two possibilities. Around thirty years ago, when linguistics ceased to be a merely descriptive science and began to reach towards some explanatory depth, one important reason for practicing it was the belief that a full understanding of language would serve as a window on the mind. But this belief implied something that was not widely recognized at the time and would not have been welcome if it had been recognized. The implication was that language permeated mind at every level. It would seem to follow from this that mind must constitute a single organism, something along the lines of the 'general problem-solving mechanism' that empiricists had often assumed.

Over the last fifteen years, the picture changed considerably. Psychobiological research suggested that what creatures in general had in their brains was not a single general-purpose organism but rather a cluster of highly task-specific modules—modules linked to one another but quasi-autonomous in their mode of operation. The concept of modularity that was derived from these studies encouraged linguists in their efforts to replace large numbers of formally similar rules by small numbers of formally distinct principles. That concept was largely responsible, too, for the claim by Chomsky that language is produced by a 'language organ'; the language organ, like the human heart or lungs, had its own function and mode of operation which did not necessarily resemble the mode and function of any other organ. This would suggest a model of mind along the lines of figure 8.2, in which language need have no effect at all on the operation of other mental modules.

Curiously enough, 'window-on-the-mind' rhetoric persisted even after modular hypotheses had made the prospect of such a window sound extremely unlikely. But modularity itself was far from problem-free. If the mechanisms of mind in general were unlike the mechanisms of language, then what were they like? A modularity approach seemed to imply an unstated number of mechanism types, perhaps a different type for each of n modules. How had each of these evolved? And how were the modules connected: were they linked one with another in series, or did several of them interface through a single larger and more generalized component? But the complete divorce of serious linguistics from evolutionary considerations meant that such problems could hardly be appreciated, let alone grappled with.

However, if the human mind evolved only as a consequence of the emergence of language, then the time-span is too short for other modules of mind, with their own unique mechanisms, to have evolved subse-

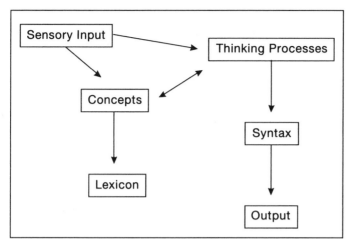

FIG. 8.2. Thinking without syntax

quently. The alternative—that other mental modules existed before language, and remained substantially uninfluenced by the development of language—could only work if almost all mental operations were independent of language, and if language, far from being a representational system, were merely a code for expressing the outputs of other modules. As we have seen, this is not the case. Moreover, such a model would predict that human intellectual capacities largely preexisted language. But if that were so, why did those capacities not begin to make an impact on the environment until around 40 Kya? The fossil record itself speaks against any such possibility.

Still, there remains the massive evidence for modular processing in other species. This is not in itself conclusive (there could be a modular PRS and a unitary SRS). But, in fact, modularity and the 'window-on-the-mind' hypothesis can still be reconciled, if we assume the type of organization shown in figure 8.3. Here, the syntactic module consists not of an isolated brain area but rather of a particular type of nervous organization that permeates and interconnects those areas devoted to higher reasoning processes, concepts, and the lexicon, a type of organization that automatically sorts material into binary-branching tree structures.

Questions such as whether the other modules developed before or after the syntactic module, or whether they contain mechanisms similar to or different from those of the syntactic module, are now moot. No matter what answer we might offer, these other modules will receive, represent, and output only material that has already been organized into   207

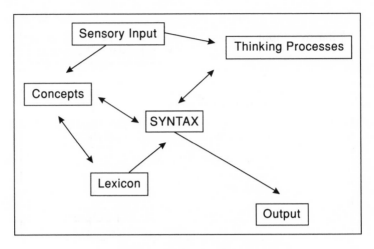

FIG. 8.3. Thinking with syntax

syntactic structures and that therefore conforms to syntactic principles. Thus, the processing that is supplied by other modules cannot, whatever it is, alter syntactic structures imposed on such material. If this model is correct, organization remains essentially modular, and yet language still constitutes our nearest and most reliable access to the workings of the mind.

It would follow from such a model that our mental processes, whether concerned with everyday trivia or with the profoundest of philosophical or scientific issues, will reflect the structural properties of language, and indeed would be impossible without them. But before we turn to these aspects of the mind we should perhaps consider what we may regard as its most striking and characteristic feature: the possession of a fully developed consciousness of the self.

LANGUAGE AND THE SELF

What seems to us most striking about our kind of consciousness is its self-reflexive nature. We can perform a series of actions and at the same time observe ourselves performing them, so to speak. Moreover, the outer and inner lives can seem at times totally divorced from one another. We can utter friendly words yet at the same time feel anger, hatred, or contempt. We can blush at our own boasting, tremble at our own rage—it really does feel as if there is a homunculus in there, pulling the strings, receiving messages, and sending answers to parts of ourselves that are somehow distinct and separate from 'the real us'. We speak of 'my arm', 'my left leg', 'my headache', 'my idea', 'my opinions', 'my brain', 'my mind'. But as with the tree in chapter 3, if you take away all the 'possessions'—the arm, the left leg, the headache, the idea, the opinions, the brain, the mind—nothing is left. The individual disappears, like an onion skinned to the limit.

This feeling of subjective consciousness is, of course, 'What it is like to be a human', and language contributes to it in a variety of ways. The most basic of these lies in its providing the infrastructure for consciousness.

You can't look at the spot you're standing on now if there is nowhere else for you to stand. A minimal prerequisite for self-consciousness is a place where you can stand and from which you can see the self—or, perhaps better, from which a part of you can look at another part of you. The SRS is such a place. The PRS provides a model of the world based on sensory input, memory, interoception, and proprioceptive feedback. The SRS provides a model of this model in which the world and your actions in it are, or potentially can be, expressed in words. The PRS feels, experiences, and behaves, the SRS puts it all into words.

This section began by noting that consciousness is self-reflexive. So is language. This can best be shown by looking at the so-called Liar Paradoxes. If statement A says 'The statement on the other side of this paper is false', then statement B on the other side must be false. But if statement B says, 'The statement on the other side of this paper is true', and B is false, then A cannot be true. But if A is not true, then B cannot be false. B is therefore simultaneously true and false, which is absurd. But this absurdity does not arise from either sentence in isolation, still less from some logical flaw at the heart of the universe. It arises because of the peculiar doubleness of language on which the duality of consciousness rests: the capacity to perform an act (in this case, make a proposition) and simultaneously comment on that act. Each sentence of a Liar Paradox is a comment on a proposition, but comments on propositions are themselves propositions.

Thus one can say *I'm writing letters* (proposition), *Writing letters makes me depressed* (comment on proposition and proposition), *It's stupid to be depressed by writing letters* (comment on comment on proposition, comment on proposition, and proposition) and so on *ad infinitum*. Each time there seems to be a different self involved: the self that writes letters, the self that looks at the self writing letters and feels depressed, the self that looks at the self feeling depressed about writing letters and thinks how stupid that self is. Thus you can think of yourself doing or feeling something, and think of yourself thinking of yourself, with infinite regress.

209

But this regress exposes the ground on which the conception of self is based. Obviously no one has an infinite number of selves. The process of 'looking at oneself' is nonfinitely recursive because the means by which the propositions are assembled is nonfinitely recursive. That is, it is syntax.

Consider again the Liar Paradox sentences above. Each sentence consists of a proposition ('There is a statement on the other side of this paper') and a comment on that proposition ('that statement is true/false'). Unlike the *writing letters makes me depressed* sentence, the comment in each of these sentences is not on the proposition in the sentence itself, but on the proposition *in the other sentence*. Moreover, since we are told only *that there is a statement on the other side of the paper*, and not any factual content for that statement, there is nothing to which we can attach the 'true/false' label except the other sentence as a whole—a proposition that, like *writing letters makes me depressed*, consists of a comment on a proposition and a proposition, but that, like all sentences, *is itself a proposition* (and thus like all propositions subject to description as either 'true' or 'false').

As such, a Liar Paradox is an elaborate linguistic artifact, possible within the schema of language and in no way anomalous *as a linguistic object*. Anomaly arises only when we try to relate it to the real world, say by trying to imagine a single proposition with content that would be at the same time true and false. We feel intuitively that a sentence should have some kind of denotation, a feeling akin to the naive realist's belief that if there is a word *unicorn* then there ought to be unicorns.

But this is not so. Occurring on the secondary level of representation, sentences do not have to be congruent with reality, nor even with the primary model of reality that they more directly represent. All representational systems have properties of their own, some of which will not be found at all in whatever is supposedly represented. If, on the lexical level, this can lead to the creation of words whose referents do not or cannot exist, it can lead, on the syntactic level, to sentences about situations that do not or cannot exist.

But the possibilities of self-reference that derive from syntactic properties cannot explain the whole story of consciousness. In simple, non-commenting propositions such as *I'm writing letters*, or even in simple noun phrases like *my ideas*, the notion of the homunculus, or some central directing force within the fleshly envelope, remains present. Other aspects of language conspire to produce these effects.

First of all, *I* is a concrete linguistic universal. Indeed in chapter 7 it was suggested that *I* may be even older than human language, since pronouns may have been a feature of protolanguage. Yet even if proper nouns were used, the choice of one's own name as subject (for instance, John saying *John feel hungry*) would involve just the same separation of observer from performer that *I* entails. The root of the issue is not so much the existence of a first-person pronoun as a pair of necessities: the necessity of sometimes talking about oneself, and the necessity of grammatical subjects.

Human language is '*cow*-and-*grazing*' language: it artificially divides entities from their behaviors. If there is a behavior, someone or something must perform it. This applies as much when the behavior is *thinking* or *hoping* or *believing* (things that are just a part of being a particular person at a particular time), as it does when the behavior is *cutting* or *building* (actions aimed at entities external to the individual). Thus *John* must *feel hungry* even if 'feeling hungry' is just part of being John at the time in question.

A similar logic accounts for expressions like *my arm*. One way in which the relation of wholes to parts can be expressed in English is by making the part the head of a phrase and placing the whole in the noun-specifier position. If that whole is a person, and if it does not represent the person *I* is speaking to (*your arm*), or anyone else (*his arm, her arm*), only two options are left: insert nothing, or insert a first-person label of some kind. The 'nothing' option is not really open. *Arm* in isolation is just a generic term for the class of all arms, so *my* must be chosen. Thus it is quite impossible in a human language to talk about oneself without using words and structures that impose dualism on their subject matter.

There would seem to be only two possible conclusions from this. If the central directing homunculus is indeed an artifact of language, then either consciousness of the kind we know is a pure illusion imposed on us solely by the structure of language, or the human organism really is divided in some way, if not necessarily in the way language suggests that it is. The second alternative should not surprise anyone who accepts a modular analysis of brain function. Moreover, it derives strong support from some recent experiments in the field of neurology.

LANGUAGE, CONSCIOUSNESS, AND THE BRAIN

In recent years, some of the most fascinating insights into the nature of consciousness have come from studies of persons who (usually in an attempt to control severe epileptic seizures) have undergone commisurotomy, an operation that cuts the nerves connecting the left and right hemispheres of the brain. In most persons, linguistic capacities exist solely in the left hemisphere.

This can be demonstrated by what is known as tachistoscopic presentation. The subject is asked to fixate a point at the center of a screen in such a way that if pictures are very briefly flashed on, say, the left-hand side of the screen, the image can be picked up only by cells in the left half of the retina. In the human visual system, nerves from the left side of the retinas of both eyes go to the right hemisphere, while nerves from the right sides go to the left hemisphere. In subjects with intact brains, both sources of information are then linked, but in 'split-brain' subjects, information from the left side reaches the right hemisphere and stays there. Thus when an object is flashed on the right side of the screen, the subject can name it immediately, but when it is flashed on the left side, most split-brain subjects are completely unable to do so.

This might suggest that only language, rather than both language and consciousness, is localized on the left side of the brain. But a medical procedure known as the Wada test, in which the left hemisphere is temporarily anesthetized, yields results that suggest something rather different. The Wada test has one advantage over commisurotomy: the intact brain can respond to questions after the usual split-brain experiments have been carried out. These responses suggest that language and consciousness are intimately linked.

In the Wada test, the right brain remains fully conscious, with complete control over the left hand. But if you place some object (a spoon, say) in that hand, remove it before the anesthetic in the left hemisphere wears off, and later ask about it, the patient will not only be unable to name the object *but will deny that anything was placed in the hand at all.* In other words, an experience that the patient 'saw' and 'felt' simply did not register in conscious experience when connections to the language centers of the brain were temporarily shut down.

In fact information of this kind *does* register in experience, it just does not register in conscious experience. This has been demonstrated in further experiments with split-brain patients. For instance, if an object is presented to the left eye, the patient will deny having seen anything, but will be able to draw, with the left hand, the object he or she 'hasn't seen'! This is very much what one would expect if experience is handled by two distinct modules: one module directly analyzes sensory information and may be largely or wholly inaccessible to consciousness; the other processes sensory and other information solely through the medium of language, and is fully accessible to consciousness.

As a result of these and similar experiments, Michael Gazzaniga came to the conclusion that "Language qua language confers little. There are other systems coincident with language that do the serious computing and decision making. Language merely reports on these other processes." This suggests a kind of modularity similar to that illustrated in figure 8.2, where language served merely to codify the output of other modules in which the real thinking is carried on. In this and other chapters, a number of reasons have been given for believing that such a picture misrepresents and trivializes the crucial role played by language in the development of our species. But Gazzaniga's work is thoughtful and thorough, and must be taken into account by any study of mental operations. His reasons for thinking that 'other systems' handle these operations lie in his belief that the right hemispheres of some split-brain patients have developed 'a rich language system', yet cannot draw simple inferences. The first of these beliefs deserves to be reviewed.

The evidence for right-brain language capacity is equivocal. In many split-brain patients there seems to be little or no such capacity. In others, single nouns can be recognized and single verbs, if uttered in the form of commands, are responded to appropriately with a frequency greater than chance. However, all patients show a radical incapacity to construct sentences with the right hemisphere, even if the materials for doing so are already assembled for them.

In an ingenious and elegant experiment, Gazzaniga presented tachistoscopically a series of slides each of which had two words on it. The words were chosen so as to constitute three sentences: *Mary Ann may come visit into the township today* (if all words on the slides were read), *Mary may visit the ship* (if only words on the left of the slides were read) and *Ann come into town today* (if only words on the right were read). When the subject was asked to recall what he had seen, he first responded with *Ann come into town today*—just the sentence composed by right-hand words and therefore fed into the left hemisphere. Under questioning he recovered *ship, Ma* (from *may?*), *visit*, and *Mary* as separate items. Finally, when asked to repeat the story, he produced *Ma ought to come into town today to visit Mary Ann on the boat.*

This experiment suggests that the right hemisphere is incapable of constructing sentences. However, two sets of subsequent experiments could be interpreted as showing syntactic capacities in the right hemispheres of at least a handful of individuals. First, Gazzaniga's two best subjects were tested on active and passive sentences. Subjects would be shown a picture (of a girl touching a boy, for instance) and immediately afterwards would hear a sentence through their left ear. For the picture of

213

the girl touching a boy, they would be expected to respond 'yes' if the sentence was *The girl touched the boy* and 'no' if the sentence was *The girl was touched by the boy.* One subject, V.P., failed to perform above chance with the right hemisphere. The other, J.W., performed well above chance on active sentences, but well below it on passives.

Gazzaniga concluded that according to J.W.'s right hemisphere, all first nouns in sentences were subjects, and that the right hemisphere can therefore 'analyze the grammatical function of lexical items'. Obviously in both types of sentence the first noun was structurally the subject. Presumably Gazzaniga meant that J.W. treated first nouns as *logical subjects* or *notional subjects*, in other words as Agents, and therefore assumed, with more than chance frequency, that in sentences like *the girl was touched by the boy,* the girl did the touching.

There is no need to take this as evidencing any awareness of grammatical function. Suppose that J.W.'s right hemisphere had access only to protolanguage. Since protolanguage has no structure, which noun comes first cannot be determined by structural criteria. First nouns in utterances are usually topics, nouns that refer to whatever in the discourse is central and/or known to both speaker and hearer. Since the PRS, whether linguistic or merely protolinguistic, sees the world in terms of Agency, Agents in protolanguage are at least as likely to be first nouns as they are in language, especially where (as here) there is no preceding context that might favor some other participant as topic.

Thus J.W.'s behavior is consonant with his having not language but protolanguage in his right hemisphere. This is exactly what we would expect if protolanguage preexisted our species, if the lexicon was not initially localized in the left hemisphere, and if the mutation that produced language affected only the left hemisphere. By using the Wada test on 'language-trained' chimpanzees, it should be possible to determine the extent to which the general capacities on which protolanguage rests are localized in that species.

The second set of experiments involved grammaticality judgments, on which both subjects performed far better than chance. (In the case of V.P., the two hemispheres performed almost equally well, but it should be noted that her corpus callosum had not been completely severed.) However, it is still questionable whether the actual task presented to the subjects required any real syntactic capacity.

Note that the issues here differ somewhat from the issues raised by those stroke victims and other 'agrammatics' who, despite their inability to produce grammatical sentences, are sometimes able to make judgments on the grammaticality of sentences presented to them. (See the final section of chapter 5 for discussion.) When speakers with undivided brains exhibit such a pattern, one explanation is readily available: production of sentences can be interfered with, since this involves localized modules, but the knowledge on which grammaticality judgments are based is widely diffused (being implicit in a type of brain organization, rather than localized in specific tissues) and therefore much harder to disrupt. However, the evidence forces us to conclude that *the language system as a whole* (the mode of neural organization that yields syntax AND the task-specific modules directly linked by that organization, including those that handle the lexicon, the sound system, and much more) is located in the left hemisphere. This conclusion predicts that the right hemisphere should have no grammatical abilities *at all*.

The experiments in question involved presenting sentences such as *Are going you to the store?*, *Harry is waiting for Mary, doesn't he?*, *Harry loves herself* mixed with the correct versions of these. Subjects were required to respond merely 'yes' to grammatical sentences and 'no' to ungrammatical ones. No grounds for making the judgments were obtained. In other words, there is nothing to show that real grammatical factors were weighed in arriving at these 'grammatical judgments'. Indeed, as anyone experienced in linguistic fieldwork knows, it is extremely difficult to tease apart judgments made on genuine grammatical grounds from judgments made on semantic, or pragmatic, or purely cultural grounds ('*We* don't say that sort of thing'). For this reason, in devising sets of sentences for judgment, it is essential to be aware of possible 'distractors', usually factors implicit in the choice of words rather than in the actual structure of the sentences, that will bias the respondent to give favorable or unfavorable judgments.

In split-brain patients a further factor may compromise such judgments. We may assume that while the language-driven SRS is restricted to the left hemisphere, the PRS must be represented in both hemispheres. Now, although the PRS cannot represent language *qua* language, it can represent *anything accessible to the senses*. Why should we assume that this 'anything' automatically excludes sentences that the subject has heard and uttered? Might it not remember *holistically* sentences of high frequency, without being able to process them, but with enough fidelity to know that there was something wrong with them when they were inaccurately reproduced? The right hemisphere is, after all, very good at remembering tunes and jingles.

If there is no real syntactic capacity in the right hemisphere, then the

215

assumption that language and inference are quite distinct from one another is undercut. It is, after all, unsurprising if a subject, confronted with the words *pin* and *finger*, fails to select *bleed* from a list of possible consequences (one of the examples cited by Gazzaniga in support of his assumption). Someone unable to construct a sentence such as 'If you stick a *pin* in your *finger* it will *bleed*' is hardly in a position to draw the required inference.

Obviously, the power to draw inferences preexisted language, otherwise apes would be unable to fetch boxes so as to reach otherwise inaccessible fruit. But although apes may be capable of constructional learning, they are capable of it only if all the relevant pieces of a puzzle are physically present. Now, drawing inferences is simply a part of learning. If apes can only draw inferences under these circumstances, the most parsimonious explanation is that they lack any abstract representational system that might enable them to draw inferences merely from the signs for, or the ideas of, the objects involved. We can therefore accept the null hypothesis: there are no mysterious 'other systems coincident with language that do the serious computing and decision making'. The power to conjoin meaningful items in systematic structures is all that we need in order to think the way we do.

WILL THE REAL 'I' PLEASE SPEAK UP?

The evidence from neurolinguistic research suggests, then, that what we are conscious of is what we are able to process linguistically. This does not, of course, mean that we have to physically express things in order to be conscious of them, or even think about them in some verbal kind of way. It merely means that information has to reach the language centers (or areas directly linked to those centers) in order for it to register in consciousness. If information passes directly from sensory or sensory-processing areas to the memory, as in the case of objects perceived with the left eye by split-brain subjects, it will not register.

The areas over which our consciousness operates form only a subset of the areas which, in the broadest sense, constitute 'ourselves'. We are aware (unless we are undergoing a Wada test or have undergone commisurotomy) of all that we see or hear, but we are not aware of the stage of digestion reached by our last meal, or indeed of anything else about our digestive processes, unless these are going badly enough to affect pain centers. Although our brains must somehow monitor the flow of blood around our bodies, we are quite unable to tell when our arteries are becoming choked by fatty products (although it would be an evolutionary advantage if we could). Thus when we say *I do this, that, and the other,* the 'I' we report on falls considerably short of the entire organism that bears our name.

At first sight this might look as if we have come full circle to a dualist position, in which the individual can be divided into an 'accessible I' (those functions performed by areas linked to the language centers) and an 'inaccessible I' (the balance of our functions). There is, however, a considerable difference between this distinction and the traditional mind-body distinction. The latter was based on a distinction between mental activities (remembering, choosing, speaking) and physical activities (breathing, walking, digesting). The accessible-inaccessible dichotomy crosscuts this distinction.

First, a great part of the motor system, though apparently physical, forms part of 'accessible I'. If this were not so, we would be unable to deliberately will ourselves to stand, sit, point, turn our heads, and so on (note however that we cannot normally will ourselves to slow down our metabolism, achieve orgasm, supply our brains with more oxygen, or perform a variety of other physical functions). Second, the processes by which we speak and think (as opposed to the content of what we speak about and think about), though apparently mental, form part of 'inaccessible I'. Indeed, in this the mind rather resembles a TV set—switch channels as you will, it will never bring you a picture of what's inside it. Third, the boundary between 'accessible I' and 'inaccessible I' is not graven in marble. Through biofeedback and certain forms of meditation, some individuals, at least, have managed to move control of some normally 'inaccessible' processes, such as the rate of the heartbeat, into the 'accessible' domain.

From this there follows perhaps the clearest distinction between the mind-body and accessible-inaccessible models. In the former, some qualitative difference between the two terms is generally assumed: body is common, everyday matter, but mind is some far more elusive medium. In the latter, the two terms are identically instantiated. They differ only with respect to the overall wiring diagram of the brain. One set of modules, that which constitutes 'accessible I', is linked to the language areas, the other set is not.

Can we say, therefore, that the 'I' to which we refer when we speak of thinking, feeling, or performing actions is none other than 'accessible I'? At first it does not seem so. If one says, 'I forced myself to memorize the number', the 'myself' that is to memorize must be 'accessible I' if it is to perform such a conscious mental action. A little earlier it was proposed that this kind of reflexivity arises from purely formal properties of language. But this cannot be the whole story, for if *I* and *myself* have identical referents, how can one force the other? And if they have distinct referents, are we not reintroducing the homunculus, some still-inexorcisable ghost in the linguistic machine?

Consider the behavior of someone under hypnosis who is given a post-hypnotic command, say to open the window. Having obeyed this command, it would be perfectly possible for the subject to answer 'I haven't the faintest idea' when asked why he or she opened the window. In fact, most subjects under these conditions respond along the lines of 'The room felt stuffy' or 'I wanted to look at something outside'. Is the hypnotic subject lying? No, almost certainly the subject believes he or she found the room stuffy, or felt an impulse to look at something outside.

Consider, too, the behavior of one of Gazzaniga's split-brain subjects whose left hemisphere saw a picture of a chicken claw while the right saw a snow scene. When asked to pick from a row of cards the objects that go with these, he chose (appropriately) a chicken and a shovel. However, when asked to explain his choice, he replied, "The chicken claw goes with the chicken and you need a shovel to clean out the chicken shed." Having no conscious memory of the snow scene, he could very easily have said, "I have no idea why I picked the shovel." But he did not.

Both the hypnotic case and the split-brain case illustrate confabulation: the invention of a logical-sounding but often totally inaccurate story designed to bridge some inexplicable gap in memory. It is as if our species were under the injunction, 'Make your representation of events absolutely complete at all times at any cost'. In the same way, as noted in chapter 2, everything we could conceivably encounter in the world has to be lexically representable in some fashion. People will say 'I saw a ghost/a UFO' or 'No you didn't, it was a hallucination/a weather balloon' sooner than they will say 'We don't know what we saw, but it sure was weird'. In the same way, something inside of us constructs a continuous history from the cradle to the present moment, and is upset at any event (blackout, fainting fit, sleepwalking) that makes a gap in that history.

Who or what is that something? In the present view, any creature (including ourselves) consists of a set of linked yet quasi-autonomous modules. Each of us is, as it were, a delegation, but there is only one microphone. This is usually in the hands of the module that, driven by the syntactic engine, forms constructional inferences; it forms them constantly, as a means of self-preservation, for if we draw all the inferences possible from our environment, we can successfully control that environment and use it to our advantage. Let us call this module, a mere part of 'accessible I', 'talking I'. 'Talking I' does not always speak out loud, of course, although as Joyce's *Ulysses* showed us, its voice seldom ceases from echoing somewhere within the vault of the brain. But from time to time some other module, thrust forward by some greater-than-normal stimulus, grabs the microphone, and instead of '. . . well, uh, then so-and-so happened, and because of that I did such-and-such, and then . . .' we hear (or feel) 'Ouch!' or 'Help me!' or 'I love you'.

What do we really mean when we say things like 'I forced myself to memorize the number'? Perhaps something along the lines of 'Information in the SRS of an individual X indicated that memorization of a number, Y, might be of future benefit to X, so that although the current state of X and/or X's immediate environment indicated that other immediate actions would be more pleasurable or beneficial to X, X memorized Y'. In other words, the incorrigibly homuncular language of 'talking I' represents a kind of shorthand by which we can describe, to ourselves and others, the motivations behind our actions and thus, to some degree, explain the actions themselves. These are functions that are essential in an advanced social species. But conversations would be far longer and more boring if it weren't for the shortcuts that 'talking I' takes.

So what, then, is the theory of mind and consciousness that follows from this analysis? Some kind of eliminative materialism? A language-driven dualism? Neither, exactly, but perhaps something that incorporates elements of both.

Eliminative materialism seeks to explain our talk of mind and what 'we' 'believe', 'think', 'want', and so on by showing that this talk simply represents a primitive theory of psychology and that this theory, like other primitive theories, is simply false. An alternative theory, based on a better understanding of the neural infrastructure of mind, would replace it with a different picture, just as our current conception of space replaced the 'starry sphere' of the ancients.

In one sense, you might regard eliminative materialism as a promissory note that the perceived role of language now offers to replace with hard cash. The shift of dichotomy from mind-body to accessible-inaccessible, and the exposure of the arbitrary and misleading things about ourselves that language forces us to say, do alter our picture of the problem, although it is unlikely that *I forced myself* will soon be replaced, in common parlance, by *Information in the SRS of.* . . . But this is an important dimension of the problem. The 'starry sphere' was just a metaphor that another metaphor could replace, but *I know, I want, I force myself*, and so on are the only, therefore the 'literal', ways we have for talking about certain phenomena essential to both our individual and our social lives.

Why is this so? Perhaps, in part at least, because desires, beliefs, fears, and all the rest of the mental apparatus are not fabrications, as the 'starry sphere' was—although thanks to the structure of language they may have been misperceived. They are things we have because, as autonomous creatures with learned rather than hard-wired responses, we need bridges between particular representations and the responses appropriate to them, if we are to fulfil our basic purpose of surviving and propagating.

Some of these bridges we call 'emotional': fears, desires, love, hatred. Some we call 'rational': belief, knowledge, thoughts, ideas. These two categories have a different subjective feel to them but they are all in some sense mental experiences and their proper descriptions may not vary so much. If X fears that Y will happen, information in X's SRS indicates that Y is both aversive and probable. If X knows that Y will happen, all information in X's SRS indicates that Y has a probability of 1. Moreover, the two categories are alike in that none of their content, whether 'emotional' or 'rational', exists for its own sake. It exists to guide the behavior of autonomous creatures toward their intrinsic goals. We fear or desire things because they seem likely to hurt or help us in the pursuit of our goals. We know or believe things because knowledge and belief are necessary for the achievement of our goals.

What makes it so hard to build machines that will behave as we do, rather than just cleverly mimick some of the things we do, is the difficulty of making machines that are goal-autonomous. Indeed, if we could really do that, we would be building a dangerous competitor for our own species. Here, however, the present approach differs from the views of at least some eliminative materialists. They, along with functionalists, believe that whatever mind *is*, it could in principle be instantiated in a machine that would replicate merely the *rational* processes of the mind. The evidence surveyed above points in a rather different direction.

The belief that mind can be machine-instantiated implies that states of mind are directly related to states of physical systems, whether those systems are biological or mechanical. The present approach suggests, instead, that language in its broadest sense, the set of principles that organize the SRS, must serve as a link, indeed as the only possible link, between brain states and states of mind. Although generated by neuronal activity, language is not a bad candidate for the kind of metaphysical stuff that dualists have felt obliged to postulate. It can be physically expressed through sound or scratches on a page, but sounds and scratches are not language, they merely represent it. And representations are incorrigibly intentional, always pointing beyond themselves to some other thing.

THE ORDERING OF NATURE

In the last section it was noted that our species strives always to make its view of the world as complete and as completely logical as possible. Faced by any array of heterogeneous phenomena, the normal human impulse is to look for regularity and order. This impulse is of course not unique to our species, although awareness of it may be. Every creature seeks to establish generalizations over some domain of experience.

Again, however, this is not done out of a spirit of disinterested inquiry, but for survival. The creature that can abstract from a set of phenomena some consistency that affects (whether negatively or positively) that creature's well-being thereby prolongs its life. It follows from this that generalizations are tightly linked to behavioral responses, while both are linked to the kind of creature you are. If something is small, round, and fast moving, and you are a frog, then it is food, and you should grab it. If something is broad winged, and hovers, and casts a shadow, and you are a chicken, then it is a hawk, and you should freeze and hope to go unnoticed. If something is round and covered with spines, and you are a dog, then it is a hedgehog or a porcupine, and you should leave it strictly alone.

Note however that the more generalizations you can make, the less you need to limit those generalizations to life-and-death issues. The hawk may be fatal to the chicken, but the porcupine will seldom be fatal to the dog. Unless blood poisoning sets in, the worst the dog can expect is a sore nose. Thus the impulse to avoid life-threatening contingencies degrades to the impulse to avoid mere unpleasantness.

In our species, the capacity to make generalizations is, at once, greatly enhanced and divorced still further from the need to survive. It is enhanced because constructional learning ends the dependence of learning on the environment and on chance. It is divorced because of the lengthened time span over which a creature with an SRS and the power of constructional learning is free to operate. A generalization might not bring any immediate benefit, but since it can be readily stored in the SRS and readily recovered, and since in the 'organized closet-space' of the SRS, storage is, for practical purposes, unlimited, then it will be kept just in case it might turn out to be useful one day.

Moreover, regardless of the value of individual generalizations, a mind stocked with a large quantity of them enjoys certain advantages. A series of well-organized generalizations constitutes a coherent world-view. A coherent worldview enables its possessor to react swiftly and appropriately to a wide variety of novel events. The more things are ordered and predictable, the more surely they can be captured, avoided, or controlled.

Thus, as soon as the hominid line had acquired an SRS (at the *erectus* stage, presumably) and had added to it a syntactic engine that would automatically construct propositions, it stood to benefit by developing as far-reaching a worldview as possible. That it began to do this at a relatively early stage is shown by the cave paintings at Lascaux, Altamira, and elsewhere. Although no one can decipher the purpose of the paintings with any certainty, they seem to express a complex cosmology in which the male and female principles and the spirits of the major animal species played significant roles.

The moon calendars that date back perhaps as far as these paintings might appear at first sight to express a rather different approach to the ordering of nature. These calendars consist of smooth pieces of bone on which have been scratched small images—round, semicircular, and crescentlike—in a regular progression which loops, in a single line, across the bone for as long as two-and-a-half lunar cycles. Speaking from a contemporary context it may seem natural to call the moon calendars 'science' and the cave paintings 'art' or 'religion', but both are essentially attempts to systematize, using slightly different approaches. Both seek for consistencies that are assumed to lie, in the case of moon calendars, only a little beneath the surface of appearances, and in the case of cave paintings, rather deeper.

This organization into systems of number or images takes the search for generalizations much further than any other creature could take it. Such systems, made possible by language, could only be interpreted through language. But this leaves open the question of whether they were *discovered in* nature or merely *imposed upon* it.

When a hypothesis about the world meets with counterevidence (for instance, when Ptolemaic astronomy fails to account for the observed motions of the planets), we can say, with all the wisdom of hindsight, that the structure was merely imposed. But of what hypothesis can we say that it represents a genuine discovery? In fact, there are only three kinds of hypothesis: those that have been disproved, those that cannot of their nature be disproved, and those that have not been disproved yet. If there are genuine discoveries, they can only fall into the third class, but it would be a rash person indeed who would undertake to select, out of all currently undisproved but potentially disprovable hypotheses, just those that constitute irrefutable certainties.

Everyone will have favorite theories which they believe to be correct (heliocentrism, evolution, and so on). But a thousand years ago, very little of what we now regard as 'knowledge' was accepted, and the bulk of what was accepted would no longer be regarded as 'knowledge'. Who could predict with any confidence what will be 'knowledge' a thousand years from now? Yet people a thousand years ago were every bit as convinced by their 'knowledge' as we are by ours, and as those a thousand years hence will be by theirs.

CONSTRAINTS ON THE ORDERING OF NATURE

In fact, in reducing the universe to order, we impose certain constraints on our representations of its phenomena. At least some of these appear identical with those that structural principles impose on language. They include the following.

Binary division. The first step we take in dealing with almost any area of knowledge is to divide its subject matter into two parts: good and evil, mind and body, animate and inanimate, conservative and liberal, *Gemeinschaft* and *Gesellschaft*, classical and romantic, extrovert and introvert, nature and nurture, realism and idealism. In a fascinating study, Mary Hesse showed that there have only ever been two ways of explaining why things are attracted to one another: a force that works without contact, or structural properties of space. Newton chose one, Einstein the other, but, stripped of their mathematical sophistication, both solutions go back as far as the earliest recorded philosophers. The fundamental role of dichotomy in human inquiry could well have the same source as the binary properties that are built into so many aspects of language structure: antonym pairs, syntactic structure, predicability trees, and the lexicon in general.

Parcellation. In proceeding with the examination of any area of knowledge, we divide up each side of the original dichotomy into smaller and smaller parcels. Two centuries ago, even though it could already be claimed that 'the proper study of mankind is man', the poet who wrote the line (Alexander Pope) would have been hard put to find a name for the field. Then the study of the individual split into 'psychology' and 'physiology' and the study of the social into 'anthropology' and 'sociol-

223

ogy'. Population pressure was not the cause of this. People still living can remember when American anthropologists could be numbered on the fingers.

Not surprisingly, these divisions separated from each other many things that, from at least some viewpoints, would have been better left connected. This book itself, forced to hop from discipline to discipline in order to pursue a single coherent theme, stands as witness to that. But instead of a remerging of fields of study, the response has been the spawning of a host of hybrids—paleoanthropology, ethnobotany, psycholinguistics—each of which in turn quickly grew to be a world unto itself. But this pattern of continual fission exactly mimics that which constantly increased the categories in the lexicon.

Exclusive class membership. A common human assumption is that all entities are either *A* or not-*A*. That is, for any entity, there is some minimal class (the smallest class to which it can belong), and it cannot then belong to any class other than a superordinate class of which that minimal class forms a proper subset. But this presupposes the existence of the hierarchical structure, illustrated in numerous figures in this book, that underlies both the lexicon and syntax.

There might seem to be counterexamples to these claims. If an entity could belong to two classes only when these were in a subordinate-superordinate relationship, the entity might have classmates in the first class that were not in the second, but could not have classmates in the second that were not in the first. Yet oilbirds and pelicans are birds, and oilbirds and bats are cave dwellers, though pelicans are not cave dwellers and bats are not birds. However, the contradiction is only apparent, since human knowledge can be organized into more than one tree. Different trees have different purposes: oilbirds and pelicans are classmates in a tree that divides creatures by type, while oilbirds and bats are classmates in a tree that divides creatures by habitat.

Exhaustiveness. The principle of exhaustiveness is a constraint on such knowledge trees. It entails that any tree will exhaust its domain. that is, if the highest node label is the set of all things, then all things must be assigned to some class in that tree. Similarly, if the highest label is the set of all animates, all animates (but no inanimates) must have a place in the tree. Domains are in no sense arbitrary. Possible domains of major knowledge trees are determined by the Keil-Sommers predicability tree discussed in chapter 2. Any node in that tree may serve as a highest-node label. Additionally, smaller trees can be constructed, but their domains will always be proper subsets of those dominated by nodes in the predicability tree.

It follows from this that no entity can be outside a tree. In chapter 2, it was noted that the lexicon, too, is governed by the principle of exhaustiveness. Everything accessible to the conscious mind could be—and not only could be, but had to be—assigned some form of linguistic label. This may be part of the reason theories constructed by our species do not have holes in them, even when some of the data they supposedly cover is in fact inexplicable at the time the theory is created.

One recent example in the history of linguistics concerns things that were known as 'filters'. At the time (around the mid-seventies) linguists wanted to exclude from grammars certain types of sentence that never, apparently, appeared in natural languages but that did not seem to be excluded by any principles that were then known. For this reason, there was proposed a set of devices that would 'filter out' the objectionable expressions. Filters were entirely ad hoc and had to be separately stipulated, and yet many linguists talked and wrote of the properties of these entities, which were in fact as mythical as basilisks. A few years later, their supposed effects could be explained in terms of general principles, and they were quietly and unceremoniously dumped.

Causal primacy. The type of generalization produced by our species commonly takes a cause-and-effect form. If 'when x happens, y happens' can be construed as 'x causes y to happen', it will be so construed. If it cannot, then the search is on for z such that 'z causes x and y to happen'. Once a species is committed to changing its environment, there are advantages to such a strategy. If y is unpleasant, remove x and y will also vanish; if y is pleasant but not procurable directly, then introduce more of x. The casting of events into a cause-effect framework has proved highly effective and underlies a large part of the spectacular difference in achievement between our own and other species.

However, the strategy is only available to a species with language. Indeed it may be linked even more intimately with language if it results from the primacy of the role of Agent. That role, as we saw in chapter 3, normally receives precedence over all other roles when thematic structure is mapped onto syntactic structure. The highest structural position in a tree, that of matrix subject, is most commonly given to an agentive noun phrase.

This may be a hen-and-egg issue, since, as was suggested in chapter 7, Agent primacy in language may derive from a purely perceptual, pre-SRS structuring of experience. One might argue, too, that language is so adaptive precisely because, by casting events into a cause-effect format, it enables us, in a sufficient number of cases, to interfere with nature in what seem to us productive ways. But it would be a risky leap to proceed from this to the claim that the world itself *really is* structured in terms of cause-effect mechanisms. The most we can say is that language mediates between the world and our species in ways that, up until now, have seemed to our advantage.

Identification. One of the consequences of causal primacy is that any event tends to be interpreted as an action with a causal agent. It thunders, and a god of thunder is evoked as the agent thereof. A person falls sick and dies, and it is supposed that some sorcerer has placed a spell upon that person. Certain sentence types fail to appear, and filters are hypothesized that act to prevent their appearance. Now thunder god, spell, and filter have one set of things in common: no one can see them, hear them, smell them, weigh them, or measure them. However, lack of sensory verification never stopped our species from hypothesizing entities.

Two distinct aspects of language conspire with causal primacy to support this power to identify 'missing agents'. The first aspect comes from the lexicon. Possession of an SRS entails the possibility that there will be words like *unicorn* or complex expressions like *the golden mountain* that refer to no actual thing. Being only a model of a model of the world, the SRS is constrained not so much by actual properties of the world as by two quite different factors: what it is possible to represent in an SRS, and what it seems to suit us, at any given moment, to choose to believe is in the world.

The second aspect comes from syntax. Syntax is characterized by the presence of null elements—structural positions that must be filled yet are not occupied by any overt form. These are acceptable so long as they can be identified. Identification may take any of several forms. Most commonly, a null element is identified by being linked, through principled processes, to some overt constituent. Where no appropriate overt constituent is available it may be identified as 'anyone', as in *It's not clear what e to do next*. However, in *They ate e and drank e*, *e* is interpreted as 'things appropriate to eat or drink', in much the same way as 'something appropriate to make thunder' gives us Jove the Thunderer.

Given that things that are physically absent can be identified through their connections or through their effects, and that the creation of words is constrained only by conceptual possibilities and not by the material universe, the way is open, especially if the principle of causal primacy is driving the inquirer, for the setting up of unlimited hypothetical entities; these hypothetical entities, whether gods, spirits, natural laws, or scientific hypotheses, may differ in the ease with which they can be empirically supported but they all belong to the same logical and linguistic types. The role played by such hypothetical entities in the history of human thought can hardly be exaggerated.

In this section we have reviewed six constraints on human thought processes, and suggested how each of them might be derived, wholly or in part, from the structure of language. The implication is that the 'intelligence' of our species differs from that of other species only through our possession of language. Both higher-mammalian 'intelligence' and language itself represent evolutionary adaptations whose primary function was not to discover secrets of the universe but simply to enable creatures to survive and reproduce within that universe. Yet many of us believe that, by virtue of our unique powers of thought, we are potentially, if not actually, capable of fully explaining those secrets. We may well ask whether such a belief is justified and why we should hold it.

The 'Search for Truth'

In the previous section it was suggested that the ways in which we seek for knowledge may be determined more by the structure of language than by the structure of reality. It may also be that properties of language determine the ends as well as the means of our inquiries. It is commonplace to speak of scientists and others as being engaged in 'the search for truth'. But what exactly is this truth for which they search? Does it, in fact, represent an achievable goal, or merely one that language by its very nature portrays as achievable?

Let us begin by examining some properties of the predicate 'is true'. Consider a proposition, such as (1), that relates to a factual event:

1. John arrived at 4:00 P.M.

Some form of 'correspondence theory' would be quite adequate to deal with (1). We might say (1) is true just in case there is a person called John and that person arrived and the time at which he arrived was 4:00 P.M. These circumstances would be easy to determine by means of eyewitnesses, videotapes, footprints, fingerprints, and so forth.

Now consider a proposition, such as (2), that relates to a quality:

2. John is brave.

Although we might still like to say that we could test the truth of (2) against some empirical circumstance that it would 'correspond with', there is in fact no equivalent manner in which the truth or falsehood of (2) can be established. No matter what evidence is produced, it is always possible for someone to say 'That wasn't brave, that was reckless', or

227

'That's just what any normal person would have done', or 'Granted he was brave on that particular occasion, but as a rule John's not brave'. Verification of (2) is impossible outside of some subjective frame of reference that will assign arbitrary conditions for the state of being brave.

Now consider a proposition that introduces the term *true* itself as a quality predicate:

3. John's theory of *x* is true.

Proposition 3 differs markedly from both propositions 1 and 2. The truth of (1) and (2) is not affected if their predicates are ascribed to other subjects: *Bill arrived at 4:00 P.M.* does not falsify (1) and *Bill is brave* does not falsify (2). But consider (4) and (5):

4. Bill's theory of *x* is true.

5. Bill's theory of *x* is not the same as John's.

Given (5), it cannot be the case that both (3) and (4) are true. Moreover, the truth of (3) cannot be established either in the way the truth of (1) is established or in the way the truth of (2) is established. The truth of (3) can perhaps be established only by social convention, so that (3) could be rewritten as 'John's theory of *x* is strongly believed in by a large majority of suitably qualified persons at time *t* and no theory accounting for the same data is so strongly believed in'.

It is possible to prove that a theory is false (by showing that it is internally inconsistent, for example). It is also possible to collect evidence suggesting that theory A is preferable to theory B (it can account for more facts, predictions based on it are confirmed more often, and so on). However, there always exists the possibility of finding facts that A cannot account for and the further possibility of finding a theory that will explain both the new facts and the facts that A explained. In the same way, no matter how many predictions of A are confirmed, it is always possible that A's next prediction will be disconfirmed. But one cannot say things like *John's theory of x is true today, but may not be true tomorrow.* True theories are supposed to be permanently as well as uniquely true.

Moreover, theories are either true or they are not. It seems to make no sense to talk about 'a half-true theory'. Despite this, one often reads remarks like this by Karl Popper: "The very refutation of a theory . . . takes us nearer to the truth.'

If this remark has any status at all, it can only relate to a special kind of truth associated with theories and suchlike, not the common or garden variety associated with expressions like (1) and (2). If (1) were true, would *John arrived at 3:57 P.M.* represent a closer approximation to the truth than *John left at 4:00 P.M.*, *Bill arrived at 4:00 P.M.*, or *John arrived at 4:05 P.M.*? The question is absurd. If (1) is true, and if only John arrived at that time, then the other propositions are not 'approximations to the truth', but simply false, and equally so.

Indeed, the 'suchlike' of the previous paragraph may well be an empty class. Other true things, even when abstract, do not have to be unique. Consider (6) through (8):

6. Mary's account of John's arrival was true.
7. Bill's account of John's arrival was true.
8. Bill's account was not the same as Mary's.

Statement 8 does not mean that either (6) or (7) is false. Suppose Mary said that John arrived at 4:00 P.M. in a rusty Volvo wearing a dark suit, while Bill said that John arrived at 4:00 P.M., parked badly, and seemed very tense. Suppose further that all parts of these descriptions are correct. Clearly, both accounts are true, albeit incomplete. Why shouldn't two theories of x be true if both contain only true statements about x (even if neither contains all possible true statements about x)?

In part this is because theories, unlike accounts, are not mere lists of separable statements. Theories, unlike statements or accounts, are expected to explain rather than describe phenomena. As noted in the previous section, the principle of causal primacy tends to impose on explanations a causal structure. For an explanation to be true, it must correctly identify the cause of a set of phenomena—in linguistic terms, it must assign the role of Agent to some argument. But Agent, like all thematic roles, can be assigned to only one argument in every proposition.

Apparent counterexamples like *Bill and John built a house* can only be interpreted as 'John and Bill built the same house together' (a single joint Agent) or 'Bill built a house and John built a different house' (two Agents, but two separate actions). However, statements, accounts, descriptions, and so forth do not require a causal structure. They can be merely lists of propositions that can then be independently true or false, as (1) and (2) were.

Note, too, that the the goal of theories is not 'true things' but rather 'the truth'. *Truth* and *true* differ in some rather interesting ways. *True* belongs to the set of adjectives that form dichotomous pairs (*hot/cold, wet/dry, dead/alive,* and so on) and to the subset of these that express absolute as opposed to scalar differences (*dead/alive, married/single, legal/illegal,* and so on). *Truth,* on the other hand, is a noun derived from *true,* that is, not a noun in its own right that denotes an independently existing class. The referents of such nouns, unlike those of most underived nouns, can have no pretence to existence outside of some Platonic no man's land where qualities are indivisible. Thus even when we are dealing with scalar adjectives, nouns derived from them resist the

229

plural form. For instance, we say *The heat of the materials was variable,* not *the heats.* In the same way we say *The evidence confirmed the truth of the accusations,* not *the truths of the accusations.* Indeed, we are even forced to say *John accepted the truth of the theories of evolution and relativity,* even though the content of these theories is completely different.

Granted that there are sentences like *the old sage on the mountaintop revealed to me many important truths.* But *truths* here refers not to quanta of the Platonic quality but rather to a set of true statements. Reference to a quality rather than to particular instantiations of it must always be a singular. While we can speak of *the prices of the books* or *the colors of the flowers,* we cannot speak of *the truths of the statements.* In other words, the word *truth* does not exist because the nature of things demands that there should be a concept with just these properties of uniqueness, permanence, and indivisibility. It exists because regular processes produce nominalized forms for adjectives and because nominalizations of dichotomous adjectives are obligatorily singular when they refer to a quality rather than to instantiations of that quality. *Truth* is simply part of the structure that we impose on, rather than discover in, the world.

But this cannot be the whole story, otherwise it might imply that if linguistic processes had not formed *truth* in the way they did, there could not have been 'truth' or any similar kind of concept. This is unlikely to be the case.

One aspect of knowledge that has not been considered here is its transmission. All young social mammals do a great deal of learning from their elders, but none do so much as the young of our species. Moreover, the young of our species run a risk that other young mammals do not. It is unlikely, for instance, that young wolves will pick up faulty information about the environment by observing some misguided elder. However, it is always possible for young humans to pick up faulty information or, at any rate, information that a majority of their elders believes to be faulty.

It becomes, therefore, important to codify what is currently believed to have a high probability of being correct and to present the results of this process as incontrovertible. For, after all, if immature minds were left without guidance, how could they arrive at the wisdom of their elders? Thus, even if there had not been *truth,* there would have had to be 'truth', and it would have achieved some label, and shown similar properties.

By looking at our 'search for truth' in this way we can make evolutionary sense out of an activity that otherwise would appear both bizarre and unique. No other species 'searches for truth', but other species, like ours, seek to extend their representations of reality in ways that will be advantageous for them. Moreover, the present analysis of that process should not be taken as a license for either absolute skepticism or absolute relativism. Some of our discoveries really do stand up better than others, some of our beliefs really do have more support. Moreover, our knowledge of the world does tend to increase over time. But it is still 'our' knowledge, the knowledge of a particular species at a particular stage of its existence, rather than some transcendental revelation of a deeper reality.

It is natural that a species with language should initially believe that it had somehow found the route to such revelations. The principle of exhaustiveness seems to tell us that our model of reality is a complete model. Our practical successes in the world seem to tell us that, with the aid of constructional learning and the principle of causal primacy, we can solve any problem that we may set ourselves and overcome any obstacle that lies in our path. But what has been called 'the search for truth' might be better and more modestly regarded as a dialogue—among ourselves, and between ourselves and nature—from which we learn whatever aspects of nature and of ourselves we may need to know in order to go on surviving and seeking—that being the mode of existence that language imposes on us.

But even if ultimate truth is unknowable, some of us may still regard our species as having freed itself from the constraints that operate on other species. Again, an evolutionary viewpoint yields a less rosy picture. If our powers are crucially dependent upon language, and if language is an evolutionary adaptation, then those powers have specific limits, just as do the powers conferred by all other adaptations. Indeed, the picture goes further than this. Every adaptation is potentially a maladaptation. That is to say, anything that fits a creature to a particular set of circumstances may become maladaptive when those circumstances change.

Since the adaptation of language seems to make us so flexible, so fitted to a variety of environments, we may believe that this last constraint does not apply in our case. Whether or not such a belief is valid will form one of the topics of the final chapter, which will try to define what kind of species a species with language really is.

9

The Nature of the Species

Since people first began to think and write about the human condition, their most pressing concern has been to answer the questions: What are we? and, What is our place in nature? It was, and is, a concern made all the more urgent by the uniqueness of the human condition. Such questions, ones that we felt forced to ask, were wholly without precedent, since even the need to ask them sprang from the very condition that was questioned. Although, from time to time, members of our species have tried to draw lessons from the lives of other species, the study of other species has not really been able to enlighten us. It is hardly surprising, then, that over time, as our knowledge of ourselves and even the selves that we knew underwent change, our questions should have received many and widely varying answers.

It would be foolish to suppose that, merely by elucidating the role of language in the life of our species, we could even approach definitive answers to those questions. Perhaps, since we are continually redefining ourselves and nature, we cannot in the nature of things ever arrive at such answers. But we can still, perhaps, learn something that will be of value to us in our struggle to know ourselves and to adjust to a world in which, as far as we know, we have no equals.

NEGOTIATING REALITY

We may perhaps begin with an idea that has recurred several times in this book: that while other species adapt to the environment, we adapt the environment to ourselves. At first sight, this might seem to conflict with what was said at the end of the last chapter. There it was noted that every adaptation is potentially a maladaptation, since the environment of a well-adapted species might change abruptly, and it might then prove impossible for that species to adapt further. Such a species may become extinct, like the vast majority of all species that have so far existed. From this it could be concluded that language, also a form of biological adaptation, might, under certain conditions, prove maladaptive too.

But surely, if language has given us the power to adapt the environment, we do not need to adapt ourselves to it. We can mold it to fit our needs, thus escaping the fate of other species, and achieving at least a kind of collective immortality.

The apparent paradox described above can be resolved, but we shall need to examine each statement with some care. Consider first the relations between creature and environment. Here we can begin to talk, with a little more confidence than before, about the nature of reality.

Note that the position of this book has not been, 'Yes, there are things out there, but we're not sure what they are'. We *are* sure what they are. The problem is that we cannot be sure of our sureness; we cannot lay claim to any knowledge of what reality is *really* like or even know whether it makes any sense to talk about 'what reality is really like' independent of any creature that may observe it. Given that other creatures perceive a reality that we believe must be different from ours, and that we cannot know the content of their version of reality, this state of affairs seems irremediable, and must be accepted as the bedrock of experience. We observe reality from a point defined by our species (and cultural, and individual) makeup, our observations can only be made through representations, and representations always both add to and subtract from what they represent.

We might want to say that all we can know of reality results from a transaction between creatures and the universe, in which properties of creatures and properties of the universe interact to produce varying models of what might be thought to be out there. However, there are times when a species can encounter reality more directly, at least through its effects.

Imagine an island on which no predators fly by night. Moths, then, have no natural enemies, and many varieties develop. Through some unfortunate chance, a pair of bats is brought to the island. They thrive and multiply. Moths begin to disappear in large quantities. To the moths themselves, the means of the departure of other moths is mysterious. Their PRS may be inadequate to give them any representation of a bat. If they cannot detect bats, they cannot practice bat-evasion, so they are quite helpless. The larger and tastier varieties go extinct quite quickly.

Thus, although in the transacted reality of their PRS no potentially lethal force is represented, a reality behind that transacted reality has the power to destroy them. What is more, regardless of whether they can perceive the danger or not, there is nothing they can do about it. Reality, for all species other than ours, may be transacted, but it is ultimately nonnegotiable. We alone can negotiate reality.

The phrase 'negotiating reality' may strike one as a strange choice of words. We tend to think of reality as an immutable rock, something as impossible for us to influence as it is for the moth to influence the bat. A somewhat different view of reality has been adopted here; according to that view, the phrase 'negotiating reality' makes sense in at least two ways. In one way, it can be taken to mean the negotiations by which we tailor the natural things around us to better fit our needs, or what we think are our needs; call this 'negotiating the environment'. In another, it can be taken to mean the negotiations between each individual and the world (which of course includes other individuals) that create the individual's model of reality; call this 'negotiating the model'. Both processes need to be examined in some depth, because they contribute to the nature of our species in complementary ways.

NEGOTIATING THE ENVIRONMENT

One might, perhaps, question whether we are in fact unique in negotiating the environment. Quite apart from exploiting it for their own sustenance, many creatures contribute to changing the face of nature. Beavers, for example, build themselves lodges, and in so doing often dam up streams and cause extensive flooding. But this behavior arises directly from the genetic program of beavers. There aren't any beavers who could sit down and decide not to build lodges. Behaviors that one's biological nature makes one perform do not count as negotiations. For a negotiation to take place, both parties must be capable of change, and at least one must want to negotiate.

Other creatures cannot even *want* to negotiate reality. Without an SRS—a second, language-driven representational system—they have nothing within which acts of negotiation can be conceived. But, within the SRS, we can conceive of things being other than as they are.

To begin to negotiate the environment does not, of course, mean that you enter the negotiation with a clear-cut goal in mind. A clear-cut goal is not needed even in purely human negotiations. Suppose you pass a stall in a market every week and notice an antique ornament for sale. At first it seems ugly, but as it grows familiar, you catch yourself wondering how it would look on your shelf. One day it rains while you are crossing the market and you take shelter in the stall. The ornament is still there; for something to do you ask its price. Even when a low price is mentioned you automatically snort in contempt, for you have no intention of buying . . . or have you? During the week that follows, you decide that the price really was low and think of a friend who has a birthday soon and might like it. Next week you stop and begin to bargain.

When did the negotiation begin? When you started to bargain? Or earlier, when you asked the price? Or earlier still, when you first noticed the ornament among an anonymous heap of others? Pointless to say, as pointless as to say where mind began. Characteristically, one drifts into negotiations, moving opportunistically from stage to stage, sometimes prompted by sheer accident (like the shower of rain), sometimes by the thought of a cunning ruse, but often without any particular goal in mind until the process is irrevocably under way.

In just such a manner our species drifted into negotiating the environment. Take a seemingly simple development like the domestication of the dog. The dog would indeed help us to change nature. It enabled us both to improve the quality of our control over the other animals we were seeking to domesticate and to increase greatly the numbers of those animals, for with its aid a child or two could manage a large flock or herd. This in turn gave us a constant source of meat, butter and cheese, allowing our population to grow. Changes in the landscape and climate followed inevitably as more and more trees and bushes were destroyed to make pasture, for another feature of the changes we negotiate is their cumulative nature.

It is inconceivable, nor is it necessary to conceive, that any ancestor of ours sat by a campfire, saw the light reflected in the eyes of a dog scavenging the perimeter of the camp, and said, either silently or aloud, "Hey, why not domesticate that animal so it can help us look after our flocks?" Almost for sure the thing began by a series of accidents. Perhaps our ancestor tossed a piece of meat to the dog, just to see what would happen. If the dog took it, he or she might have tossed another piece a little closer to see if this shy and savage creature could be persuaded to approach. Or perhaps it began with children finding an abandoned puppy and bringing it into camp. Or, perhaps all these things and others happened at different times and places.

Such events may seem accidental, but they are not the kinds of accident that happen to members of other species. Suppose that the first motive was simply to play with the dog or see if it could be played with. A chimpanzee might play with a dog, but the chimp would soon lose inter-

235

est—and the fact that the playing was successful wouldn't spell anything out to the chimp. It probably wouldn't even perceive the next stage in the negotiation: if the strange, snarling, suspicious animal can be made to play with you, perhaps you could do still more with it, make it come to you when you called, for instance. To do things like that you need persistence and for persistence you need a representation that will keep a goal alive in your mind even when the dog gets restless and starts to snarl and snap at you. This is so even if that goal is not an ultimate goal but just an immediate one, one like 'making the dog obey you'.

We are not alone in domesticating animals. Some species of ants keep aphids in their nests, and milk them for their secretions. But this was not an alternative chosen by ants who might otherwise have been leaf-cutters and grown fungi, if they had felt like it. Both ant-herders and ant-farmers are the ends of long lines of evolution, processes, spread over millions of years and several speciations, in which the various fixed action patterns required for aphid-herding and fungus-growing were built up gradually, and gradually assembled in the mosaic fashion in which evolution works. Only a species equipped with language and all its representational powers could have developed pastoral or agricultural behaviors without first having undergone some genetic change.

Moreover, at the end of their long and laborious process, leaf-cutter ants could only grow fungi. We, in a minute fraction of the time, learned how to grow most of the plant species that exist. Again, things doubtless fell into place accidentally. People camped or perhaps even settled permanently near natural sources of wild grain, noted how the seeds fell to earth and sprouted, remembered these things and turned over and over in their minds representations of them, until it occurred to someone that if seeds from the best plants were collected and if competing species were weeded out, then there would be more to eat. But without an SRS, within which to manipulate these objects and these ideas about them, the chains of action that followed on such thoughts could never have occurred.

As should be apparent from the dog example, the fruits of our negotiations are both cumulative and self-generating. We tame sheep and dogs, and the dogs help us look after the sheep, so we can breed more sheep, which creates a surplus that can be traded to other people, and so on and so forth. But that cannot be the whole story, if what we are doing is really negotiating. In a negotiation, the one who gets must also give.

This is perhaps something that our hunting forebears knew better than we do. Among some surviving hunter-gatherers it is customary to conduct rituals which, in effect, ask pardon for taking the lives of the creatures they must kill in order to eat. At least some interpretations of early cave paintings suggest that our ancestors of 30 Kya had similar rituals and a similar attitude toward nature. But the very success of our negotiations changed all that, so that in recent times it became commonplace to speak of 'taming the wild', of 'the conquest of nature', as if you could conquer something of which you yourself formed a part.

In fact, every negotiation is a trade-off. We may change the environment, but changes in our environment also change us, sometimes in ways that we neither expected nor desired.

TERRITORIALITY AND SOCIAL CONTROL

In the popular wisdom, species are immutable: 'A leopard can't change his spots'. Such adages are often appealed to in order to show that human nature, too, cannot change. Now it may well be the case that we cannot change ourselves into the species that we might wish ourselves to be, and it is also true by definition that species in general can't undergo really radical changes—if they do, we just call them new species. But that doesn't mean that a species that has language cannot change radically, without any of the differences in outward form that would force us to say, 'This is a new species'.

Consider two things, territoriality and social control. In both these areas, our species has changed massively in the very recent past. Both changes arose directly from our abandonment of the hunting-gathering way of life and our adoption of agriculture.

In general, the extent to which a species is territorial is determined by a cost-benefit analysis. If a creature is a member of a species that exploits highly predictable food sources found in a limited area, the creature will be highly territorial; this is because the expenditure of energy used to defend that area against competitors is less than the energy to be gained from exploiting the area. If a creature is a member of a species that exploits food sources of varying predictability spread over a wide area, it will rank low on the scale of territoriality, because the energy needed to defend that area against competitors would be greater than the energy gained from exploiting it.

Of course no conscious cost-benefit analysis was ever carried out, even by our own ancestors. It is simply the case that, if an individual creature with predictable, local food sources does not defend them, it runs the risk of being squeezed out by those conspecifics who do annex and exploit territories (including that of our pacifistic creature) and who will exclude the latter altogether if they can. On the other hand, if an individual creature with unpredictable, scattered food sources insists on defending them, it will spend most of its feeding time patrolling its territory while its competitors happily exploit the areas next door. Thus the genes of 'inappropriately territorial' and 'inappropriately nonterritorial' creatures would alike tend to die out.

Some writers, projecting backward from modern societies with their hedges, fences, guards, frontiers, and 'No Trespassing' signs, have assumed that some 'territorial instinct' is part of our genetic inheritance. The previous paragraph suggests that there is, and indeed can be, no such thing as a 'territorial instinct'. Thus, no creature is innately territorial or nonterritorial; the degree of territoriality, like so much else, arises through a transaction between the creature's needs and the ability of the environment to supply them. A cost-benefit analysis suggests that our ancestors, whether remote or quite recent (that is, up to about 10 Kya), ranked fairly low on the scale of territoriality.

Those ancestors extracted a wide variety of often seasonal and unpredictable foods from wide ranges of savanna—where water supplies, vital to a species such as ours, were widely scattered and seasonal as well. At a later stage, some of our ancestors were predominantly hunters, following game herds regardless of where they led. We know that among most modern hunters and hunter-gatherers the idea of real property is unknown. People own only the things they make and can carry with them. At most, a particular family may have a right to the produce of particular trees, but the land itself is common, and (depending on local conditions) other bands, too, may be permitted to forage over it.

Agriculture changed the picture completely. Where a small plot of land could provide food for an entire family, it now made good ecological sense to defend that land. However, the time that has elapsed since the birth of agriculture is too short for there to have been significant changes in genetic distribution. If we are now territorial, it cannot be that 'territorial' genes in our population have completely replaced 'nonterritorial' ones. Becoming a territorial species was simply part of the price we had to pay nature for the privilege of more closely controlling our own food supply. It was not the whole price, however. Our system of social control, too, had to change.

Every species has some kind of internal organization that, like territoriality, may not be directly determined by any single genetic factor, but derives at least in large part from the interaction between its biological nature and its environment. Such an organization may involve structured masses of individuals, as it does among the social insects. It may involve unstructured masses of individuals, as are found among rabbits or penguins. It may involve small groups that are tightly organized and permanent (like wolves) or loosely organized groups that dissolve and reform over time (like chimpanzees). Or there may simply be single individuals, with or without spouses and offspring (robins, foxes).

If modern hunter-gatherers resemble, at least in their social organization, the hunting-gathering groups of antiquity, we can conclude that our species was originally organized into bands of fewer than fifty individuals. These groups were permanent or semi-permanent, without any internal organization other than a loose and rather flexible pecking-order based primarily on kinship relations, and secondarily on individual age, experience, and skill. This kind of organization is not uncommon among other primates and indeed among social mammals in general. However, what happened to our species after the advent of agriculture was rather like the conversion of a social mammal into a social insect.

Over the period from the birth of agriculture to the present, human social organization has increasingly converged on a type of structure that bears some eerie resemblances to both the structure of the hive and the structure of language. Most often we think of this kind of organization in the context of the state. But the state does not monopolize the type of organization at issue here. The same type can nowadays be found in large businesses, schools, universities, jails, hospitals, monasteries, churches, armies, and indeed any large-scale human enterprise, as well as in the overall structure of all types of state, whether monarchic, oligarchic, theocratic, democratic, fascistic, or communistic.

In contrast to earlier forms of organization, this new system is hierarchical in structure, with a chain-of-command system by which orders are passed down from one level to another. It is compartmentalized, that is, divided into sections (ministries, offices, departments) each of which is semi-autonomous, with a head whose powers are limited to the unit he or she commands and do not extend to units on lower levels. Each compartment is staffed with individuals each of whom performs a single specific role, without sharing, alternating, or mixing roles with others. Power in the hierarchy derives from the position held rather than the qualities of the holder, while relationships between positions are permanently asymmetrical and nonreversible. Despite this, individuals can be advanced from one position to another, if the two positions are of the same type, and if each move is to the level immediately above.

Granted, the change from acephalous kinship-groups to rational bureaucracies took what may seem a considerable length of time, around ten thousand years. That may be a long time in human terms, but in evolutionary terms it is only a moment. If the period from Lucy, our earliest identified ancestor, to the present is represented by a year, the change has taken no more than a day. Granted, too, that the gap between the two social-control systems was bridged by charismatic leaders, kings who were killed if they fell sick, and other phenomena that do not belong in either system. But all of these forms appear to be transitional, that is we do not revert to them. If one exemplar of the modern system is overthrown, we replace it by another, and even modern charismatics (Hitler, de Gaulle) are forced to work though its machinery.

Again, such a change could come about in other species only after a long series of developments. Nowadays, for instance, we find both social bees and solitary bees. Since more complex forms tend to evolve out of simpler ones, rather than vice versa, we may suppose that the remote ancestors of today's social bees were solitaries. However, that change took perhaps millions of generations to bring about. Moreover, like the changing of ants into herders and farmers, it resulted from specific genetic changes in the species involved. No species other than our own has ever revolutionized its social organization in midcareer, so to speak.

The roles that language played in the creation of a new system of social control perhaps exceed, in both variety and importance, those it played in the creation of territoriality. However, nothing can be said about either, for the moment, because they involve the second kind of negotiation, negotiating the model. First we need to look a little more closely at the price we paid for adapting the environment to ourselves.

TECHNOLOGY, INEQUALITY, AND VIOLENCE

It was noted just now that our successes are cumulative. But prices can escalate too.

This chapter began with a seeming paradox: although language, as an evolutionary adaptation, might be expected in certain circumstances to prove maladaptive, it should, at the same time, by virtue of our power to negotiate the environment, be able to preserve us indefinitely against the fate of other species. Now this paradox can be resolved.

It may now seem that in 'adapting the environment to ourselves', we are not 'dominating nature' but rather negotiating with nature to adjust reality in our favor. But even if we replace 'dominating nature' by 'negotiating with nature', the words can still mislead us. The situation recalls that in chapter 8 where 'I' forced 'myself', although 'I' and 'myself' refer to the same creature. Once again, '*cow*-and-*grazing*' language forces us to divide what cannot be divided, for we ourselves form merely a part of the 'nature' that we try to dominate or negotiate with. If we are negotiating with ourselves, we cannot expect the negotiation to leave us unchanged, and we have seen that it does not.

But the changes we undergo do not necessarily all resemble the two changes examined above. Those two, territoriality and new means of social control, fitted us for the new life of agriculture, population increase, and settled dwelling. Nothing, however, dictates that all the results of negotiations will always fit together so well.

In the wake of agriculture, and as a direct consequence of it, came three new things, three things that have shaped the world our species now inhabits: technology, inequality, and violence. To many, technology seems good, inequality undesirable but unavoidable, and violence of any kind a shameful blot on a supposedly rational species. Moreover, many would dispute that these things are new. Technology, they might argue, we have had with us ever since *habilis*, accidentally or on purpose, chipped the first flint, while inequality, like the leopard's spots, forms an inevitable part of our nature, and violence, far from being a novelty, represents the mark of the beast that we are trying to extirpate from our lives.

Unfortunately, things are not quite as simple as that.

Differences in quantity, if great enough, pile up imperceptibly and topple into differences in quality. We and our immediate ancestors were indeed tool-using, toolmaking creatures. But a principled difference can be made between the kind of tool kit anyone can make and carry about and the kind that only specialists can make and that is far too vast and complex to be held in the hands. There is a big gap between hand axes and burins on the one hand, and wheeled chariots, seagoing galleys, stone forts, and siege engines on the other. The first kind of technology had existed for countless millennia, and still exists, barely changed or added to, among the few hunter-gatherers who survive today. The second, only two or three millennia from the birth of agriculture, stood already in place.

To produce this new kind of technology, even the skills of a specialist, honed in an unvarying lifetime, were not enough. It required the concentrated activity of many individuals to build a war galley, let alone a pyramid. It required another cumulative effect: that the new forms of social control be applied to the work. The result of this was *organized technology* and that is what was new.

As for inequality, its status depends on what we mean by the word. If we mean simply that no two members of any species have exactly equal powers, and that some come off better than others in the struggle for the good things of life, then, given genetic variability and a variable world, inequality is simply an inevitable condition of existence. Again, what was new was the application of social control to this condition, so as to yield *organized inequality*.

In a hunting-gathering band, inequalities may exist but they are alleviated by two factors. First, there is little to be unequal *with*—so few possessions and so little power that no matter how great one's ambition, one can hardly exceed one's fellows in wealth, or exercise any lasting control over them. Second, the situation fluctuates, as band members mature or age and alliances between close kin form and reform, so that one need not remain throughout life in an inferior position. New skills can be acquired or old ones improved, advantage can be taken of feuds between others—there are a dozen ways in which status can be improved.

Agriculture institutionalized inequality. Differences in the size of a holding or its fertility, coupled with skill, foresight, energy, luck, or their opposites, served in the space of a few generations to build into society inequalities of wealth and influence that became permanent states and all-but-inescapable traps for individuals. Not every society carried these divisions to their logical limit by setting up a caste system in which inequalities were legally enforced. But most societies with an organized technology created a slave class, all postagricultural societies at one time or another have had institutionalized ranks, and all such societies (including, ironically, even those for which 'social equality' is a stated goal) have privileged elites who are insulated from the masses by power, or wealth, or both.

The third new thing that has shaped our world in the wake of the development of agriculture is violence. Violence seems to some as natural as inequality, and as ancient. It is seen as the product of some 'aggressive instinct' or of 'emotions' that 'reason' could, and should, control. To others, it has seemed a blemish peculiar to our species. This viewpoint became popular a few decades ago, when studies by early ethologists seemed to suggest that ours was the only species in which disputes between individuals were taken to the limit, resulting in the death of at least one participant. In other species, what was observed seemed very different: lots of threatening postures, little physical violence, and a ritual act of submission by the vanquished that the victor always accepted.

Unfortunately, it turned out that this picture came from sampling errors. Few species had been observed for long enough to make sure that lethal combat was really rare, and no one had taken the obvious step of treating murder and manslaughter as a fraction of the innumerable arguments, shouting matches, brawls, tussles, and other sublethal encounters between humans that end, if not with ritual submission, at least with one or both participants backing off. When other species were studied over longer periods, it turned out that many of them, from lions to doves, quite frequently killed one another.

If we are a species that frequently kills its own kind, that is in part due to organized technology. It is hard to kill someone with your bare hands, not much easier with a hand ax (especially if the other person has one too), rather easier with a sword, quite easy with a pistol, and almost unavoidable with a semiautomatic assault rifle. But what makes us really lethal is the application of social control to violence. Unorganized violence, whether between individuals in any era or beween foraging bands in hunter-gatherer times, was and is of its nature impulsive, sporadic, and short-lived. Organized violence, on the other hand, is applied generally, is executed rationally, and persists over long periods. Unorganized violence seldom aims at the destruction of other groups or the enslavement of other individuals; organized violence very frequently does just that.

Anyone who believes that violence comes from within the individual human psyche should first work out the following equation:

Total number of humans killed by violence
minus total killed in wars
minus total killed by own government
minus total killed in revolts against inequalities and injustice
equals total killed by individual violence

It would involve some research to work out the figures. One source suggests that, during the present century alone, 40 million have been killed in wars (the first line to be subtracted) and a staggering 119 million have been killed by their own governments (the second subtraction). But we can be reasonably certain that the figure on the bottom line would be a relatively small proportion of the figure on the top line.

You might say that the number on the bottom line, though relatively small, would still be quite large in absolute terms, and moreover that states could not conduct wars, slaughter their own dissidents, and suppress revolts if a majority of their population did not actively or at least passively support this violence. That must be granted, but we might well ask how such support is achieved—for it is a compliance that often works against the biological interests of the individuals concerned.

The question of compliance cannot be answered until we come to examine how we negotiate our models of reality. And before that, the inter- 243 actions of territoriality, social control, organized technology, organized inequality, and organized violence should be briefly noted, especially as they operate to produce this, the fourth phase of our species' sojourn on earth.

THE FOURTH PHASE

In the beginning, in the first phase, from maybe 200 Kya to around 40 Kya, we were hunters and gatherers in tropical and subtropical regions, distinguished from previous hominid species only by our possession of language and a modest blade technology.

The second phase, from 40 Kya to 10 Kya, began when we (or rather some of us) went north, beat the Neanderthal, and became king of the icy steppes. The constraints of a less friendly environment, as well as competition with a better-equipped rival, led to us to begin negotiating that environment, eventually achieving the domestication of plants and animals that triggered the third phase.

The third phase, from 10 Kya to around four hundred years ago, turned us from loosely organized, nonterritorial creatures to tightly controlled, highly territorial ones; it introduced technology, inequality, and violence, in their *new, postagricultural, organized form.*

Thus each phase contained in itself, as it were, the seeds of the next. For, having once begun to negotiate the environment, humans received the immediate payoff of that process; life became easier and safer (for some at least) and an ever-increasing supply of material objects became available (for some at least), causing the process to continue, and gradually, almost imperceptibly at first, to intensify. Our powers expanded in the same way the language-driven brain had expanded. For each invention, each discovery enlarged the store of information on which constructional learning was based, and this in turn led to new discoveries and new inventions.

Our numbers, too, increased. Normally, a species' numbers wax and wane with the rise and fall of the food supply and with variations in the numbers and strength of its competitors and predators. We no longer had competitors or predators, and apart from occasional droughts and famines, we had a food supply that kept pace with our growing numbers.

The specialization of labor that agriculture brought about meant that some people could now spend their whole lives, not just fleeting parts of them, improving their models of reality. Even if they could never know how things really were, they could surely broaden the store of information on which behavior was based. And, once writing had been invented, this learning too became cumulative. The library at Alexandria might burn, the barbarians might sweep down on Rome, but the processes unleashed by language and husbandry, though they might be delayed and frustrated, had eventually to reach a critical mass.

Suppose you had been born in Elizabethan London. If you had then been given a time machine and the freedom to roam wherever you chose, past or future, you would probably have found yourself (language problems apart) more at home in Babylon or Ur of the Chaldees than you would in your own city a mere half-dozen lifetimes later. For around four hundred years ago, things began to change much more rapidly than before.

Before then, the level of development among agricultural societies had not varied dramatically. Early European visitors to West Africa wrote about its towns and states much as they would have written about the towns and states of some unfamiliar part of Europe, with nothing of the superior tone that later travelers adopted. But, by Elizabeth's time, the inequalities that already existed *within* states began to appear *between* states. A relatively small edge in technology could now be converted into global conquest.

The wealth unleashed by this conquest served as a catalyst. It flowed back into a continent where a model of the universe unchallenged for over a millennium was disintegrating under the blows of schismatic strife, a novel cosmology, and a Baconian and Cartesian approach to knowledge that exalted the practical craftsman over the metaphysician.

Cumulative effects take time, although the time they take is constantly shortening. At first the practical craftsman was hardly aware that the philosophers had espoused him. The tinkerers went on negotiating the environment while the scientists searched for basic principles. These two currents did not merge until about the middle of the last century, and not until this century did Newton and Stephenson meet aboard Apollo. By then, the fourth phase was already well under way.

We have, seemingly, adapted the world to our own needs. All major predators and even many microscopic ones have been tamed or extirpated. Such hunger as remains exists only because of tolerated inequalities between and within nations. Within a few hours we (or some of us) can travel to any corner of the globe and find, almost everywhere, the material riches to which we have grown accustomed. Yet all of this, achieved under the primary drive to ensure our own survival, has brought with it perils never before seen.

Organized technology has brought us weapons able to shatter the biosphere, and organized violence means that we live permanently under

245

the threat of their use. Organized technology, plus the numbers our success as a species created, has polluted our air and water, destroyed our forests, radically changed earth's ecology by massive elimination of other species, punched holes in the protective ozone layer, choked our cities with garbage, and threatened to change earth's climate—with potentially disastrous effects on our densely inhabited coastal plains and on our food supplies. Organized inequality ensures that, in this highly unstable environment, there will be persistent causes of dissension within and between nations. Organized violence, on any level from terrorism to nuclear engagement, will seem to some a natural and quite legitimate self-protective response.

It may suit us to think of these ills as merely due to bad management or individual errors of judgment that can be individually corrected. Such hopes are likely to prove false with regard to some of them, perhaps all. They are simply the consequences of doing the things we have done. Given the power to negotiate reality, and proceeding in the opportunistic manner characteristic of our species, we have tried to adapt the environment to ourselves without first understanding either the environment or ourselves.

By now, perhaps, we are beginning to be aware that we cannot adapt the environment to ourselves without at the same changing both ourselves and the environment in ways whose consequences cannot be foreseen and that, in all likelihood, would not be desired if they could be foreseen. We cannot manipulate reality, we can only negotiate it, and in any negotiation, the more you want to take the more you have to give. These are constraints that not even a species with language can escape. Even our chances of alleviating them are sharply reduced by the some of the ways in which we negotiate our models of reality.

SOME PROBLEMS WITH MODELS

If other creatures cannot negotiate reality, neither can they negotiate their models of reality. A creature with only a PRS has at first only a species model, a model the parameters of which are set by its powers to perceive the world and to process what it perceives into the categories appropriate to the kind of creature it is. Individual experience and learning can add to or modify that model somewhat, but they can neither change it radically nor cause it to be substantially different from that of other members of the species.

Moreover, a creature with only a PRS is more responsible to the environment. It lives one level of representation closer to reality than we do, and though its PRS can only give it a partial and biased view, that view cannot stray too far from the surface of things-as-they-are. If it did, if the PRS presented its owner with counterfactual evidence, the creature would quickly starve or be killed and eaten.

But in a species with an SRS (ours, and perhaps our immediate ancestors') the SRS makes only a selection from the PRS, just as the PRS makes only a selection from the phenomenal world. At first that selection must have been quite a small one, as the selections made from the phenomenal world by early PRSs were quite small ones (remember our flatworms, frogs, and sea anemones). The protolanguage of *erectus* cannot have represented much, in the beginning at least, and the PRS probably steered the behavior of *erectus* much more than it steers ours. (This may be one reason *erectus* developed so slowly and so little, as compared to us.) But the SRS grew far faster than the PRS, and expectedly so: a transaction between two areas of the same nervous system is easier to set up, when one area exists already, than is a transaction between a nervous system and an entire material universe.

The advent of language made it possible for the SRS to represent anything that we could perceive. In the beginning, that representation might not have varied much from one individual to the next, even across wide distances and periods of time, any more than the PRSs of members of other species had varied, and for the same reason. The information that any neurological system contains will be determined in part by individual experience, but the individual experiences of hunter-gatherers do not, and presumably did not, vary very much.

Yet some of the means that would change this state of affairs already existed. Consider how models are acquired. It may be convenient to speak of our creating models for ourselves, but the implication that we do this as single individuals must be resisted. As social animals, we learn far more from those around us than we do from our own efforts. As children, the little information that we can garner by our own puny powers amounts to far less than what our parents, siblings, playmates, and teachers supply. Some of this information is factual, but that may be the least important part. What we learn also are attitudes, emphases, biases, assumptions—things that provide our individual model of reality with a particular structure, and so create the molds into which future information will be poured.

The trouble is, of course, that many things in this input to our model conflict with one another.

Contradictions in a model of reality are something no other species could have had to contend with, because the models of other creatures

contain only *perceptions of* the world, while ours contain both perceptions of the world and *opinions about* it. We saw, in chapter 8, how we
are driven by the nature of secondary representations to actively increase
our knowledge of the world. But knowledge does not lie around like ripe
fruit waiting to be picked. It has to be distilled from a continuous processing and reprocessing of raw information. These procedures, driven
by the consciousness language gave us, and based inevitably on only a
selection of the data that the PRS furnishes us with, become more and
more a matter of *interpretation.*

For our lives are short, and we cannot wait for certainty. (We would
have to wait for ever, anyway.) If we had what we desired, doubtless the
one true and unimpugnable explanation of the world would be available
to all, in a freshman course perhaps. But it is not, so each of us arrives at
his or her best guess, so to speak, of what the world is like. The trouble
is, we do not regard our view of the world as just our best guess. Indeed,
it would be very hard for us to do so, for it is the only reality we will
ever know.

Each model of the world is slightly different from every other model,
and must be, because of the way in which models are constituted. All
models of the world are radical constructions in which three distinct
layers can be distinguished: a species layer, derived from our genetic
heritage; a sociocultural layer, derived from whatever society the accident of birth has placed us in; and an individual layer, derived from our
own unique experiences. As the phases of our species's existence (described in earlier sections of this chapter) began to unroll, the second
and third layers of the model began to diversify. As societies diverged
from one another, and as the divisions within them grew, members of one
group would experience a reality different from that of other groups and
would interpret that reality in different ways. And from this there springs
one of the most salient features of our inner life: the conflict of
representations.

NEGOTIATING THE MODEL

Consider children as they grow. They have to understand the world if
they are to make sense of it and guide their behavior in it. From the moment they become aware that there is a world outside of themselves they
are constantly, and for the most part quite unconsciously, building their
model. It is not a passive process. They do not absorb information passively, as a computer does. They come with their own wants and needs

and they look for a world that will satisfy them, but of course they have to settle for what there is. That is why building the model is a negotiation. They will negotiate the best reality they can, the one that best fits their personalities and their goals.

But isn't this premature? Can we yet say that they have a personality, or goals? Much may be determined by their genetic heritage, but much remains to be formed. Like any negotiation, building one's reality is a two-way street. The negotiating process *forms the individual* even as the individual forms a model of the world. The processes interpenetrate and interact.

Quite early in those processes, children may begin to be aware that the input to their models is not quite homogeneous. Even the parents may disagree on some issues, and children are quick to exploit this and play one off against the other, as best they can. For they need every advantage they can get. They are negotiating, but not from strength—rather, from a great weakness, an inevitable ignorance of the world they are entering that puts them wholly at the mercy of others. They cannot, for the most part, seek information themselves but must depend on what they are given.

Within the circle of the family, particularly within the narrow circle of the nuclear family that has become the norm in developed societies, there is likely to be a fair degree of unanimity about what the world is like. Children negotiate their best adjustment to the family's view. But no sooner have they done this than they are sent to school, and they rapidly become aware, if they have not done so already, that there are other ways of modeling the world.

Conflicts of representation are painful for a variety of reasons. On a very practical level, it is painful to have a model of reality that conflicts with those of the people around you. The people around you soon make you aware of that. But why should this conflict worry people, if a model is only a model, a best guess at reality that each of us makes? Because nobody thinks of it in that way. If the model is the only reality you can know, then that model *is* reality, and if there is only one reality, then the possessor of a different model must be wrong. Besides, models guide behavior, and in a social species, any differences in behavior are a potential cause of friction. It is the odd one in the pack who gets mobbed.

But conflicts of representation are painful for more abstract reasons as well. Since we believe that there is true knowledge to be had somewhere, then there really *should* only be one model, if only we could find out what it is. In fact, as in any negotiation, we sooner or later settle for what

Chapter Nine

we can get: we negotiate a model of the world that fulfils some of our goals, satisfies some of our needs, and reconciles us to at least some of those with whom we must spend our lives. That becomes reality, for us.

Yet despite the provisional, almost contractual basis of what we come to believe about the world, few of us see things as provisional. An individual, A, sincerely believes that his or her model of the world represents the world as it really is. If A were right, and if it turned out that B's model differed from A's, then A would be justified in concluding that B could not or would not see reality as it should be seen. Several possible explanations present themselves to A. B might be too stupid to see things correctly, in which case B should be instructed. B might be too devious and selfish to admit that A is right, in which case B should be confronted and forced to face the facts. Or B might reject the right view because B is evil, in which case B should be fought and overcome.

But A's logic, which would be impeccable if its major premise were correct, is gravely flawed. A's model merely represents what A has negotiated on the basis of personal experience and in response to personal needs, needs formed in part by precisely that experience. Meanwhile B, having arrived through slightly different experiences at a different model, has followed an identical chain of argument to precisely the same conclusions about A. How can A and B hope to avoid conflict?

They could, if they would both regard the creation of a model as an ongoing negotiation that lasts all of one's life. But this is like saying that you must spend your whole life rehearsing for a performance that will never come. We do not have models for the sake of having models, and though we may believe that their purpose is to give us a true picture of reality, that purpose can, at best, only take second place to the purpose of getting us through life. That is why all animate creatures have representations: not so that they should know the truth about the world, but so that they should be able to survive and function effectively in the world.

So, we have to settle as soon as we can for the best model we can get. And sometimes that model may be strange indeed. For, as already noted, the bonds that tie secondary representations to the world of biological reality are loose and indirect.

DYSFUNCTIONAL REPRESENTATIONS

A soldier advances across a barren plain into withering machine-gun fire. A heretic refuses to recant and goes up in flames. A sacrificial victim, wreathed in flowers, mounts the stone platform and bares his breast

250

for the knife. A young man, torn by imagined guilt, castrates himself. Another, rejected by a lover, drives his car off a bridge.

Whether we approve or disapprove of some or all of these actions, we have to agree that no creature other than ourselves could perform them. One hears occasional anecdotes of animals that kill themselves, but these are dubious at best. Other creatures obey their biological imperatives: to survive and to breed if they can. But what we have here are cases of *antibiological conduct*. How is this possible?

It is possible because while we are, within limits, free to negotiate what we believe, we are not free to negotiate the representations on which our beliefs are based. The content of those representations is determined for us by the society we enter and the experiences we undergo. And once we have accepted what the world is like, we do not welcome the thought of changing our assumptions again. Even though it may cost us our lives, we are unable (if there seems to be no alternative) or unwilling (even if there are highly visible alternatives) to abandon the certainties we have bargained for so hard. We may resist doing so to the very end, or until (as happened to Saul on the road to Damascus) our very bodies rebel against our choice.

Nothing could speak the power of linguistic representations so forcefully as antibiological acts. You may think that the five cases with which this section opened are not really all of the same type. Some involve a sacrifice of the self for others, or for an ideal, which some of us may see as admirable, even if we ourselves would not perform it. Others look more personal and misguided, even selfish: the self-castrator and the suicide-for-love. This may be so, but on a deeper level all are indeed acts of the same kind.

For to commit any of them you would first have had to derive, from the minds of others or from your own mind, linguistic representations of these acts as the desirable or the only possible ones, given the circumstances in which you found yourself. Acts of self-destruction can only seem desirable or unavoidable within a given context, a special view of the world from which certain factors have been edited out and certain others heavily underlined. If we say 'we can see no way out' or 'we can do no other', this simply means that there is no acceptable alternative within that view.

Three of our cases were 'social', two were 'individual'. In the last two, society is just as much outraged as biology. In the first three, some society or other would have been proud, not ashamed of the victims.

Thus some questions raised earlier in the chapter can now be an-

251

swered: How can people adjust to systems of social control that are alien to their original natures? How can they actively support or passively condone the organized slaughter of other species members? It is because they must negotiate their reality, and in this negotiation, as asymmetries of power and status increase, the bargaining position of most of us is gravely weakened. Part of being powerful is getting the best of negotiations, that is, imposing your reality on other people.

Those who have power in a society control its myths, which is to say the linguistic constructs that supposedly enshrine the common purposes of the society. Even if these myths are not formally taught, they are quickly absorbed from those around us. Perhaps no alternatives will be presented to us, or the only alternatives offered may identify us, if we choose them, with despised and persecuted minorities. And we cannot say, 'We don't like any of this, we will stand aside, we won't negotiate'. We have to negotiate. We have to have *some* model of the world, or—if we can get around the language of 'we' and 'having'—some model of the world has to be part of us, and grow in us, and guide our conduct, if we are to be creatures at all.

Our Place in Nature

Thus it seems that despite the vast and unprecedented powers that language has bestowed on us, some of the consequences of having it may indeed threaten our continued existence on earth. We might overcome the consequences of our too rapid rise—the threats of nuclear destruction and a deteriorating biosphere—if we could understand one another and work effectively together to overcome them. But, though our models of reality differ inevitably from one another, we find it hard to accept that they are merely models and therefore negotiable. Moreover, in a world of organized inequality, we often cannot get to build models that are truly our own; often, without realizing it, we have to accept the models of others, built not for our benefit but to ensure that those others continue in all their power and privilege.

In this predicament, we might wish that we had someone to counsel us—some other species, perhaps, that shared our doubts and uncertainties. Indeed a part of our predicament might seem to be our very aloneness. It is hardly surprising, then, that we look up at the stars on clear nights and wonder if around any of them there circles a planet on which beings as perplexed as we are could be found.

Over recent years, many people have wondered why, if in the universe there are countless other planets, and if on at least some of these planets there is what is called 'intelligent life', no inhabitant of such a planet has as yet made contact with us. The lack of such contact has led others to claim that we may, after all, constitute the only 'intelligent life' in the universe.

As yet, there is simply not enough evidence to determine who is right. But if there are no other beings like us, a sinister reason may suggest itself for their absence. Perhaps language is, after all, terminally dysfunctional. Perhaps any species that achieved language would seek to take control of its planet, just as we have done. However, a biosphere irreparably damaged, whether accidentally through reckless use of it, or deliberately through conflicts fought with hyperdestructive weapons, might, in a relatively short time, bring any such species to extinction.

This suggestion is pessimistic and purely speculative, but it does contain one plausible assumption: that wherever life evolves, it will sooner or later produce creatures that think and communicate—even if they do not look like us—more or less as we do.

This suggestion runs counter to mainstream evolutionary theory, which has consistently regarded evolution as lacking any particular goal. Nature throws up a profusion of forms, evolutionary necessity selects those that function best under current circumstances, and there does not seem to be anything that might be taken for an overall plan. But mainstream evolutionary theory has concentrated on the more purely material aspects of life, and it has failed to grasp the evolutionary role of representational systems.

Teleological views of evolution have acquired a bad name in the business. However, a teleology based on the progressive growth of representations, culminating in the representational system of language, is proof against the arguments that are commonly raised against other teleologies.

For instance, the fact that most living creatures have poor representational systems and yet function efficiently, or that some have persisted for hundreds of millions of years without changing or improving their representational equipment, has no relevance here. All that is required is that *some* creatures should improve their representations. And since more efficient representations paid off in terms of survival and gene transmission, creatures with better representations were bound to prosper. Moreover, given the conservatism of neural structures, representational gains were bound to be passed on to successor species, thereby eventually providing a basis for further advances.

Such has certainly been the case on earth. But since it is hard to imagine a planet on which ignorance of one's environment and failure to take advantage of its opportunities would lead to longer life and greater fecundity than their opposites, we may assume, until we are in a position to test it empirically, that on other planets, too, the forces of evolution tend to produce better and better representational systems, and will eventually yield creatures whose ways of dealing with reality are not unlike ours.

If evolution has a direction, and if that direction leads inevitably to conscious creatures capable of moral choice, what, if anything, does that tell us about the world we inhabit? Could the world of material forces that our rational inquiries seem currently to reveal turn out to be just another layer of illusion? Could some spiritual world still underlie appearances?

It could indeed. If there did exist, behind the transacted reality that we know, behind the brute evolutionary reality that we can only guess at, some other and yet deeper reality, there is no way in which creatures such as ourselves could rationally apprehend it. Mystics are well aware of this, more so perhaps than others, who, whether secular or religious, have all too often exaggerated the potential scope of human reason. But no attempt will be made here to answer questions about ultimate realities. Perhaps in the nature of things they cannot ever be satisfactorily answered, although this does not mean that they should not be asked.

Indeed, we may have to resign ourselves to never knowing, with any degree of certainty, what our true place in the universe is or what we may eventually become. But we can at least achieve one indispensible prerequisite for such knowledge. We can know how we came to be, how we achieved both power over the rest of nature and an awareness of our own being. We can recognize the frail foundations on which human reason is built: language, added to reasoning powers that we largely share with other primates. Eventually, with a modest acceptance of our own fallibility, we may even learn how to live in balance with a world that we cannot change without changing, even perhaps destroying, ourselves.

Epilogue

This has been a book about language and what language has meant to our species. As noted both in the introduction and at the beginning of the final chapter, language, for all its importance, cannot account for every aspect of our behavior. Moral and ethical issues, human emotions, and much else that is sometimes subsumed under the heading of 'heart' or 'soul' or 'spirit' cannot be so easily explained by language alone, despite the fact that, without language, these issues and emotions could not be expressed.

For instance, a glib equation of morality with 'what society puts into our SRS' or religion with 'the need to believe in a single, nonvisible, causative Agent' simply will not do. There are too many awkward counterexamples. Some highly moral acts may run dead counter to social injunctions, may be only too clearly the product of a single active conscience. Similarly, not all religions feature a single omnipotent creator, yet religions of one sort or another have existed in every human society. If this fact arises from a human need to reverence something outside of, and greater than, oneself, then language alone cannot explain such a need.

However, our possession of language *is* sufficient to account for what may seem to many the most salient and distinctive aspects of our nature: our 'rational' capacities, our 'intelligence', our ability to control our environment, our elusive yet ever-present consciousness of self, and the force that drives at least some of us constantly to seek a better understanding of the world. These are what forged the gulf that now seems to divide us from other species. They are also the things most responsible for the subjective feeling of 'what it is like to be a human'.

For, more than any other factor, language created our species, and created too the world that our species sees. Only language could have broken through the prison of immediate experience in which every other

255

creature is locked, releasing us into infinite freedoms of space and time. Only language could have refined the primitive categories of other creatures and built them into complex systems that could describe and even seem to explain the world. Only language could have given us the power to manipulate those systems through the power of constructional learning, designing futures different from our past and then seeking to make those imagined futures real.

Yet we cannot flatter ourselves that language was a discovery born of our own superior skills. On the contrary, it is a feature of our species biology written into the genetic code. Its more superficial aspects—the particular sounds and words used by the particular groups that each of us belongs to—must be learned, but that part which enables us to link words meaningfully together grows in us as naturally as do our physical powers.

For the foundations of language lie far back in the evolutionary history of animate creatures, creatures with goals and purposes derived from their own needs. Most of those foundations we share with other species. Only evolutionary chance triggered, in our ancestors, the emergence of the first stumbling attempts at language. And even these were no more than a haphazard stringing together of meaningful elements, effective in helping our forefathers to exploit the environment more efficiently, but still not adequate to change that environment in any significant way. True language had to wait on a further evolutionary accident, but one of a different kind: not a change in behavior, but rather a change in neural organization that caused us to slot meaningful symbols into formal structures and to do so quite automatically, without any conscious effort in either production or comprehension.

The result was an adaptation of a type never before seen. Language bestowed on its possessor powers that yielded far more than mere survival, powers that effectively conferred on our species the stewardship of earth. Yet, formidable as those powers were, they carried within them the seeds of destruction. Language had given us, not enough, but too much: not just the stewardship of earth, but the capacity to destroy species weaker than ourselves, and even features of the environment on which our own survival might depend.

Yet language is at the same time the nurturer and facilitator of all that is best in us, all that seeks to avoid such a fate and to bring us back into unity with the rest of creation. It is language, and language alone, that makes it possible for us to dream of a world of peace, freedom, and justice where we might live in harmony with that nature of which, after all, we form only a dependent part. If we are ever to realize such dreams, if we are even to survive as a species at all, we must as a very minimum first understand how it is that we think and behave as we do.

For the position in which we find ourselves is rather like that of a speaker at a scientific congress who describes findings made with the help of some novel machine. How does the machine work? the others present will want to know. What are its specifications? What parameters can it measure, and with what margins of error? If to these and similar questions the only answer is, 'I don't know', or 'Pretty well anything, I guess', the speaker will be hooted from the podium.

Yet that novel machine of which we can say so little is simply the human mind. It is a mind that pretends to be at least potentially able to reveal the profoundest mysteries of the universe, yet it cannot solve the simplest social problems that our species constantly creates for itself. Indeed, the machine may consist of little more than powers common to a wide range of creatures, but focused and amplified by the single evolutionary adaptation of language. Seeming to us no more than the glass through which we see our world, language is in fact the subtle, many-layered lens that created that world—the lens without which all that we know would dissolve into chaos.

What difference does it make, our utter dependence on language? No one can deprive us of it, and the ordered world that it shows us seems very convincingly to exist. Why should language concern us, why should we not simply ignore it and proceed undisturbed with the serious business of our lives?

It makes a great deal of difference. If our nature is indeed as it has been described here, we can understand neither ourselves nor our world until we have fully understood what language is and what it has done for our species. For although language made our species and made the world we inhabit, the powers it unleashed drove us to understand and control our environment, rather than to explore the mainspring of our own being. We have followed that path of control and domination until even the most daring among us have begun to fear where it may lead. Now the engine of our quest for power and knowledge should itself become the object that we seek to know.

Notes

Introduction

Evidence for the closeness of the genetic relationship between humans and chimpanzees comes from a variety of sources, for example, Yunis, Sawyer, and Dunham (1980) and Chiarelli (1985) on chromosomal resemblances; King and Wilson (1975) on similarities in macromolecules; and Deninger and Schmid (1976) on the relationship between human and chimpanzee DNA. This material suggests a relatively recent common ancestry. For estimates of the recentness of the split, see Sarich and Wilson (1967), Szalay and Delson (1979), Sibley and Ahlquist (1984), and Pilbeam (1986), among many others.

An exceedingly generous estimate of what animals might be able to experience in terms of consciousness is found in Griffin (1981). The whole issue of 'animal consciousness' is of course simply an extra dimension of the 'other minds' problem in philosophy (see, for example, Nagel 1974).

Opinions vary on the precise relationship between brain size and human evolution. Claims that sheer brain size produced human capacities, rather than vice versa, tie in with 'naive continuist' attitudes towards language origins (see chapter 1); for instance, Passingham (1979) argues that a certain level of brain size may have been necessary for the '*intellectual* achievement' of '*inventing* language' as a 'tool' (emphasis added). Godfrey and Jacobs (1987) contains a useful discussion of three hypotheses on brain-size increases among hominids: gradual and uniform development; punctuated development at species breaks; and autocatalytic development (increased brain size led to new selectional pressures, which in turn favored greater brain size). They find the first hypothesis 'flawed', and the evidence as yet inadequate to decide between the second and third. However, Grusser and Weiss (1985) conclude that the evidence does not support a punctuated equilibrium hypothesis. The issue is murky, in large part due to the patchy nature of the fossil evidence (see references cited in notes on chapter 6), but a language-driven autocatalytic model is supported by Falk (1987).

The quotation from Darwin is taken from the Princeton (1981) edition of *The Descent of Man*, 105. It is remarkable that even avowed followers of Darwin never developed or even acknowledged such insights as these; Richards (1987), a thorough study of Darwin's impact on late nineteenth and early twentieth-century thinking, shows that the only aspect of Darwin's ideas on language that interested Darwin's contemporaries was his comparison of the evolution of species with the evolution of languages—a connection between 'language and species' that will emphatically not be pursued in these pages! Typical of more recent work on the development of Darwinian ideas is Jacobs (1985), which contains *no mention at all* of language as a distinguishing human characteristic.

The example of the snowy mountain among grassy hills is taken from the introduction to Lumsden and Wilson (1983). The belief that only an appropriate degree of size and/or complexity in natural or artificial information-processing machinery is needed to produce consciousness is implicit in much recent work in artificial intelligence (e.g., Dennett 1978, Churchland 1988).

For a good survey of developments in linguistics over the past few decades, see Newmeyer (1986). A convenient summary of the earlier history of linguistics can be found in Robins (1967).

Chapter One

The 'official' Neo-Darwinian position on evolution (and the human place in it) is generally agreed to have been expressed by Dobzhansky (1955, 1962) and Mayr (1963). (See also Monod 1971.) For a more recent summary (with some perhaps overly acerbic comments on rival views) see Dawkins (1987). This 'gradualist' account, with its emphasis on slow and relatively regular change at an individual level, has been challenged by a theory of 'punctuated equilibrium' (Eldredge and Gould 1972, Gould and Eldredge 1977). The theory proposes that species undergo long periods of relative stagnation followed by relatively brief periods of rapid evolution.

For animal communication in general see Sebeok (1977), and Griffin (1982); for primate communication, see Snowden et al. (1982), and Harre and Reynolds (1984). Plooij (1978) attempts to establish links between chimpanzee communication and human language.

For the anti-formalist case see, for example, Hockett (1968), which is reviewed from a formalist viewpoint in Lakoff (1969), and Givon (1979), especially chapter 1. The formalist case is expressed by Chomsky (1968, 1975, 1980) and Lightfoot (1982), among others.

Examples of fairly explicit continuist scenarios are to be found in Hockett and Ascher (1964), Parker and Gibson (1979), and Browne and Greenwood (1988). The general issues involved are discussed from a continuist viewpoint in Steklis and Raleigh (1979) and Sarles (1988). For a variety of scenarios, some overtly continuist, see Harnad et al. (1976). Gyori (1988) provides a sometimes insightful, but overly functionalist, review of the issues.

Vervet communication is described in Seyfarth, Cheney, and Marler (1980), Seyfarth and Cheney (1982), and Cheney (1984). (The latter deals specifically with the development of categorization in vervet infants.) For a review of deceptive practices among primates, including the use of alarm calls to deceive conspecifics (reported anecdotally for vervets, guenons, and chimpanzees), see Whiten and Byrne (1988).

Russell's approach to meaning and reference is discussed in Ayer (1972, especially chapter 2) and Jager (1972); see also Donellan (1966). De Saussure (1966, first published in French in 1915) gave a clear account of word-concept relations that was largely ignored by contemporary (and some later) philosophers, with the significant exception of Ogden and Richards (1923). However, de Saussure advances a position ("There are no pre-existing ideas, and nothing is distinct before the appearance of language," p. 112) that is incompatible with the material surveyed in chapter 4 below.

The concept of mental activity as representational modeling was first developed by Craik (1943). For a somewhat different psychological approach to representation in our species, see Fodor (1975, 1981). A good discussion of the representational systems of other species, relevant also to the material in chapter 4, is found in Roitblatt (1982), which also contains critical comment from a variety of viewpoints. However, while Roitblatt recognises that representations do not include all the features of things represented, he does not draw sufficient attention to the fact that they must, necessarily, *add* properties.

Exactly how a painting 'represents' is discussed from a philosopher's viewpoint by Ziff (1960); predictably, it turns out to be more complex than it seems!

For the decline of the sense of smell among primates see Fobes and King (1982). References for the Sommers-Keil predicability tree are cited in the notes on chapter 3. The perceptual system of frogs was first described in detail in Lettvin et al. (1955); similar work on toads is reported in Ewert (1976, 1987).

The debate on 'innate' ideas goes back at least as far as Locke and Descartes. For some negative responses to the idea that the principles underlying language are innate, see Goodman (1972), and Putnam (1975, ch. 5). Further discussion of 'innateness' in species generally is found in Chapter 4 of this book.

For avoidance behavior and other fear indicators in primates, see Yerkes and Yerkes (1936), and Hebb (1946). However, Kortlandt (1962) observed chimpanzees in the wild who, under natural conditions, evinced no fear symptoms at the sight of live snakes (although they did give them a wide berth!).

Chapter Two

Many of the issues dealt with in this chapter are covered (from a rather different perspective) by Jackendoff (1983).

The idea of language as a map was first elaborated, although quite differently, by Korzybski (1958). The introductory chapters of a good technical work on the principles of cartography, such as Fisher (1982), should serve as a corrective to simplistic ideas of how maps represent. The history of how maps developed out of pictorial images (Harvey 1980) is equally instructive in this respect.

That there is not necessarily any formal distinction between human concept formation and animal responses to categories of stimuli was recognised by Lenneberg (1967). The reactions of frogs to real and bogus bugs are described in Grusser and Grusser-Cornelis (1968, cited in Guthrie 1980, 98–99.

Much even among recent literature (e.g., Medin et al. 1987) assumes that object categories are based on perceptual rather than functional criteria. Categories chosen for examination are often higher order abstractions like *tree* or *bird*. Work by Berlin et al. (1973) and Brown et al. (1976) strongly suggests that the initial human vocabulary operated at about the level of the genus, rather than that of the order, family, or species (see further discussion in chapter 6).

For perspectives on 'mental illness' that differ dramatically from the 'medical model', and hence from standard definitions of conditions such as 'paranoia', see, among others, Laing (1967), Ruitenbeek (1972), Szasz (1961).

A linguist's account of the 'classical', bundles-of-criteria theory of meaning is provided by Katz and Postal (1964). For the prototype theory of object categorization, see Rosch (1973), and Rosch and Lloyd (1978). Medin et al. (1987) reviews prototype theory along with other categorization theories. Neurologically based approaches are discussed in Haber and Hershenson (1980). A convenient summary of linguistic thinking on semantics can be found in Palmer (1976). Hierarchical structures in semantics are treated by Baldinger (1980) and Hervey (1979); the latter applies the principle to an analysis of Chinese vocabulary. There is little disagreement among linguists, however, with the notion that our understanding of semantics is by far inferior to our understanding of syntax.

The very limited extent to which sign language can be said to be iconic is indicated in works such as Stokoe (1978) and Kyle and Woll (1985). Klima and Bellugi (1979, ch. 3) explicitly addresses the issue of iconic versus abstract representation, showing that even where signs are originally iconic they rapidly become more formal and abstract.

The original hypothesis concerning linguistic constraints on the naming of colors is found in Berlin and Kay (1969); for a recent criticism, see McLaury (1987). The 'opponent' theory of color discrimination was first developed by Hering (1920) and confirmed neurologically for primates by de Valois and Jacobs (1968). The relationship between neurological and linguistic approaches to color vision is described in Kay and McDaniel (1978); see also Stephenson (1973).

The classic work on 'bee language' is von Frisch (1967). For robins and their territorial behavior see Lack (1965).

The lexical expression of the semantic area 'location-possession-existence' is discussed in Bickerton (1981), based on data originally collected by Clark (1970).

Chapter Three

Chomsky (1957) was perhaps the first to distinguish systematically between semantically anomalous sentences such as *colorless green ideas sleep furiously* (as opposed to *revolutionary new ideas occur infrequently*) and syntactically anomalous sentences such as *new occur revolutionary infrequently ideas.* See also comments in Putnam (1961; and 1975, ch. 4).

Wittgenstein's 'meaning as use' doctrine is found in Wittgenstein (1951).

The predicability tree was developed by Keil (1979, 1981) based on work by Sommers (1959, 1963).

The definition of *any* in Webster's Third International Dictionary begins: "one indefinitely out of more than two; one or some indiscriminately of whatever kind; one or another; this, that or the other—used as a function word especially in interrogative and conditional expressions to indicate one that is not a particular or definite individual of the given category but whichever one chance may select. . . ." The definition continues for another *twenty-five lines.*

Quine's opinions on tense are given in Quine (1960, 170). The idea that grammatical particles express topological relations, and thus provide a conceptual framework for our analysis of nature, is developed thoroughly in Talmy (1986); see also Talmy (1977, 1983). The claim that Hopi and English make different analyses of reality can be found in Whorf (1956).

The model of syntax described in these chapters is developed principally in Chomsky (1981, 1982, 1986). However, it represents the logical extension of trends begun by Ross (1967), and it incorporates ideas developed by Cattell (1976), Emonds (1976), and Reinhart (1976), among others. X-bar theory was first developed by Jackendoff (1977); Stowell (1981) first clearly showed how it rendered obsolete the clumsy 'phrase structure rules' that had been a feature of all previous generative models. The motivation for assuming binary branching as a universal principle is found in Kayne (1984). The germs of a theory of thematic roles are to be found in Gruber (1965), and were further developed in Jackendoff (1972). Other works relevant to the model discussed include Aoun and Sportiche (1983) and Williams (1980).

For a pre-Chomskyan treatment of case in English, see, among others, Gleason who states that "In English case is restricted to pronouns" (1955, 162).

Chapter Four

Roitblatt (1982), in common with many psychologists, restricts use of the term 'representation' to '*remnants* of *previous* experience' that affect '*later* behavior'. In his well-known attack on representational theories, it is clear that Gibson (1979, especially 279–80) assumed a concept of 'representation' very different from that proposed here. The present approach owes much to the seminal work of Craik (1943). The definition of information is from Bateson (1979, 62–3).

For general information about nervous systems, one highly accessible source is the special September, 1979 issue of the *Scientific American,* which is devoted to the brain. Sarnat and Netsky (1974) provide a general account of the phylogeny of nervous systems. Although devoted mainly to the human brain, Young (1978) has much useful information about brain functions. Churchland (1988) includes a brief but lucid account of some of the aspects of neural evolution and neurophysiology most relevant to the topics of this book; see also Camhi (1984, ch. 3).

There is, perhaps, still no better account of sundews and other carnivorous plants than that of Darwin (1875). For the behavior of sea anemones, see Sund (1958) and Ward (1962).

The way in which creatures represent and respond to their environment falls into the domain of neuroethology; two useful introductions to this field are Guthrie (1980) and (easier reading) Camhi (1984). Neuroethology is in part an attempt to account for the observations of ethology, for which the work of Tinbergen (1951, 1972a) is still basic; for a critical (if far from consensual) account of how well this goal has been fulfilled, see Hoyle (1984). In fact much of our knowledge of sensory and motor cell functioning is derived from the study of the "behaviorally boring glob of squishy protoplasm" (Hoyle 1984, 377), the marine mollusk *Aplysia* (Kandel 1976; Kandel and Schwartz 1982).

The escape mechanisms of the cockroach are described in Camhi et al. (1978) and Camhi (1980). For heat sensing in pit vipers, see Barret et al. (1970). The classic description of mammalian visual systems is provided by Hubel and Wiesel (1960, 1963, 1968, 1977).

Neurons intermediate between sensory and motor neurons (interneurons) are dealt with from a variety of viewpoints in Brazier (1969). For a detailed discussion of neurons that monitor internal states, see Chernigovskiy (1966). Thresholds and habituation are described in most introductory texts in zoology and neurophysiology; various aspects of habituation are discussed in much greater detail in the two volumes of papers edited by Peeke and Herz (1973). The neural mechanisms that raise and lower thresholds are lucidly described by Camhi (1984, ch. 3). Crayfish habituation is dealt with by Krasne (1969).

Data on stalking behavior in lizards is derived from the author's own observations of common house-dwelling species in the Caribbean and West Africa; for some of the constraints on lizard behavior, particularly limitations on energy expenditure, see Huey et al. (1983).

The gaping behavior of thrushes and the range of stimuli that will elicit it are given by Tinbergen (1951, ch. 4).

Sutra 42 of the Tao Teh Ching, as cited by Givon (1979), reads:

> From Tao, one is born.
> From one, two;
> From two, three;
> From three, all.

For the categorization capacities of pigeons, see Herrnstein (1979, 1985).

How *Philanthus* orients itself is described by Tinbergen (1951, chs. 4 and 6) summarizing a more detailed study originally published in German and reprinted as Tinbergen (1972b). Original work on 'provisioning' by *Ammophila*, carried out by Dutch naturalists, is described in Tinbergen (1958). For the use of echolocation by bats for orienting purposes, see Griffin (1958). Knudsen et al. (1987) provide a general discussion of internalized maps. That maps do not need to be visual is shown in studies of how owls map auditory space (Knudsen 1982, 1984).

Data on the responses of individual monkey cells are from Perrett et al. (1982), Perrett, Smith, Potter, et al. (1985), and Perrett, Smith, Mistlin, et al. (1985). See also work by Kendrick and Baldwin (1987) on the recognition capacities of temporal cortex cells in sheep. Aspects of the social life of primates that may have been shared by our remote ancestors are discussed by Ghiglieri (1987); see Krebs and Davies (1987) for a more general view of the behaviors of social mammals.

On the vexed question of intelligence in other creatures, see Thomas (1980), who tries to establish some eight levels of difference between the most primitive creatures and primates. McPhail (1987) holds that the mechanisms of intelligence are uniform across species; however, see Thomas (1987) and other critical responses to the McPhail article. Bickerton (1987) suggests that the word 'intelligence' itself may be the problem.

Teilhard de Chardin (1959) represents an attempt to reconcile Christianity with Darwinian evolution; McMullin (1985) develops a similar approach in a variety of ways. For an uncommonly hostile review of the first-named work, see Medawar (1961).

The lack of directionality in evolution is emphasized in many standard evolutionary texts, such as Dobzhansky (1955) and Hardin (1959). The reference to Monod's work is again to Monod (1971). The 'smart dinosaur' possibility originates from Russell and Seguin (1981), and is further discussed in Wilford (1985).

Chapter Five

The title of the chapter is owed to Begley (1982).

Reference to a 'language organ' is found in Chomsky (1975) and much subsequent work by the same author; see also Harnad et al. (1976, 57) for a significant exchange between Chomsky and Steven Harnad, discussed in Bickerton (1981, ch. 4, fn. 1); see also Lenneberg (1967). The reference to 'fossilism' is from Bickerton (1985).

For the length of time since the common ancestor of chimpanzees and humans, see references in notes on the introduction.

Early work on ape 'language' is described readably but rather uncritically by Linden (1975). Premack (1985) and Savage-Rumbaugh (1986) incidentally cover much of the same ground but from a more critical perspective. Hoban (1986) discusses ape 'language' experiments from a more linguistic viewpoint, and includes a thorough demolition of the popular belief that 'apes can learn sign language'. There were always those who were sceptical about the entire research program (see, e.g., Sebeok and Umiker-Sebeok 1980), but the deathblow to the more extreme claims about ape 'language' was given by Terrace et

265

al. (1979), who proved to most people's satisfaction that syntax lay beyond the capacity of apes. (See also Terrace (1979) for a fuller background to these findings, including the sixteen-item string cited in this chapter.) The use of an 'if-then' symbol and other aspects of chimpanzee Sarah's vocabulary are described in Premack (1972). The experiments designed to test whether apes are capable of true reference are described in Savage-Rumbaugh (1986).

Parallel work on other species is described in Schusterman and Krieger (1984) for sea lions, Herman et al. (1984) for dolphins, and Pepperburg (1987) for the African grey parrot. For the communicative behavior of chimpanzees in the wild, Lawick-Goodall (1971) is still a good introduction.

The examples of ape utterances are taken from Terrace (1979). The examples of Seth's utterances are from a recording made by Robert Wilson (see Wilson (1985) for further information about Seth).

An explicitly Haeckelian approach to language origins was first adopted by Lamendella (1976), with the appropriate qualifications (see also Parker and Gibson (1979)). Haeckel's recapitulationism is discussed in more general terms by Gould (1977).

The literature on child language acquisition is immense, although surprisingly little of it is directly relevant to the issues raised here. (For an observational treatment, see Brown (1973); for more theoretical approaches see Pinker (1984), and Berwick (1985)). Problems that children have with passives have been discussed by Bever (1970); problems with questions are dealt with by Klima and Bellugi (1966), among others. On the early development of syntax, see Bowerman (1973).

Prelinguistic regularities at the two-word stage are well documented cross-linguistically by Bowerman (1973). She, however, interprets such regularities as evidence for the existence, at this stage, of a grammar more primitive than, but substantially along the lines of, the mature adult's grammar. For a thorough account of early child vocabulary, its concrete nature, and its tendency to overgeneralize see Clark and Clark (1977, chs. 8 and 14)

The comparison of child and ape (Washoe's) utterances is taken from Gardner and Gardner (1974).

The strange case of Genie is described in Curtiss (1977), from which the examples of Genie's speech are taken. For feral children in general, see Malson (1972).

The Russonorsk example is from Broch (1930), cited by Fox (1983). For pidgins and pidginization, see Bickerton (1981, ch. 1). Rather different approaches are found in Hall (1966), and Muhlhausler (1986), to mention two.

The example sentence *Bill is too crazy e to live with e* is a case of 'null operator movement', for which see Chomsky (1985), and Browning (1987). The claim that all subcategorized arguments must appear somewhere in surface structure must be modified by the case of what one might call 'null generic' complements, for instance, *he ate e*, where *e* clearly indicates 'something unspecified but edible'. By no means all two-argument verbs will allow this; compare *he ate* with *he convinced*.

The first example of agrammatic speech is from Goodglass (1973); the second is from Schwartz et al. (1985). The grammatical status of speech by Broca's aphasics is discussed in Grodzinsky (1986). Caramazza (1988) supports the conclusion that aphasia studies can tell us relatively little about normal language functioning and the human language faculty. However, it reports work (e.g. Hart et al. (1985)) which confirms that cerebral trauma can occasion highly class-specific lexical losses (subject could not name or sort fruits and vegetables).

Chapter Six

A variety of texts (e.g. Howells 1967; Pilbeam 1972; Washburn and Moore 1974; etc.) provides a general view of hominid development. For an excellent summary of more recent developments in the field, see Foley (1987a), which includes a discussion of 'straight-line' versus 'adaptive radiation' models of hominid development.

Jerison (1973, 1977) deals with brain size in evolutionary perspective and establishes the 'encephalization index' and EQ. The 'constant of cephalization' was designed by Hemmer (1971). Figures of hominid brain sizes are taken from Tobias (1987), updating a number of previous sources cited therein. With regard to brain content, fossil hominids show more marked hemispheric asymmetries than contemporary apes (Holloway and de la Coste-Lareymondie 1982). Tobias (1987) considers that the development, in *habilis*, of the inferior parietal lobule, in conjunction with other features, indicates that language could have emerged at this stage. On the other hand, Bradshaw (1988), surveying a wide range of evidence, concurs with the present volume in supposing that "*some* form of 'language' began with *erectus*, but that true language is confined to our own species." In a review of recent work in paleoneurology, Falk (1987) concurs with this volume in thinking that the likeliest cause of increases in brain size was the development of language (see also Falk 1980).

An overview of human tool development is given by Washburn (1960). Various approaches to the relation between tools and language are dealt with in Miller (1964), Hewes (1973a), Kitahara-Frisch (1978), and Frost (1980), among many others. More recently, Ingold (1988) considers 'technology' and 'language' too ill defined to allow any definite conclusions, while Wynn (1988), who is responsible for the 'string-of-beads' analogy, finds 'nothing comparable' to syntax in toolmaking behavior. That a contemporary 'Stone Age' people do not employ language in teaching toolmaking skills is shown by White et al. (1977).

At what stage home bases developed remains uncertain; see Foley (1987a, ch. 7) for discussion and references. For the early appearance of fire, see Gowlett et al. (1981) and Yellen (1986).

Hewes (1973b, 1976) has argued for a signing phase in the development of human language.

Chimpanzees were once thought to lack cortical control over their vocalizations; that this is far from being the case is shown by studies such as Aitken (1981) and Sutton (1979).

For discussion of *afarensis*, see Johanson and Edey (1981).

The restructuring of the primate vocal tract in hominids is discussed in detail by Lieberman (1984); see also Laitman (1985). Development of language by *erectus* would be impossible if one accepted the claim—first made in Lieberman and Crelin (1971)—that even Neanderthals were incapable of speech. However, this claim was disputed by several authors (see, e.g., Carlisle and Siegal (1974), Falk (1975), and LeMay (1975)). For an overview of the controversy, see Spuhler (1977).

The claim that you have to know a language in order to learn a language is found in Fodor (1975).

For the evolutionary development of primate vision, see Noback and Moskowitz (1963).

On the extent to which our ancestors might have remained at least partially arboreal, see Foley (1987a), especially ch. 7. For reconstructions of some typical paleoenvironments, see Isaac (1984). The competitors of early hominids are discussed by Maglio (1978).

A corrective to the widely held concept of 'Man the hunter' (as expressed, e.g., in Lovejoy (1980)) and an alternative 'scavenging' hypothesis is provided by Binsford (1981, 1987); Binsford points out that the hunting hypothesis served to integrate brain size, radiation, loss of estrus, and other typically human features into a single coherent account of hominization which, without it, simply disintegrates.

The role that endurance hunting may have played in the development of hominids is discussed by Bortz (1985), while Schaller (1973, 248 ff.) describes an interesting attempt to reconstruct the scavenging and hunting opportunities of early hominids, which included his running down and grappling with a sick zebra. The connection between representational systems and the development of exploratory behavior is stressed by Campbell (1979) in an insightful study that (surely almost alone in the evolutionary literature) cites the seminal work of Craik (1943).

Harnad et al. (1976) represents perhaps the richest and most varied collection to date of essays relating to the origins of human language; continuist assumptions, however, are usually present in one form or another. (See also Hamilton (1974)—unusual in that it emphasizes the advantages of language for problem solving—Parker and Gibson (1979), and Dingwall (1979).) Hockett and Ascher (1964) specifically propose mutations of existing calls as an originating device.

The quotation from Rachel Kupepe is from the introduction to Bickerton and Odo (1976).

The use of water by Japanese macaques to sort grain from sand is described by Kawai (1965) and the opening of milk-bottle tops by British bluetits by

Hinde and Fisher (1952). A similar process would account for chimpanzee 'termiting' behavior (van Lawick-Goodall (1971), Nishida (1973)). For problem solving by captive apes, Kohler (1927) and Yerkes and Yerkes (1929, chs. 27–30) have not really yet been superceded. For the problem-solving capacities of apes that have had some exposure to 'language' training, see Premack (1983).

Chapter 7

The genetic arguments in favor of the view that a unique speciation event in Africa gave rise to our species is advanced in Cann et al. (1987), Cann (1988), and Stringer and Andrews (1988). For an alternative view of the genetic evidence, see Spuhler (1988). Paleoanthropological arguments are found in Smith and Spencer (1984), Rightmire (1984), and Braun (1984)—all in favor of unique speciation; Wolpoff et al. (1984)—against it.

For the Seth data, as well as first language acquisition in general, see references in chapter 5. On creole languages and their origins, see Bickerton (1981, 1983, 1984, 1988). The topic is far from uncontroversial; alternative views are found in Alleyne (1980) and Muhlhausler (1986).

Tools of early 'anatomically modern' *sapiens* are compared with those of previous hominid species in Oakley (1972). Bricker (1976) suggests that the transition is less abrupt than has been supposed, but his data refer to toolmaking *techniques* rather than to the *diversity* of tool types *and functions*. Foley (1987b) shows by a cladistic analysis of tools that there is a sharp break between our species and all other hominids. For a broader view of the contrasts on the *sapiens-erectus* interface see White (1982), Klein (1985), and Tattersall (1986).

Chimpanzee use of stones to smash palm nuts is documented in Struhsaker and Hunkeler (1971); see Kortlandt (1986) for arguments that this behavior is *not* homologous with early hominid tool use.

Wolpoff et al. (1984) makes the case for continuities across the *erectus-sapiens* divide in East Asia; see also Trinkhaus and Smith (1985) for events in Europe, and Wolpoff (1988) for an overview of the 'anti-Eve' argument. Milo and Quiatt (1988) review the Neanderthal literature and conclude that there were significant linguistic as well as morphological and cultural differences between *sapiens* and *neandertalensis;* Rightmire (1988) provides a more general account of the *erectus-sapiens* interface. For controversy over Neanderthal speech capabilities, see notes on chapter 6.

The hypothesized 'interlanguages' discussed in this chapter were proposed by Premack (1985), developing ideas initiated in Premack (1983); for discussion, see Bickerton (1986), and for a response to that discussion, Premack (1986).

For the typical course of development in negative sentences for children learning English, see Klima and Bellugi (1966).

See chapter 3 for references concerning thematic roles.

Newmeyer (1986) describes the early stages of development in generative grammar.

For the presumed language capacities of Neanderthals, see notes on chapter

6; also Milo and Quiatt (1988). Laitman (1985) concludes that although there was some development toward a modern upper-respiratory tract in *homo erectus*, the major change took place between *erectus* and ourselves.

The first attempt at a unified 'locality theory' was that of Koster (1978). Koster (1984) develops these ideas within the framework of Chomsky (1981); see also Williams (1980). A similar reductionism motivated Chomsky (1986) to set the boundaries of movement and government in terms of the same set of mechanisms.

The data on twin languages is taken from Bakker (1986).

Gregory (1970) suggested that syntax might actually derive in some way from visual processing. The suggestion that all complex structures must be hierarchical was first made by Simon (1962). For data on brain localization and aphasia, see references cited in notes to chapter 6. Fodor (1983) proposes a modular-cum-central-processing approach to cerebral macroarchitecture not unlike the approach adopted here, although, for Fodor, thinking processes rather than syntax serve to connect the modules.

Leigh (1988) compares the skulls of *erectus* and *sapiens* with respect to the rate of development in their cranial content. Stringer (1987) distinguishes 'anatomically modern humans' from archaic *sapiens*, *erectus*, *neandertalensis*, and other hominids on the basis of cladistic analysis. Tattersall (1986) cites the autapomorphies (unique structural features) of our species: all of these but one, 'gracile limb bones,' relate to various dimensions of the skull.

See Ebbeson (1984) for development of the claim that parcellation processes are central to brain development.

Chapter Eight

Einstein (1949, 7–9) himself declared it to be the case that a great deal of thinking is done without words; he failed to comment on whether it is done without syntax. On this topic, see also Goodman (1984).

On the impossibility of determining the subjective experiences of another species, see Nagel (1974).

A readily accessible discussion of the varieties of monism and dualism is found in Fodor (1981): Margolis (1984) discusses various psychological approaches, while Churchland (1988) provides a lucid summary of recent developments. For updated varieties of dualism, see Eccles (1986). For an unusually broad-minded behaviorist view, see Lashley (1949). A way of regarding 'mind' itself as a linguistic artifact while saving various kinds of 'mental operations' is provided by Hunter (1986).

Whether machines could develop anything one could call 'mind' or 'consciousness' has been widely (and sometimes acrimoniously) debated by (among others) Searle (1980, 1984), Dennett (1978, 1984, 1987), Dreyfus (1979) and Churchland (1988). Hookway (1984) contains a fair spectrum of views from both philosophers and AI specialists. Two of the prerequisites mentioned here (autonomy, and the possession of a dual representational system) are, curiously enough, seldom if ever referred to in this literature. The robot that thinks dialing a number may change the number is from McCarthy and Hayes (1969). The idea that we are merely vehicles for genes comes from Dawkins (1976).

'Liar Paradoxes' have been discussed by philosophers since the ancient Greeks; for some more recent views, see Martin (1970), Bunge (1979), Chihara (1979), and the *Journal of Philosophic Logic* (1984, vol. 13, no. 2), which is devoted exclusively to this issue. The example given here belongs to the type known as the 'Strengthened Liar', but is so designed as to create problems for the most recent, 'Austinian' solution by Barwise and Etchemendy (1987).

Work on the linguistic consequences of hemispherectomy, along with other 'split-brain' phenomena, is in Gazzaniga (1985). For a more detailed technical account, see Gazzaniga (1987). Baynes and Gazzaniga (1988) deals more specifically with the linguistic aspects; see also Linebarger et al. (1983), Zurif and Grodzinsky (1983), and Goodman and Whitaker (1985).

On the status of entities unconfirmed (and unconfirmable) by the senses, see Maxwell (1980). The 'obsessive' nature of our search for causal explanations, even when these entail 'unobservable entities', is noted by Pearl and Tarsi (1986).

For discussion of the significance of early cave paintings and other human artifacts, see Campbell (1988). Moon calendars and other examples of early human computational capacity are described by Marshack (1984).

The view presented here, that what is assumed to be 'knowledge' is highly time- and culture-specific, has much in common with the so-called strong programme in the sociology of knowledge (Bloor 1976, Barnes 1974, 1977); see Manicas and Rosenberg (1985) for discussion.

Hesse (1961) shows ingeniously how only two views about the nature of 'attraction' have alternated over nearly three millennia of inquiry.

For 'filters', see Chomsky and Lasnik (1977).

On 'truth' and its functions, see Unwin (1987); for other views of what 'truth' might mean, see Sellars (1962), Dummett (1972), Bonjour (1985), and Putnam (1987) among countless others. For the quotation on 'approximating to truth' see the preface to Popper (1963) wherein the characteristic 'Popperian' approach to philosophy of science is developed. Popper (1976) provides some useful background to this.

Chapter Nine

Again, the strong programme of Barnes and Bloor (see references in chapter 8) has strongly influenced this chapter.

The agricultural practices of ant species are described in Wilson (1971). Early phases of human agriculture are discussed by Reid (1977), Rindos (1984), and others. Approaches that link agriculture with climatic and vegetational changes are discussed in Leakey (1981, ch. 12).

Basic principles governing territoriality in species were worked out by Brown (1964); see also Foley (1987a). For dominance systems and other forms of group organization in other species see Krebs and Davies (1987). Territorality is erroneously attributed to our ancestors in a number of semipopular works beginning with Morris (1967).

A useful (if a little outdated) overview of the development of early forms of government is provided by Mair (1962). 'Government' among hunter-gatherers is discussed by Service (1966); for more recent views see Layton (1986). Maisels (1987) discusses the various paths to statehood (some emerging directly from an egalitarian society); see also Fried (1967), Service (1962, 1966), and Wright (1977) for early stages in the development of government.

The effects of predators on prey species, and vice versa, are reviewed in Lack (1954).

For a somewhat outdated view of the differences between aggression in our species and others see Lorenz (1966). Schaller (1972) gives statistics for the high number of lion deaths in combat. The figures for twentieth-century war dead and victims of government are from Rummel (1987).

For the nondirectionality of evolution, see references in chapter 4.

Estimates on the distribution of 'intelligent' (that is, language-using) life forms in the universe vary widely from Churchland (1988), who estimates 10,000 "concurrently intelligent planets in our galaxy at any given time," to some of the contributors to Billingham (1981) who estimate none. See also Hart and Zuckerman (1987).

For a fine analysis of the mystic's approach to these issues, the anonymous author of *The Cloud of Unknowing* can hardly be improved on (see Wolters 1961).

References

Aitken, P. G. 1981. Cortical control of conditioned and spontaneous vocal behavior in rhesus monkeys. *Brain and Language* 13:171–84.

Alleyne, M. C. 1980. *Comparative Afro-American*, Ann Arbor, Mich.: Karoma.

Aoun, J., and D. Sportiche. 1983. On the formal theory of government, *The Linguistic Review* 3:211–35.

Ayer, A. J. 1972. *Bertrand Russell*. New York: Viking Press.

Baker, G. P., and P. M. S. Hacker. 1984. *Language sense and nonsense*. Oxford: Basil Blackwell.

Bakker, P. 1986. Twin languages. Ph.D. diss., Univ. of Amsterdam.

Baldinger, K. 1980. *Semantic theory*. New York: St. Martin's Press.

Barnes, B. 1974. *Scientific knowledge and sociological theory*. London: Routledge and Kegan Paul.

—————. 1977. *Interests and the growth of knowledge*. London: Routledge and Kegan Paul.

Barret, R., P. A. F. Maderson, and R. M. Meszler. 1970. The pit organs of snakes. In *Biology of the reptilia*, vol. 2, ed. C. Gans and T. S. Parsons, 217–314. New York: Academic Press.

Barwise, J., and J. Etchemendy. 1987. *The liar: An essay on truth and circularity*. New York: Oxford Univ. Press.

Bateson, G. 1979. *Mind and nature*. New York: Dutton.

Baynes, K., and M. S. Gazzaniga. 1988. Right hemisphere language: Insights into normal language mechanisms? In *Language, communication and the brain*, ed. F. Plum. 117–26. New York: Raven Press.

Begley, S. 1982. The fossils of language. *Newsweek*, 15 March, 80.

Berlin, B., D. E. Bredlove, and P. H. Raven. 1973. General principles of classification and nomenclature in folk biology. *American Anthropologist* 75:214–42.

Berlin, B., and P. Kay. 1969. *Basic color terms*. Berkeley: Univ. of California Press.

Berwick, R. C. 1985. *The acquisition of syntactic knowledge*. Cambridge: MIT Press.

Bever, T. G. 1970. The cognitive basis for linguistic structures. In *Cognition and the development of language*, ed. J. R. Hayes, 279–352. New York: Wiley and Sons.

Bickerton, D. 1981. *Roots of language*. Ann Arbor: Karoma.

———. 1983. Pidgin and creole languages. *Scientific American* 249(1): 116–22.

———. 1984. The language bioprogram hypothesis. *Behavioral and Brain Sciences* 7: 173–221.

———. 1985. Review of *The biology and evolution of language*, by P. Lieberman. *American Anthropologist* 87: 691–92.

———. 1986. More than nature needs? A reply to Premack. *Cognition* 23: 73–79.

———. 1987. The supremacy of syntax. *Behavioral and Brain Sciences* 10: 658–59.

———. 1988. Creole languages and the bioprogram. In *Linguistics: The Cambridge survey*, vol. 2, ed. F. J. Newmeyer, 267–84. Cambridge: Cambridge Univ. Press.

Bickerton, D., and C. Odo. 1976. *General phonology and pidgin syntax*. Vol. 1 of final report on NSF grant no. GS-39748. Honolulu: Univ. of Hawaii. Mimeo.

Billingham, J., ed. 1981. *Life in the universe*. Cambridge: MIT Press.

Binsford, C. R. 1981. *Bones: Ancient man and modern myths*. New York: Academic Press.

———. 1987. The hunting hypothesis, archeological methods and the past. *Yearbook of Physical Anthropology* 30: 11–20.

Bloor, D. 1976. *Knowledge and social imagery*. London: Routledge and Kegan Paul.

Bonjour, L. 1985. *The structure of empirical knowledge*. Cambridge: Harvard Univ. Press.

Bortz, W. M. 1985. Physical exercise as an evolutionary force. *Journal of Human Evolution* 14: 145–55.

Bowerman, M. 1973. *Early syntactic development*. Cambridge: Cambridge Univ. Press.

Bradshaw, J. L. 1988. The evolution of human lateral asymmetries. *Journal of Human Evolution* 17: 615–37.

Braun, G. 1984. A craniological approach to the origin of anatomically modern *homo sapiens* in Africa and implications for the appearance of modern Europeans. In *The origins of modern humans: A world survey of fossil evidence*, ed. F. H. Smith and F. Spencer, 327–410. New York: Alan R, Liss Inc.

Brazier, M. A. B., ed. 1969. *The interneuron*. Berkeley: Univ. of California Press.

Bricker, H. M. 1976. Upper Paleolithic archaeology. *Annual Review of Anthropology* 5: 133–48.

Broch, O. 1930. Russenorsk textmateriale, Maale og Minne. *Norske Studier* 1930:113–40.

Brown, C., J. Kolar, R. J. Torrey, T. Truong-Quang, and P. Volkman. 1976. Some general principles of biological and nonbiological 'folk classification'. *American Ethologist* 3:73–85.

Brown, J. L. 1964. The evolution of diversity in avian territorial systems. *Wilson Bulletin* 76:160–9.

Brown, R. 1973. *A first language.* Cambridge: Harvard Univ. Press.

Browne, J. C., and W. Greenhood. 1988. Paternity, jokes and song: A possible evolutionary scenario for the origin of language and mind. Paper read at the International Conference on the Biology of Language, Rydzyna, Poland, 1–4 December.

Browning, M. 1987. *Null operator constructions.* Ph.D. diss., Massachusetts Institute of Technology.

Bunge, J. 1979. Semantical paradox. *Journal of Philosophy* 76:169–98.

Camhi, J. 1980. The escape system of the cockroach. *Scientific American* 243(6):158–72.

———. 1984. *Neuroethology.* Sunderland, Mass.: Sinauer Associates.

Camhi, J., W. Tom, and S. Volman. 1978. The escape behavior of the cockroach *Periplaneta americana:* Detection of natural predators by air displacement. *Journal of Comparative Physiology* 126:203–12.

Campbell, B. G. 1979. Ecological factors and social organisation in human evolution. In *Primate ecology and human origins,* ed. I. J. Bernstein and E. O. Smith, 291–312. New York: Garland.

Campbell, J. 1988. *Historical atlas of world mythology.* Vol. 1, pt. 1, Mythologies of the primitive hunter gatherers. New York: Harper and Row. *Anthropology* 17:127–43.

Cann, R. L., M. Stoneking, and A. C. Wilson. 1987. Mitochondrial DNA and human evolution. *Nature* 325:31–36.

Caramazza, A. 1988. Some aspects of language processing as revealed through the analysis of acquired aphasia. *Annual Review of Neuroscience* 11:395–421.

Carlisle, R. C., and M. I. Siegel. 1974. Some problems with regard to Neanderthal speech capabilities: A reply to Lieberman. *American Anthropologist* 76:319–22.

Cattell, R. 1976. Constraints on movement rules. *Language* 52:18–50.

Cheney, D. L. 1984. Category formation in vervet monkeys. In *The meaning of primate signals,* ed. R. Harre and V. Reynolds, 58–76. Cambridge: Cambridge University Press.

Chernigovskiy, V. N. 1966. *Interoceptors.* Washington, D.C.: American Psychological Association.

Chiarelli, B. 1985. Chromosomes and the origins of man. In *Hominid evolution: Past, present and future,* ed. P. V. Tobias, 457–64. New York: Alan R, Liss Inc.

Chihara, C. 1979. The semantic paradoxes: A diagnostic investigation. *Philosophical Review* 88:590–618.

Chomsky, N. 1957. *Syntactic structures*. The Hague: Mouton.

———. 1968. *Language and mind*. New York: Harcourt, Brace and World.

———. 1975. *Reflections on language*. New York: Pantheon Books.

———. 1980. *Rules and representations*. New York: Columbia University Press.

———. 1981. *Lectures on government and binding*. Dordrecht: Foris.

———. 1982. *Some concepts and consequences of the theory of government and binding*. Cambridge: MIT Press.

———. 1985. *Knowledge of language: Its nature, origin and use*. New York: Praeger.

———. 1986. *Barriers*. Cambridge: MIT Press.

Chomsky, N., and H. Lasnik. 1977. Filters and control. *Linguistic Inquiry* 8:425–504.

Churchland, P. M. 1988. *Matter and consciousness*. 2d. ed. Cambridge: Bradford/MIT Press.

Clark, E. V. 1970. Locativeness: A study of 'existential', 'locative' and 'possessive' sentences. *Working papers in Linguistics* (Stanford University) 3:L1–L36.

Clark, H. H., and E. V. Clark. 1977. *Psychology and language*. New York: Harcourt Brace Jovanovich.

Craik, K. J. W. 1943. *The nature of explanation*. Cambridge: Cambridge Univ. Press.

Curtiss, S. 1977. *Genie: A psycholinguistic study of a modern-day 'wild child'*. New York: Academic Press.

Darwin, C. 1875. *Insectivorous plants*. London: Murray.

Dawkins, R. 1976. *The selfish gene*. Oxford: Oxford Univ. Press.

———. 1987. *The blind watchmaker*. Harlow: Longmans.

Day, M. H., and C. B. Stringer. 1982. A reconsideration of the Omo-Kibish remains and the *erectus-sapiens* transition. In *Premier Congrès International de Paléntologie Humaine*, vol. 2, 814–46.

Deninger, P. L., and C. W. Schmid. 1976. Thermal stability of human DNA and chimpanzee DNA heteroduplexes. *Science* 194:846–48.

Dennett, D. 1978. *Brainstorms*. Montgomery, Vt.: Bradford.

———. 1984. Cognitive wheels: The frame problem of AI. In *Minds, machines and evolution*, ed. C. Hookway, 129–52. Cambridge: Cambridge Univ. Press.

———. 1987. *The intentional stance*. Cambridge: MIT Press.

De Saussure, F. 1966. *Course in general linguistics*. New York: McGraw-Hill.

de Valois, P. L., and G. H. Jacobs. 1968. Primate color vision. *Science* 162:533–40.

Dingwall, W. O. 1979. The evolution of human communication systems. In

Studies in Neurolinguistics, vol. 4, ed. H. Whittaker and H. A. Whittaker, 1–95. New York: Academic Press.

Dobzhansky, T. G. 1955. *Evolution, genetics and man.* New York: John Wiley and Sons.

———. 1962. *Mankind evolving: The evolution of the human species.* New Haven: Yale Univ. Press.

Donellan, K. 1966. Reference and definite descriptions. *Philosophical Review* 75(3):281–304.

Dreyfus, H. 1979. *What computers can't do: The limits of artificial intelligence.* New York: Harper and Row.

Dummett, D. [1959] 1972. Truth. In *Truth and other enigmas*, 1–24. Cambridge: Harvard Univ. Press.

Ebbeson, S. O. E. 1984. Evolution and ontogeny of neural circuits. *Behavioral and Brain Sciences* 7:321–66.

Eccles, J. C., ed. 1986. *Brain and conscious experience.* New York: Springer-Verlag.

Einstein, A. 1949. Autobiographical notes. In *Albert Einstein: Philosopher-scientist*, ed. P. A. Schilp, 3–95. Evanston, Ill.: Library of Living Philosophers.

Eldredge, N., and S. J. Gould. 1972. Punctuated equilibrium: An alternative to phyletic gradualism. In *Models in paleobiology*, ed. T. J. M. Schopf, 82–115. San Francisco: Freeman and Cooper.

Emonds, J. 1976. *A transformational approach to modern syntax.* New York: Academic Press.

Ewert, J. P. 1976. The visual system of the toad: Behavioral and physiological studies on a pattern recognition system. In *The amphibian visual system*, ed. K. V. Fyte. New York: Academic Press.

———. 1987. Neuroethology of releasing mechanisms: Prey-catching in toads. *Behavioral and Brain Sciences* 10:337–405.

Falk, D. 1975. Comparative anatomy of the larynx in man and the chimpanzee: Implications for language in Neanderthal. *American Journal of Physical Anthropology* 43:123–32.

———. 1980. Hominid brain evolution, the approach from paleoneurology. *Yearbook of Physical Anthropology* 23:93–107.

———. 1987. Hominid paleoneurology. *Annual Review of Anthropology* 16:13–30.

Fisher, H. T. 1982. *Mapping information.* Cambridge, Mass.: Abt Books.

Fobes, J. L., and J. E. King. 1982. Auditory and chemoreceptive sensitivity in primates. In *Primate behavior*, ed. J. L. Fobes and J. E. King, 245–70. New York: Academic Press.

Fodor, J. A. 1975. *The language of thought.* New York: Thomas Crowell & Co.

———. 1981a. 'The mind-body problem'. *Scientific American* 244:114–23.

———. 1981b. *Representations.* Cambridge: MIT Press.

————. 1983. *Modularity of mind.* Cambridge: MIT Press.

Foley, R. 1987a. *Another unique species: Patterns in human evolutionary ecology.* London: Longman Group.

————. 1987b. Hominid species and stone tool assemblages: How are they related? *Antiquity* 61:380–92.

Fox, J. A. 1983. Simplified input and negotiation in Russenorsk. In *Pidginization and creolization as language acquisition,* ed. Roger W. Andersen. Rowley, Mass.: Newbury House.

Fried, M. H. 1967. *The evolution of political society.* New York: Random House.

Frost, G. T. 1980. Tool behavior and the origins of laterality, *Journal of Human Evolution* 9:447–59.

Gardner, B. T., and R. A. Gardner. 1974. Comparing the early utterances of child and chimpanzee. In *Minnesota symposium on child psychology,* vol. 8, ed. A. Pick, 3–23. Minneapolis: Univ. of Minnesota Press.

Gazzaniga, M. S. 1985. *The social brain.* New York: Basic Books.

————. 1987. *Cognitive and neurologic aspects of hemispheric disconnection in the human brain.* Discussions in Neurosciences, vol. 4, no. 4. Geneva: Foundation for the Study of the Nervous System.

Ghiglieri, M. P. 1987. Sociobiology of the great apes and the hominid ancestor. *Journal of Human Evolution* 16:319–57.

Gibson, J. J. 1979. *The ecological approach to visual perception.* Boston: Houghton Mifflin.

Givon, T. 1979. *On understanding syntax.* New York: Academic Press.

Gleason, H. A. 1955. *Introduction to descriptive linguistics.* New York: Holt, Rinehart and Winston.

Godfrey, L., and K. Jacobs. 1987. Models of human brain evolution. *Journal of Human Evolution* 10:255–72.

Goodglass, H. 1973. Studies on the grammar of aphasics. In *Psycholinguistics and aphasia,* ed. H. Goodglass and S. Blumstein, 183–215. Baltimore: Johns Hopkins Univ. Press.

Goodman, N. 1972. The emperor's new ideas. In *Problems and projects,* 76–79. Indianapolis: Bobbs-Merrill.

————. 1984. *Mind and other matters.* Cambridge: Harvard Univ. Press.

Goodman, R. A., and H. A. Whitaker. 1985. Hemispherectomy: A review (1928–1981) with special reference to the linguistic abilities and disabilities of the residual right hemisphere. In *Hemispheric function and collaboration in the child,* ed. C. T. Best, 121–55. New York: Academic Press.

Gould, S. J. 1977. *Ontogeny and phylogeny.* Cambridge, Mass.: Belknap Press.

Gould, S. J. and N. Eldredge. 1977. Punctuated equilibria: The tempo and mode of evolution reconsidered. *Paleobiology* 3:115–51.

Gowlett, J. A. J., J. W. K. Harris, D. Walton, and B. A. Wood. 1981. Early archaeological sites, hominid remains and traces of fire from Chesowanja, Kenya. *Nature* 294:125–29.

Gregory, R. 1970. The grammar of vision. *The Listener* (19 Feb.): 242–44.

Griffin, D. R. 1958. *Listening in the dark*. New Haven: Yale Univ. Press.

———. 1981. *The question of animal awareness*. Rev. ed. New York: Rockefeller Univ. Press.

———, ed. 1982. *Animal mind—human mind*. Berlin: Springer Verlag.

Grodzinsky, Y. 1986. Language deficits and the theory of syntax. *Brain and Language* 27:135–59.

Gruber, J. S. 1965. *Studies in lexical relations*. Ph.D. diss., Massachusetts Institute of Technology.

Grusser, G. L., and L.-R. Weiss. 1985. Quantitative models on phylogenetic growth of the hominid brain. In *Hominid evolution: Past, present and future*, edited by P. V. Tobias, New York: 457–64. New York: Alan R, Liss Inc.

Grusser, O. J., and U. Grusser-Cornelis. 1968. Visual behavior of frogs in the field (in German). *Zeitschrift fur Vergleichende Physiologie* 59:1–24.

Guthrie, D. M. 1980. *Neuroethology: An introduction*. New York: Wiley and Sons.

Gyori, G. 1988. Animal communication and human language: A search for their true relationship. Paper presented at the International Conference on the Biology of Language, Rydzyna, Poland, 1–4 December.

Haber, R. N., and M. Hershenson. 1980. *The psychology of visual perception*. New York: Holt, Rinehart and Winston.

Hall, R. B. 1966. *Pidgin and creole languages*. Ithaca, N.Y.: Cornell Univ. Press.

Hamilton, J. 1974. Hominid divergence and speech evolution. *Journal of Human Evolution* 3:417–24.

Hardin, G. J. 1959. *Nature and man's fate*. New York: Rinehart.

Harnad, S. R., H. D. Steklis, and J. Lancaster. 1976. *Origins and evolution of language and speech*. Annals of the New York Academy of Science, vol. 280. New York: New York Academy of Science.

Harre, R., and V. Reynolds, eds. 1984. *The meaning of primate signals*. Cambridge: Cambridge Univ. Press.

Hart, H. M., and B. Zuckerman. 1987. *Extraterrestrials: Where are they?* New York: Pergamon Press.

Hart, J., R. S. Bendt, and A. Caramazza. 1985. Category-specific naming deficit following cerebral infarction. *Nature* 316:439–40.

Harvey, P. D. A. 1980. *The history of topographical maps*. London: Thames and Hudson.

Hebb, D. O. 1946. On the nature of fear. *Psychological Review* 53:259–76.

Hemmer, H. 1971. Beitrag zur Erfassung der progressiven Cephalization bei

Primaten. In *Proceedings of the 3rd International Congress of Primatology*, ed. J. Biegart and W. Leutenegger, vol. 1, 99–107. Basel: Karger.

Hering, E. 1920. *Outline of a theory of the light-sense*. Cambridge: Harvard Univ. Press.

Herman, L. M., D. G. Richards, and J. P. Wolz. 1984. Comprehension of sentences by bottle-nosed dolphins. *Cognition* 16:129–219.

Herrnstein, R. J. 1979. Acquisition, generalization, and discrimination reversal of a natural concept. *Journal of Experimental Psychology (Animal Behavior Processes)* 5:116–29.

———. 1985. Riddles of natural categorization. In *Animal intelligence*, ed. L. Weiskrantz. Oxford: Clarendon Press.

Hervey, S. G. J. 1979. *Axiomatic semantics*. Edinburgh: Scottish Academic Press.

Hesse, M. 1961. *Forces and fields*. London: Nelson.

Hewes, G. W. 1973a. An explicit formulation of the relationship between tool-using, tool-making and the emergence of language. *Visible Language* 7:101–27.

———. 1973b. Primate communication and the gestural origin of language. *Current Anthropology* 14:5–24.

———. 1976. The current status of the gestural theory of language origins. In *Origins and evolution of language and speech*, ed. S. R. Harnad, H. D. Steklis, and J. Lancaster, 482–504. New York: New York Academy of Science.

Hinde, R. A., and J. Fisher. 1952. Further observations on the opening of milk-bottles by birds. *British Birds* 44:393–6.

Hoban, E. 1986. *The promise of animal language research*. Ph.D. diss., Univ. of Hawaii.

Hockett, C. F. 1968. *The state of the art*. The Hague: Mouton.

Hockett, C. F. and R. Ascher. 1964. The human revolution. *Current Anthropology* 5:135–68.

Holloway, R. L., and M. C. de la Coste-Lareymondie. 1982. Brain endocast asymmetry in pongids and hominids: Some preliminary findings on the palaentology of cerebral dominance. *American Journal of Physical Anthropology* 58:101–10.

Hookway, C. 1984. *Minds, machines and evolution*. Cambridge: Cambridge Univ. Press.

Howells, W. 1967. *Mankind in the making: The story of human evolution*. New York: Doubleday.

Hoyle, G. 1984. The scope of neuroethology. *Behavioral and Brain Sciences* 7:367–412.

Hubel, D. T., and T. N. Wiesel. 1960. Receptive fields of single neurons in the cat's striate cortex. *Journal of Physiology (London)* 150:91–104.

————. 1963. Shape and arrangement of columns in the cat's striate cortex. *Journal of Physiology (London)* 165:559–68.

————. 1968. Receptive fields and functional architecture of monkey striate cortex. *Journal of Physiology (London)* 195:215–43.

————. 1977. Functional architecture of macaque monkey visual cortex. *Proceedings of the Royal Society of London*, series B. 198:1–59.

Huey, R. B., E. R. Pranka, and T. W. Schoener. 1983. *Lizard ecology.* Cambridge: Harvard Univ. Press.

Hunter, J. F. M. 1986. The concept, 'mind'. *Philosophy* 61:439–51.

Ingold, T. 1988. Tool-using, toolmaking and the evolution of language. Paper presented at the International Conference on the Biology of Language, Rydzyna, Poland, 1–4 December.

Isaac, G. 1984. The archeology of human origins: Studies of the lower Pleistocene in East Africa. *Advances in World Archeology* 3:1–79.

Jacobs, K. H. 1985. Human origins. In *What Darwin began*, ed. L. R. Godfrey. Boston: Allyn and Bacon.

Jackendoff, R. 1972. *Semantic interpretation in generative grammar.* Cambridge: MIT Press.

————. 1977. *X-bar syntax: A study of phrase structure.* Cambridge: MIT Press.

————. 1983. *Semantics and cognition.* Cambridge: MIT Press.

Jager, R. 1972. *The development of Bertrand Russell's philosophy.* London: Allyn and Bacon.

Jardine, N. 1975. Model theoretic semantics and natural language. In *Formal semantics of natural language*, ed. E. L. Keenan, 219–40. Cambridge: Cambridge Univ. Press.

Jerison, H. J. 1973. *Evolution of the brain and intelligence.* New York: Academic Press.

————. 1977. The theory of encephalization. In *Evolution and lateralization of the brain*, ed. S. J. Diamond and P. A. Blizard. Annals of the New York Academy of Science, Vol. 299:601–6. New York: New York Academy of Science.

Johanson, D. C., and M. Edey. 1981. *Lucy: The beginnings of humankind.* New York: Simon and Schuster.

Kandel, E. R. 1976. *The cellular basis of behavior.* San Francisco: Freeman.

Kandel, E. R., and J. H. Schwartz. 1982. Molecular biology of learning: Modulation of transmitter release. *Science* 218:433–42.

Katz, J. J., and P. M. Postal. 1964. *An integrated theory of linguistic descriptions.* Cambridge: MIT Press.

Kawai, M. 1965. Newly-acquired pre-cultural behavior of the natural troop of Japanese monkeys on Koshima Islet. *Primates* 6:1–30.

Kay, P., and C. K. McDaniel. 1978. The linguistic significance of the meanings of basic color terms. *Languages* 54:610–46.

Kayne, R. 1984. *Connectedness and binary branching*. Dordrecht: Foris.

Keil, F. 1979. *Semantic and conceptual development*. Cambridge: Harvard Univ. Press.

———. 1981. Constraints on knowledge and cognitive development. *Psychological Review* 88:197–227.

Kendrick, K. M., and B. A. Baldwin. 1987. Cells in temporal cortex of conscious sheep can respond preferentially to the sight of faces. *Science* 236:448–50.

King, M.-C., and A. C. Wilson. 1975. Evolution at two levels in humans and chimpanzees. *Science* 188:107–16.

Kitahara-Frisch, J. 1978. Stone tools as indicators of linguistic ability in early man. *Kagaku Kisoron Gakkai Annals* 5:101–9.

Klein, R. E. 1985. Breaking away. *Natural history* 94(1):4–7.

Klima, E. S., and U. Bellugi. 1966. Syntactic regularities in the speech of children. In *Psycholinguistics papers*, ed. J. Lyons and R. J. Wales, 183–208. Edinburgh: Edinburgh Univ. Press.

———. 1979. *The signs of language*. Cambridge: Harvard Univ. Press.

Knudsen, E. I. 1982. Auditory and visual maps of space in the optic tectum of the owl. *Journal of Neuroscience* 2:1177–97.

———. 1984. Synthesis of a neural map of auditory space in the owl. In *Dynamic aspects of neocortical function*, ed. G. M. Edelman, W. M. Cowan, and W. E. Gall, 375–96. New York: Wiley and sons.

Knudsen, E. I., S. du Lac, and S. D. Esterley. 1987. Computational maps in the brain. *American Review of Neuroscience* 10:41–65.

Kohler, W. 1927. *The mentality of apes*. New York: Harcourt, Brace.

Kortlandt, A. 1962. Chimpanzees in the wild. *Scientific American* 206(5):128–38.

———. 1986. The use of stone tools by wild chimpanzees and earliest hominids. *Journal of Human Evolution* 15:77–132.

Korzybski, A. 1958. *Science and sanity*. Lakeville, Conn.: International Non-Aristotelian Library.

Koster, J. 1978. *Locality principles in syntax*. Dordrecht: Foris.

———. 1984. On binding and control. *Linguistic Inquiry* 15:417–43.

Krasne, F. B. 1969. Habituation of crayfish responses. *Journal of Experimental Biology* 50:29–46.

Krebs, J. R., and N. B. Davies. 1987. *An introduction to behavioural ecology*. 2d ed. Oxford: Blackwell.

Kyle, J. G., and B. Woll. 1985. *Sign language*. Cambridge: Cambridge Univ. Press.

Lack, D. L. 1954. *The natural regulation of animal numbers*. Oxford: Clarendon Press.

———. 1965. *The life of the robin*. London: Weatherby.

Laing, R. D. 1967. *The politics of experience*. New York: Ballantine Books.

Laitman, J. T. 1985. Evolution of the hominid upper respiratory tract: The fossil evidence. In *Hominid evolution: Past, present and future*, ed. P. V. Tobias, 281–86.

Lakoff, G. 1969. Empiricism without facts. *Foundations of Language* 5: 118–27.

Lamendella, J. 1976. Relations between the ontogeny and phylogeny of language: A neo-recapitulationist view. In *Origins and evolution of language and speech*, ed. Harnad et al., 396–412. New York: New York Academy of Science.

Lashley, K. S. 1949. Persistent problems in the evolution of mind. *Quarterly Review of Biology* 24:28–42.

Lawick-Goodall, J. van. 1971. *In the shadow of man*. Boston: Houghton Mifflin.

Layton, R. 1986. Political and territorial structures among hunter-gatherers. *Man* 95:18–33.

Leakey, R. E. 1981. *The making of mankind*. New York: E. P. Dutton.

Leigh, S. R. 1988. Comparison of rates of evolutionary change in cranial capacity in *homo erectus* and early *homo sapiens*. *American Journal of Physical Anthropology* 75(2):237–38.

LeMay, M. 1975. The language capability of Neanderthal man. *American Journal of Physical Anthropology* 42:9–14.

Lenneberg, E. 1967. *Biological foundations of language*. New York: Wiley and Sons.

Lettvin, J. Y., H. R. Maturana, W. S. McCulloch, and W. H. Pitts. 1955. What the frog's eye tells the frog's brain. *Proceedings of the Institute of Radio Engineering* 47:1940–51.

Lieberman, P. 1984. *The biology and evolution of language*. Cambridge: Harvard Univ. Press.

———, and E. S. Crelin. 1971. On the speech of Neanderthal man. *Linguistic Inquiry* 2:203–22.

Lightfoot, D. 1982. *The language lottery*. Cambridge: MIT Press.

Linden, E. 1975. *Apes, men and language*. New York: Dutton.

Linebarger, M., M. F. Schwartz, and E. M. Saffran. 1983. Sensitivity to grammatical structures in so-called agrammatic aphasics. *Cognition* 8:1–71.

Lorenz, K. 1966. *On aggression*. New York: Harcourt, Brace & World.

Lovejoy, C. O. 1980. The origin of man. *Science* 211:341–50.

Lumsden, C., and E. O. Wilson. 1983. *Promethean Fire*. Cambridge: Harvard Univ. Press.

Maglio, J. V. 1978. Patterns of faunal evolution. In *Evolution of African mammals*, ed. V. J. Maglio and H. B. S. Cooke, 603–20. Cambridge: Harvard Univ. Press.

Maisels, C. K. 1987. Models of social evolution: Trajectories from the neolithic to the state. *Man* 22:331–59.

Mair, L. 1962. *Primitive government*. Harmondsworth: Penguin Books.

Malson, L. 1972. *Wolf children and the problem of human nature.* New York: Monthly Review Press.

Manicas, P. T., and A. Rosenberg. 1985. Naturalism, epistemological individualism and the 'strong programme' in the theory of knowledge. *Journal for the Theory of Social Behavior* 15:76–101.

Margolis, J. 1984. *Philosophy of psychology.* Englewood Cliffs, N.J.: Prentice-Hall.

Marshack, A. 1984. The ecology and brain of two-handed bipedalism: An analytic, cognitive and evolutionary assessment. In *Animal cognition,* ed. H. L. Roitblat, T. G. Bever, and H. S. Terrace, 491–511. Hillsdale, N.J.: Erlbaum.

Martin, R., ed. 1970. *The paradox of the liar.* New Haven: Yale Univ. Press.

Maxwell, G. 1980. The ontological status of theoretical entities. In *Minnesota Studies in the Philosophy of Science,* vol. 3, ed. H. Feigl and G. Maxwell, 3–14. Minneapolis: Univ. of Minnesota Press.

Mayr, E. 1963. *Animal species and evolution.* Cambridge: Harvard Univ. Press.

McCarthy, J., and P. Hayes. 1969. Some philosophical problems from the standpoint of artificial intelligence. In *Machine intelligence,* ed. B. Meltzer and D. Mitchie. New York: Elsevier.

McLaury, R. E. 1987. Color category evolution and Shuswap yellow-with-green. *American Anthropologist* 89:107–24.

McMullin, E., ed. 1985. *Evolution and creation.* Notre Dame, Indiana: Univ. of Notre Dame Press.

McPhail, E. M. 1987. The comparative psychology of intelligence. *Behavioral and Brain Sciences* 10:645–95.

Medawar, P. 1961. Review of *The phenomenon of man,* by P. Teilhard de Chardin. *Mind* 70:99–106.

Medin, D. C., W. P. Wattenmaker, and S. E. Hampson. 1987. Family resemblance, conceptual cohesiveness and category construction. *Cognitive Psychology* 19:242–79.

Miller, G. A. 1964. Communication and the structure of behavior. In *Disorders of communication,* ed. D. M. Rioch and E. A. Weinstein. Baltimore: Williams and Wilkins.

Milo, R. G., and D. Quiatt. 1988. Group selection in the biocultural evolution of language: Fate of the Neanderthals revisited. Paper presented at the International Conference on the Biology of Language, Rydzyna, Poland, 1–4 December.

Monod, J. 1971. *Chance and necessity.* New York: Knopf.

Morris, D. 1967. *The naked ape.* New York: McGraw-Hill.

Muhlhausler, P. 1986. *Pidgin and creole linguistics.* Oxford: Basil Blackwell.

Nagel, T. 1974. What is it like to be a bat? *Philosophical Review* 83:435–50.

Newmeyer, F. 1986. *Linguistic theory in America.* 2d ed. New York: Academic Press.

Nishida, T. 1973. The ant-gathering behavior by the use of tools among wild chimpanzees of the Mahali mountains. *Journal of Human Evolution* 2:357–70.

Noback, C. R., and N. Moskowitz. 1963. The primate nervous system: Functional and structural aspects in phylogeny. In *Evolutionary and genetic biology of primates*, vol. 1, ed. J. Buettner-Janusch, 131–77. New York: Academic Press.

Oakley, K. P. 1972. *Man the toolmaker.* London: Trustees of the British Museum.

Ogden, C. K., and I. A. Richards. 1923. *The meaning of meaning.* London: Routledge and Kegan Paul.

Palmer, F. R. 1976. *Semantics: A new outline.* Cambridge: Cambridge Univ. Press.

Parker, S. T. and K. R. Gibson. 1979. A developmental model for the evolution of language and intelligence in early hominids. *Behavioral and Brain Sciences* 2:367–408.

Passingham, R. E. 1979. Specialization and the language areas. In *Neurobiology of social communication in primates*, ed. H. D. Steklis and M. J. Raleigh, 221–56.

Pearl, J., and M. Tarsi. 1986. Structuring causal trees. *Journal of Complexity* 2:60–77.

Peeke, H. V. S., and M. J. Herz, eds. 1973. *Habituation*, vols. 1–2. New York: Academic Press.

Pepperberg, I. M. 1987. Acquisition of the same/different concept by an African Grey parrot *psittacus erithacus*. *Animal Learning and Behavior* 15:423–32.

Perrett, D., E. T. Rolls, and W. Cann. 1982. Visual neurons responsive to faces in the monkey temporal cortex. *Experimental Brain Research* 47:329–42.

Perrett, D., P. A. J. Smith, A. J. Mistlin, A. J. Chitty, A. S. Head, D. D. Potter, R. Broenniman, A. P. Milner and M. A. Jeeves. 1985. Visual analysis of body movements by neurones in the temporal cortex of the macaque monkey. *Behavior and Brain Research* 16 (2–3):153–70.

Perrett, D., P. A. J. Smith, D. D. Potter, A. J. Mistlin, A. S. Head, A. P. Milner, and M. A. Jeeves. 1985. Visual cells in the temporal cortex sensitive to face view and gaze direction. *Proceedings of the Royal Society of London*, series B. 223:193–317.

Pilbeam, D. 1972. *The ascent of man: An introduction to human evolution.* New York: Macmillan.

———. 1986. Hominoid evolution and hominoid origins. *American Anthropologist* 88:295–312.

Pinker, S. 1984. *Language learnability and language development.* Cambridge: Harvard Univ. Press.

Plooij, F. X. 1978. Some basic traits of language in wild chimpanzees? In *The emergence of language*, ed. A. W. Lock, 111–31. New York: Academic Press.

Popper, K. R. 1963. *Conjectures and refutations: The growth of scientific knowledge.* London: Routledge and Kegan Paul.

———. 1976. *Unended quest: An intellectual biography.* London: Collins.

Potts, T. C. 1975. Model theory and linguistics. In *Formal semantics of natural language*, ed. E. L. Keenan, 241–50. Cambridge: Cambridge Univ. Press.

Premack, D. 1972. Language in the chimp? *Science* 172:808–22.

———. 1983. The codes of men and beasts. *Behavioral and Brain Sciences* 6:125–68.

———. 1985. 'Gavagai!' or the future history of the animal language controversy. *Cognition* 19:207–96.

———. 1986. Pangloss to Cyrano de Bergerac: "Nonsense, it's perfect"; a reply to Bickerton, *Cognition* 23:81–88.

Putnam, H. 1961. Some issues in the theory of grammar. *Proceedings of Symposia in Applied Mathematics* 12:25–42.

———. 1975. *Mind, language and reality.* Cambridge: Cambridge Univ. Press.

———. 1987. *The many faces of realism.* La Salle, Ill.: Open Court.

Quine, W. 1960. *Word and object.* New York: Wiley and Sons.

Reid, C. A., ed. 1977. *Origins of agriculture.* The Hague: Mouton.

Reinhart, T. 1976. *The syntactic domain of anaphora.* Ph.D. diss., Massachusetts Institute of Technology.

Richards, R. J. 1987. *Darwin and the emergence of evolutionary theories of mind and behavior.* Chicago: Univ. of Chicago Press.

Rightmire, G. P. 1984. *Homo sapiens* in sub-Saharan Africa. In *The Origins of modern humans: A world survey of fossil evidence*, ed. F. H. Smith and F. Spencer, 295–325.

———. 1988. *Homo erectus* and later middle Pleistocene humans. *Annual Review of Anthropology* 17:239–59.

Rindos, D. 1984. *The origins of agriculture: An evolutionary perspective.* New York: Academic Press.

Robins, R. H. 1967. *A short history of linguistics.* Bloomington: Indiana Univ. Press.

Roitblatt, H. L. 1982. The meaning of representation in animal memory. *Behavioral and Brain Sciences* 5:353–406.

Rosch, E. 1973. Natural categories. *Cognitive Psychology* 4:328–50.

Rosch, E., and B. B. Lloyd, eds. 1978. *Cognition and categorization.* Hillsdale, N.J.: Erlbaum.

Ross, J. R. 1967. *Constraints on variables in syntax.* Ph.D. diss., Massachusetts Institute of Technology.

Ruitenbeek, H. M., ed. 1972. *Going crazy.* New York: Basic Books.

Rummel, R. J. 1987. Deadlier than war. *IPA Review* 41(2):24–30.

Russell, D. and R. Seguin. 1981. Reconstruction of the small cretaceous theropod *Stenonychosaurus inequalis* and a hypothetical dinosauroid. National Museum of Natural Sciences Syllogeus No. 37, Ottawa.

Sarich, V. M., and A. C. Wilson. 1967. Immunological time scale for hominoid evolution. *Science* 158:1200–3.

Sarles, H. B. 1988. The biology of language: Essentialist versus evolutionist in the nature of language. Paper read at the International Conference on the Biology of Language, Rydzyna, Poland, 1–4 December.

Sarnat, H. B., and M. G. Netsky. 1974. *Evolution of the nervous system.* Oxford: Oxford Univ. Press.

Savage-Rumbaugh, E. S. 1986. *Ape language: From conditioned response to symbol.* New York: Columbia Univ. Press.

Schaller, G. 1972. *The Serengeti lion.* Chicago: Univ. of Chicago Press.

———. 1973. *Golden shadows, flying hooves.* New York: Knopf.

Schusterman, R. J., and K. Krieger 1984. California sea lions are capable of semantic comprehension. *The Psychological Record* 34:3–23.

Schwartz, M. F., M. C. Linebarger, and E. M. Saffran. 1985. The status of the syntactic deficit theory of agrammatism. In *Agrammatism*, ed. M.-L. Kean, 83–124. New York: Academic Press.

Searle, J. 1980. Minds, brains and programs. *Behavioral and Brain Sciences* 3:417–57.

———. 1984. *Mind, brains and science.* Cambridge: Harvard Univ. Press.

Sebeok, T. A., ed. 1977. *How animals communicate.* Bloomington, Ind.: Indiana Univ. Press.

———, and J. Umiker-Sebeok, eds. 1980. *Speaking of Apes.* New York: Plenum Press.

Service, E. R. 1962. *Primitive social organisation.* New York: Random House.

———. 1966. *The hunters.* Englewood Cliffs, N.J.: Prentice-Hall.

———. 1975. *Origins of the state and civilization.* New York: Norton.

Seyfarth, R. M., and D. L. Cheney. 1982. How monkeys see the world: A review of recent research on East African vervet monkeys. In *Primate communication*, ed. C. T. Snowdon, C. H. Brown, and M. R. Petersen, 239–57.

Seyfarth, R. M., D. L. Cheney, and P. Marler. 1980. Monkey responses to three different alarm calls: Evidence for semantic communication and predator classification. *Science* 210:801–3.

Sellars, W. 1962. Truth and 'correspondence'. *Journal of Philosophy* 59: 29–56.

Sibley, C., and J. Ahlquist. 1984. The phylogeny of hominoid primates as indicated by DNA-DNA hybridization. *Journal of Molecular Evolution* 20: 2–15.

Simon, H. A. 1962. The architecture of complexity. *Proceedings of the American Philosophical Society* 106:467–82.

Smith, F. H., and F. Spencer, eds. 1984. *The origins of modern humans: A world survey of fossil evidence.* New York: Alan R, Liss Inc.

Snowdon, C. T. 1982. Linguistic and psycholinguistic approaches to primate communication. In *Primate communication*, ed. C. T. Snowden, C. H. Brown, and M. R. Petersen, 212–38.

Snowdon, C. T., C. H. Brown, and M. R. Petersen. 1982. *Primate communication*. Cambridge: Cambridge Univ. Press.

Sommers, F. 1959. The ordinary language tree. *Mind* 68:160–85.

———. 1963. Types and ontology. *Philosophical Review* 72:327–63.

Spuhler, J. N. 1977. Biology, speech and language. *Annual Review of Anthropology* 6:509–61.

———. 1988. Evolution of mitochondrial DNA in monkeys, apes and humans. *Yearbook of Physical Anthropology* 31:15–48.

Steklis, H. D., and M. J. Raleigh. 1979. Requisites for language: Interspecific and evolutionary aspects. In *Neurobiology of social communication in primates*, ed. H. D. Steklis and M. J. Raleigh, 283–314. New York: Academic Press.

———, eds. 1979. *Neurobiology of social communication in primates*. New York: Academic press.

Stephenson, P. H. 1973. The evolution of color vision in the primates. *Journal of Human Evolution* 2:379–86.

Stokoe, W. C. 1978. *Sign language structure*. Silver Spring, Md.: Linstock Press.

Stowell, T. 1981. *Origins of phrase structure*. Ph.D. diss., Massachusetts Institute of Technology.

Stringer, C. B. 1987. A numerical cladistic analysis for the genus *homo*. *Journal of Human Evolution* 16:135–46.

Stringer, C. B., and F. Andrews. 1988. Genetic and fossil evidence for the origin of modern humans. *Science* 239:1263–68.

Struhsaker, T. T., and P. Hunkeler. 1971. Evidence of tool-using by chimpanzees in the Ivory Coast. *Folia Primatologica* 15:212–19.

Sund, P. N. 1958. A study of the muscular anatomy and swimming behavior of the sea anemone *Stomphia coccinea*. *Quarterly Journal of Microbiological Science* 99:401–20.

Sutton, D. 1979. Mechanisms underlying vocal control in nonhuman primates. In *Neurobiology of social communication in primates*, edited by H. D. Steklis and M. J. Raleigh, 45–68. New York: Academic Press.

Szalay, F. S., and E. Delson. 1979. *Evolutionary history of the primates*. London: Academic Press.

Szasz, T. S. 1961. *The myth of mental illness*. New York: Dell Publishing.

Talmy, L. 1977. Rubber-sheet cognition in language. In *Papers from the 13th regional meeting, Chicago Linguistic Society*, ed. W. Bead, et. al. Chicago: CLS.

———. 1983. How language structures space. In *Spatial orientation: Theory, research and application*, ed. H. Pick and L. Acredolo. New York: Plenum Press.

———. 1986. The relation of grammar to cognition. LAUDT occasional papers, series A, no. 165. University of Duisburg.

Tattersall, I. 1986. Species recognition in human palaentology, *Journal of Human Evolution* 15:165–75.

Teilhard de Chardin, P. 1959. *The phenomenon of man*. New York: Harper and Row.

Terrace, H. S. 1979. *Nim*. New York: Knopf.

Terrace, H. S., L. A. Petitto, R. J. Sanders, and T. G. Bever. 1979. Can an ape create a sentence? *Science* 206:891–900.

Thomas, R. K. 1980. Evolution of intelligence: An approach to its assessment. *Brain, Behavior and Evolution* 17:456–72.

———. 1987. Overcoming contextual variables, negative results and McPhail's null hypothesis. *Behavioral and Brain Sciences* 10:680–81.

Tinbergen, N. 1951. *The study of instinct*. Oxford: Clarendon Press.

———. 1958. *Curious naturalists*. New York: Basic Books.

———. 1972a. *The animal and its world*. Cambridge: Harvard Univ. Press.

———. [1932–38] 1972b. On the orientation of the digger wasp. In *The animal and its world*, 103–96. Cambridge: Harvard Univ. Press.

Tobias, P. V. 1987. The brain of *homo habilis*: A new level of organization in cerebral evolution. *Journal of Human Evolution* 16:741–61.

Trinkhaus, E., and F. H. Smith. 1985. The fate of the Neandertals. In *Ancestors: The hard evidence*, ed. E. Delson, 325–333. New York: Alan R, Liss Inc.

Unwin, N. 1987. Beyond Truth: Towards a new conception of knowledge and communication. *Mind* 96:299–317.

von Frisch, K. 1967. *The dance language and orientation of bees*. Cambridge: Harvard Univ. Press.

Ward, J. 1962. A further investigation of the swimming reaction of *Stomphia coccinea*. *American Zoologist* 2:567.

Washburn, S. L. 1960. Tools and human evolution. *Scientific American* 203(3): 63–75.

Washburn, S. L., and R. Moore. 1974. *Ape into man*. Boston: Little, Brown.

Wenke, R. J. 1984. *Patterns of prehistory*. 2d ed. New York: Oxford Univ. Press.

White, J. P., N. Modeska, and I. Hipuya. 1977. Group definitions and mental templates: An ethnographic experiment. In *Stone tools as cultural markers*, ed. R. V. S. Wright. Canberra: Australian Institute of Aboriginal Studies.

White, R. 1982. Rethinking the middle-upper Paleolithic transition. *Current Anthropology* 23:169–92.

Whiten, A., and R. W. Byrne. 1988. Tactical deception in primates. *Behavioral and Brain Sciences* 11:233–73.

Whorf, B. L. 1956. *Language, thought and reality*. Cambridge: MIT Press.

Wilford, J. N. 1985. *The riddle of the dinosaur*. New York: Knopf.

Williams, E. 1980. Predication. *Linguistic Inquiry* 11:203–38.

Wilson, E. O. 1971. *The insect societies*. Cambridge: Harvard Univ. Press.

Wilson, R. 1985. The emergence of the semantics of tense and aspect in the language of a visually impaired child. Ph. D. diss., Univ. of Hawaii.

Wittgenstein, L. 1951. *Philosophical investigations*. Oxford: Basil Blackwell.

Wolpoff, M. H. 1988. Multiregional evolution: The fossil alternative to Eden. In *The origins and dispersal of modern humans*, ed. C. B. Stringer and F. Andrews. New York: Cambridge Univ. Press.

Wolpoff, M. H., and W. X. Zhi, and A. G. Thorne, 1984. Modern *homo sapiens* origins: A general theory of hominid evolution involving the fossil evidence from South-East Asia. In *The origins of modern humans: a world survey of fossil evidence*, ed. F. H. Smith and F. Spencer, 411–83.

Wolters, C., ed. 1961. *The cloud of unknowing*. London: Penguin Books.

Wright, H. T. 1977. Recent research on the origin of the state. *Annual Review of Anthropology* 6:379–97.

Wynn, T. 1988. Stone tools and language. Paper presented at the International Conference on the Biology of Language, Rydzyna, Poland, 1–4 December.

Yellen, J. E. 1986. The longest human record. *Nature* 322:744.

Yerkes, R. M., and A. W. Yerkes. 1929. *The great apes*. New Haven: Yale Univ. Press.

———. 1936. Nature and conditions of avoidance (fear) response in chimpanzees. *Journal of Comparative Psychology* 21:53–66.

Young, J. Z. 1978. *Programs of the brain*. Oxford: Oxford Univ. Press.

Yunis, J. J., J. R. Sawyer, and K. Dunham. 1980. The striking resemblance of high-resolution G-banded chromosomes of man and chimpanzee. *Science* 208:1145–48.

Ziff, P. 1960. On what a painting represents. *Journal of Philosophy* 57:647–54.

Zurif, E. B., and Y. Grodzinsky. 1983. Grammatical sensitivity in agrammatism: A reply to Linebarger et al. *Cognition* 15:207–13.

Index

Adaptations, evolutionary, 146–47, 231
Adaptive radiation, 133, 267 n
Agent (thematic role), 66–68, 186, 225, 229
Aggression. *See* Violence
Agreement (grammatical), 54, 64
Agriculture, 236, 238, 241, 242, 271 n
Alarm calls, 141–43, 155; used deceptively, 14–15, 261 n; of vervet monkeys, 12–13
Analysis of nature, 50, 53, 204
Animal communication. *See* Communication, animal
Animals, domestication of, 235–36
Ant lion, 161
Antibiological conduct, 250–51
Ants, 236, 240
Any, meaning of, 53, 263 n
Apes, 1, 140; and constructional learning, 159–60; and 'language', 106–10, 265 n, 266 n; and syntax, 108–9; vocabularies of, 107–8
Aphasia, 127–28; and grammatical judgments, 128, 214–15; language in, 127, 168, 194, 267 n
Argument structure, 65–69, 124–25, 195–96; and phrase structure, 67; universality of, 66–67, 185. *See also* Thematic roles
Attributes, 40, 42, 49
Austin (ape), 107
Australopithecines, 138
Australopithecus afarensis, 134–36, 142–43, 268 n

Autonomy, 203; of creatures, 85, 90, 101, 220; of representations, 31

Bateson, Gregory, 77
Bats, 95–96, 204–5, 233
Battle of Lepanto (painting), 17–19
Beavers, 234
Bees, 153, 154, 240, 262 n
Behavior, 204; changes in, 146–47, 160, 172–73, 177; representation of, 39–40; plasticity in, 84
Binary branching, 52, 207, 263 n
Binary division, 223
Binary opposition, 42
Bipedalism, 149, 151
Body weight, of hominids, 134
Brain: mapping within, 45–46, 193–94; modularity in, 4, 206–7, 211, 212, 270 n; of primates, 149; reorganization of, 196–97; hemispheres of, 212–13; size of hominid, 3, 4, 133–36, 161, 259 n, 267 n
Broca's area, 127, 128, 137, 194
Burglar, concept of, 32–35
Bush, concept of, 34, 36

Case (grammatical), 69–70, 263 n
Categories, 88, 157, 262 n; criteria for, 30, 33; definition of, 93; formation of, 21, 29, 88, 90–92; prototypical, 26. *See also* Concepts
Categorization, 87, 92, 114; and behavioral responses, 91; and perception, 87–88. *See also* Concept formation; Identification